The Backbenchers

by the same author
published by Allen and Unwin
PARLIAMENT AND FOREIGN AFFAIRS
THE NEW LOCAL GOVERNMENT SYSTEM
PARLIAMENT AND CONSCIENCE
DELEGATION IN LOCAL GOVERNMENT
PATRONAGE IN BRITISH GOVERNMENT

The Backbenchers

PETER G. RICHARDS

Professor of British Government
University of Southampton

FABER AND FABER, LONDON

First published in 1972 by Faber and Faber Limited
3 Queen Square London W.C.1
Printed in Great Britain at The Pitman Press, Bath

ISBN 0 571 09752 9

to Ann Lesley

CONTENTS

PREFACE 9

1. MEMBERS OF PARLIAMENT: WHO ARE THEY? 11
Legal Qualifications—Social Experience

2. CONDITIONS OF SERVICE 24
Members' Pay and Pensions—Accommodation for
Members—Information Services

3. MEMBERS AND PARTY 45
Party Meetings and Committees—The Whips and
Party Discipline

4. THE FRAMEWORK OF PARLIAMENTARY
BUSINESS 69
The Speaker and Chairmen—The Pattern of
Parliamentary Behaviour

5. THE CHALLENGE TO THE EXECUTIVE—(1)
BY THE WHOLE HOUSE 89
Members and Ministers—Parliamentary Debates—
The Passage of Legislation—Questions and
Statements—Adjournment and Private Members'
Motions

6. THE CHALLENGE TO THE EXECUTIVE—(2)
BY COMMITTEES 115
Legal and Financial Committees—Nationalised
Industries—Specialised Committees—Regional
Committees—Members and Civil Servants

7. NON-GOVERNMENT LEGISLATION 142
Private Members' Bills—Private Bills—Church of
England Measures

8. MEMBERS AND THEIR CONSTITUENCIES 153
The Impact of Local Opinion—The Welfare Officer Role

9. MEMBERS AND THEIR INTERESTS 172

10. MEMBERS AND THE PUBLIC 185
Parliamentary Privilege—The Mass Media

11. POLITICAL PROMOTION 206

7

12. WHAT FUTURE FOR BACKBENCHERS?   218
    The Threat to Parliamentary Institutions—The Tasks of
    the Commons and the Purpose of Reform—The Future
    and the Status of Members

SELECT BIBLIOGRAPHY   235

INDEX OF MEMBERS   237

GENERAL INDEX   241

PREFACE

My earlier book on the backbencher in the House of Commons, *Honourable Members*, was published in 1959. A second edition followed in 1964. As a further edition became necessary it was clear that a wholly fresh book was required as the changes at Westminster over the past few years have been so considerable. Just a few passages of the original work remain, e.g. the physical description of the Commons' Chamber. The rest is a new attempt to explain how backbenchers fulfil their duties in the political climate of 1971.

Twelve years ago I argued that the individual Member was more than a pawn in the game of party politics, that backbenchers acting in unison could exercise significant influence over public policy. Since then backbenchers have become much more active. The results have been manifold. Members have obtained major improvements in the facilities available to them; executive action is now subject to much fuller scrutiny by select committees; procedural changes permit more efficient use of parliamentary time; private members' legislation has become more important; Members have displayed more independence in the division lobbies. By 1968 it was possible to hear complaints from a variety of sources that Members had become too free. Ten years earlier such an idea would have been manifestly ridiculous. In my view the added vigour of Members has improved the health of Parliament and this book endeavours to provide detailed justification for optimism.

To assist identification of backbenchers, the party affiliation and constituency are given for those mentioned in the text. These citations have sometimes been omitted to avoid repetition and are not given for party leaders or for leading statesmen of the pre-war period.

Acknowledgement is due to Messrs. George Allen and Unwin for permission to reproduce a passage from Harold Laski's *Grammar of Politics*.

I am deeply grateful to those who have assisted me with the provision of information. My friends in the Study of Parliament Group have never failed to answer my questions. Members and ex-Members of the House have been willing to discuss their personal experiences with me. My research assistant, John Seagrave, collected much detailed material, especially that of a quantitative nature. Miss Diana Marshallsey has supervised the construction of the indexes. Mrs. Dunn and Mrs. Powell have typed my drafts with care and accuracy. Ann Lesley has checked the figures. And my wife has devoted her usual selfless care to the final version sent to the publisher. Finally, the responsibility for error is mine.

Red Lodge, Chilworth
December 1971   PETER G. RICHARDS

CHAPTER I

MEMBERS OF PARLIAMENT: WHO ARE THEY?

The United Kingdom is divided into 630 constituencies. Each returns one Member to the House of Commons: England elects 511 Members, Wales 36, Scotland 71 and Northern Ireland 12. These 630 men and women have the power to change the character of public policy and, indeed, to change the government. If the Cabinet fails to command a majority in the Commons on a vote of confidence, then the Cabinet must resign or the Prime Minister must appeal for public support at a general election. In fact, the Commons does not destroy governments, due to the strength of party loyalty and party discipline. But the threat is still there. In a less stable political situation it could become crucial. Meanwhile, the 630 Members are a vital link in the connecting chain between government and governed. They transmit opinions and help to shape attitudes. They form the pool of talent from which national leaders are chosen. They elect these leaders, either directly or indirectly. The individual backbencher is generally unimportant; collectively, backbenchers can be all-important.

What sort of people are these 630 Members? Obviously they are not, like a jury, a typical cross-section of the community. Powerful filters ensure that only certain types of individual arrive at Westminster. These filters are political, social and legal. An initial requirement is a keen interest in politics, a willingness to take up a political career and to devote much leisure time to the affairs of a political party. Such voluntary activity may lead to nomination as a parliamentary candidate. The next limitation arises from the lack of any element of proportional representation in a single-member constituency system, so political minorities are at a disadvantage and the overwhelming majority of Members are sponsored by one of the two major parties, Conservative or Labour. These parties have certain preferences as to the qualities they seek in their representatives—preferences to be analysed in the second section of this chapter. The first section considers the legal obstacles to entering the House of Commons which raise fundamental questions concerning the nature of the British Constitution—about the relationship between the legislature and the judiciary, the legislature and the executive, the legislature and the Established Church and between the two Houses of the legislature.

Legal Qualifications

Some of the legal qualifications for membership of the Commons can be stated briefly; others require more extended discussion. Members must not be aliens, but citizens of the Republic of Ireland are not excluded. The minimum age requirement is 21 years; the minimum age for voting was lowered to 18 in 1969, but this change did not extend to the elected Members. Mental patients are excluded; by the Mental Health Act, 1959, if a Member is detained in a mental hospital as being of unsound mind for more than six months, the seat is vacated. Bankrupt persons are excluded until five years after discharge from backruptcy, unless the discharge is accompanied by a certificate that the bankruptcy was not due to misconduct. Corrupt practices at an election are a further source of disqualification: the last Member to be unseated for an election offence was the Liberal contender at Oxford in 1923.[1] Formerly persons convicted of treason or felony and sentenced to twelve months' imprisonment were debarred from the Commons until their punishment had been completed.[2] The position now is that a Member sentenced to imprisonment may be expelled by the House. Nothing was done in the case of Miss Bernadette Devlin (Ind. Mid-Ulster) who was sentenced in 1970 to six months' jail arising out of her part in disturbances in Londonderry, nor was action taken in 1971 when Frank McManus (Ind. Fermanagh and South Tyrone) was jailed for six months for his part in an illegal march through Enniskillen. Should the House decide on expulsion in such a case, the Member would still be entitled to offer himself—or herself—for re-election. The House also claims the right to expel a Member felt to have been guilty of dishonourable conduct even although the Member may not have been convicted of a crime in a regular Court: the last such expulsion was that of Garry Allighan (Lab. Gravesend 1945–47).[3]

All the stipulations outlined in the above paragraph are designed to ensure that Members of the Commons are suitable persons of good character. The other disqualifications, which exclude people of the utmost integrity, are all thought necessary to uphold some constitutional principle.

---

[1] Corruption at elections was notorious during the nineteenth century. The Corrupt and Illegal Practices Prevention Act, 1883, now re-enacted in the Representation of the People Act, 1949, was passed to 'clean up' elections and, indeed, make them less expensive for candidates.

[2] The last case of this kind was in 1954 when Captain Baker (Con. Norfolk, South, 1950–54) was convicted of forgery.

[3] Allighan's offence was that he had published an article in the *World's Press News* alleging that Members received payments from newspapers for revealing confidential information. It was shown that Allighan was himself guilty of this malpractice. See the Report of the Committee of Privileges: 1946–47 (138) ix.

The first of these principles is the separation of powers. It has been widely believed that if the tasks of government can be divided between separate groups of people then the chances of arbitrary, despotic or oppressive rule are greatly reduced. The separate groups act as a check on each other. An elected assembly of substantial size cannot undertake the day-to-day business of government; nor is it a suitable body to adjudicate when it is alleged that the law has been broken. The rule-execution function and the rule-adjudication function are separate from the rule-making function: this tripartite division demands a legislature, an executive and a judiciary. Strictly applied, the separation of powers theory requires that those engaged in these three tasks should be independent of each other. The constitution of the United States is based upon this model.

In Great Britain the concept is of far less importance. The Lord Chancellor is head of the judiciary, a senior member of the Cabinet which directs the executive and he also presides over the Upper House of Parliament. Members of the Government, except perhaps the Scottish Law Officers, belong to either the Commons or the Lords. Through party loyalty and party discipline the Cabinet dominates the Commons. Nevertheless some disqualifications for membership of the Commons reflect a desire to separate it from the other branches of government in order to safeguard its independence. Holders of full-time judicial offices and many part-time judicial posts including those associated with minor tribunals are disqualified from entering the Commons. (Recorders of Crown Courts are an exception to this principle).[1] Since the reign of Queen Anne there has been a restriction on the number of Ministers who may sit in the Commons. If the Prime Minister were able to distribute unlimited patronage among Members of the Commons, he could purchase support for his administration through the use of public funds. Before 1926 those appointed to some ministerial offices were required to seek re-election if they belonged to the Lower House: this rule was repealed because it tended to restrict appointments to Members sitting for 'safe' constituencies. The House of Commons Disqualification Act, 1957, limited the holders of Government office in the Commons to 70; within this figure the number of Ministers, including Ministers of State, could not exceed 27. The Ministers of the Crown Act, 1964, raised the overall limit from 70 to 91[2] and abolished the

---

[1] However, they may not represent a constituency within the area where they exercise judicial authority. The Recorders of London, Liverpool and Manchester are completely disqualified.

[2] This increase is not quite so big as it seems. Before 1964 four or five unpaid Government whips were appointed. Being unpaid, they were excluded from the total of 70 but were still regarded as belonging to the Government. Since 1964 assistant whips have been paid and are included in the limit of 91.

limit on Ministers. Since the Government needs little more than 315 supporters in the Commons to retain office, nearly 30% of these supporters may be included in the Ministry. It is arguable that this proportion is so high as to absorb most of the talent on the Government benches with consequent damage to the independence of thought and action in the Commons.

The general rule is that offices of profit under the Crown are closed to Members of the Commons with the exception of the restricted number of ministerial posts. In the nineteen forties and fifties there were a number of cases where Members were disqualified for utterly trivial reasons, e.g. occasionally sitting on a tribunal for a negligible fee. This occurred largely through ignorance of the law: to prevent further cases the law was codified in 1957 by the House of Commons Disqualification Act which lists the judicial and administrative posts that are barred to Members. The list grows steadily with the establishment of further state-sponsored organisations—nationalised industries and supervisory boards of various kinds. Regular members of the armed forces are disqualified. So are the police. So are permanent civil servants. The latter are disqualified not merely to restrain ministerial patronage and to divide the executive from the legislature, but also to preserve the anonymity and impartiality of the civil service. Ministers rely heavily on the advice of their permanent servants. Their confidence in the civil service would be fatally undermined if some of the latter were associated with their political opponents. So a civil servant, a policeman and a serviceman who wishes to enter Parliament must leave his job before standing for election.

A Member cannot be appointed to a disqualifying office against his will and a Prime Minister cannot force his critics to leave the Commons. Nor can a Member resign from the Commons: if he wishes to leave he must be appointed to a disqualifying office. Two sinecure offices have been retained in order to enable Members to escape from Parliament— the Steward and Bailiff of the Chiltern Hundreds and of the Manor of Northstead. One possible gap in the legal restraints on patronage is that there is nothing to prevent a Prime Minister from appointing Members who have given him loyal support to highly paid posts outside the Government. Such a move would immediately remove a Member from the Commons: a by-election would be caused unless the appointment came immediately before a general election. In fact, few Members are appointed to disqualifying offices. Those that are include Opposition supporters, normally ex-Ministers. Under the Wilson Government Aubrey Jones (Con. Birmingham, Hall Green 1950–65) was nominated as Chairman of the Prices and Incomes Board: under the Heath Government Richard Marsh (Lab. Greenwich 1959–71) became Chairman of British Rail. There is no evidence that this form of patronage is used for political purposes.

An English or Scottish peerage is another disqualification. Irish peers may sit in the Commons. Before 1963 a Member who was also heir to a peerage was unable to escape translation to the Lords when he succeeded to the title. He was deprived of the opportunity of staying in the main centre of political life, not through an adverse popular vote, but through the operation of an antique constitutional rule. This was widely felt to be a hardship and some elder statesmen are known to have refused peerages out of consideration for their sons. On the other hand the rule was defended not merely in the name of tradition but also by the argument that a flow of fresh younger blood from the Commons was important for the vigour of the Upper House. Two Members tried to have the law changed when they came to be moved to the Lords. In 1950 Quintin Hogg unsuccessfully asked the Labour Prime Minister Clement Attlee to introduce legislation to permit him to stay in the Commons.[1] The second Member Wedgwood Benn (Lab. Bristol S.E.) was successful. He had tried during the lifetime of his father, Viscount Stansgate, to avoid the Upper House through a Personal Bill. This move was rejected by the Lords. When his father died in 1960 Benn signed an Instrument of Renunciation of his peerage and petitioned the Commons to allow him to remain a Member. The Committee of Privileges considered the matter but rejected Benn's plea: the view of the Committee was upheld by the House.[2] A by-election was then held in his Bristol constituency which Benn won by a handsome majority. The Commons refused to admit him[3] and an Election Court awarded the seat to his defeated Conservative opponent, Malcolm St. Clair. The Government then agreed to the appointment of a Select Committee of both Houses to consider the future composition of the Lords. The subsequent Report[4] became the basis of the Peerage Act, 1963, which allows an inherited peerage to be renounced, and disclaiming a title allows a peer to vote at parliamentary elections and be elected to the Commons. A peerage cannot be given up by its first holder nor by any peer who, subsequent to the passage of the Act, applies for a writ of summons to the Upper House. A surrendered peerage goes into cold storage and on the death of the erstwhile holder becomes available for his heir. Anyone who inherits a peerage has a year from the date of succession to decide whether to disclaim it or, in

---

[1] See correspondence in *The Times*, September 8th 1950. Quintin Hogg has had a unique parliamentary career. He was Conservative Member for Oxford 1937–50, Viscount Hailsham in the Lords 1950–63, upon renunciation of his peerage, Con. St. Marylebone 1963–70 and became Lord Chancellor and a life peer in 1970.

[2] H.C. Deb., Vol. 638, cols. 565–636. The Report of the Privileges Committee is 1960–61 (142) vi.

[3] H.C. Deb., Vol. 640, cols. 34–164.   [4] 1962–63 (38) vi.

the case of a minor, the decision must be made before his twenty-second birthday. Similarly, Members of the Lords at the date when the Act came into effect—other than first-generation peers—who wished to disclaim were given a year within which to do so. A Member of the Commons who succeeds to a peerage is in a different position. He has but one month to make up his mind. During this period he is not disqualified from the Commons, but he may not sit or vote until he has renounced the title. Thus in 1970 Antony Lambton (Con. Berwick) renounced the Earldom of Durham.

The Peerage Act was a notable personal triumph for Wedgwood Benn. As soon as it became law, St. Clair resigned and Benn was re-elected at Bristol. Benn succeeded where Hogg had failed, largely because he campaigned with far greater energy but also because the hereditary character of the Lords had been undermined by the introduction of life peers in 1958. Public opinion was prepared to accept further change in the constitutional position of the peerage and by fighting his cause by every legitimate means Benn succeeded. Yet the most dramatic consequence of the Act came elsewhere. The fourteenth Earl of Home was enabled to return to the Commons in 1963 as Conservative Member for Kinross and West Perthshire and to become the Prime Minister.

One other category of disqualification relates to the church. The established church, the Church of England, is represented in Parliament through the presence of bishops in the House of Lords. But the disqualification of clergy from the Commons extends beyond the Church of England to the Church of Scotland and to Roman Catholic clergy. In 1950 after the election of the Rev. J. G. MacManaway for Belfast, West, the Judicial Committee of the Privy Council advised that ordination in the Church of Ireland was a disqualification.[1] However, the Welsh Church Act, 1914, ended the disqualification of its clergy, and priests and deacons of the established church may also become Members if they have been divested of their orders. All other non-conformist clergy can enter the Commons. This discrimination is impossible to justify but there has been no significant demand to amend the law. The problem was considered by Select Committees of the Commons in 1941 and 1953 but no changes were recommended.[2] The 1957 Disqualification Act specifically left the status of clergy unchanged.[3] More recently the report of the Archbishop's Commission on *Church and State*[4] recommended that no one should be excluded from the

---

[1] 1950 Cmd. 8067 xviii. Earlier a Commons' Select Committee failed to reach a decision on the matter: 1950 (68–1) v.

[2] 1940–41 (120) iii and 1952–53 (200) vi.

[3] Section 14 (3). An attempt to end disqualification of clergy was defeated by 160 votes to 38: H.C. Deb., Vol. 565, col. 1194.

[4] Church Information Office, 1970, p. 58.

Commons through being a minister in *any* church: even so, this document leaves a feeling that the idea of a political priest is regarded without favour.

Two other causes of disqualification were, however, removed in 1957—Crown pensions and Crown contracts. The number of Crown pensioners is now negligible but Crown contracts are a more serious problem. Clearly, it is undesirable that a Member should use his parliamentary status to advance his financial interests or that Ministers should be able to attract political support through the award of contracts. Nevertheless before 1957 the law was anomalous and indefensible. It was framed in an age when trade was carried on by individuals acting singly or in partnership, not by large companies: in consequence a Member with financial interest in an engineering firm with valuable state contracts could sit in the Commons without hindrance while a Member who supplied a small quantity of furniture or stationery to a Government department could have been ejected from Parliament. No Member had been disqualified under the contracts rule since 1924 and there was no real purpose in keeping this safeguard.

Any query on whether a person is entitled to be a Member is settled after his election, either by a Court or by the Commons itself. If a candidate is nominated in accordance with the law—if he has sufficient valid signatures on his nomination form and deposits £150— a returning officer has no power to prevent him from standing, even if it is abundantly clear that he is not qualified to take a seat. A candidate, however, must make a statement that to the best of his knowledge and belief he is not disqualified.[1] Should a dispute arise over the conduct or result of an election, the issue will be determined by an aggrieved party presenting an election petition to a Court.[2] An allegation that a person elected to the Commons is ineligible can be submitted to the Judicial Committee of the Privy Council.[3] But the House also retains the right to judge the fitness of its Members and may declare any seat to be vacant.[4] Alternatively, it may direct that the previous occupancy of a

---

[1] This did not prevent Wedgwood Benn from standing at the 1961 Bristol by-election because he argued that, in law, his peerage was not a disqualification.

[2] The procedure for the hearing is governed by the Representation of the People Act, 1949, together with the Election Commissioners Act, 1949.

[3] House of Commons Disqualification Act, S.7.

[4] The alternative procedures are well illustrated by the outcome of the election of two Sinn Fein candidates in 1955. The Sinn Feiners, P. Clarke (Fermanagh and South Tyrone) and T. Mitchell (Mid-Ulster), were both at the time of the election serving a ten-year prison sentence in Belfast Gaol for their part in a raid on the depot of the Royal Inniskilling Fusiliers. Mitchell was unseated by a resolution of the Commons, but Clarke was replaced as a consequence of an election petition. For further discussion of these incidents see 'The Controverted Elections in Northern Ireland' in *The Table*, Vol. 24.

disqualifying office shall be disregarded, provided that the cause of disqualification is first removed. The result is some overlapping in the jurisdictions of the Courts and the Commons. A clash of authority is prevented by two stipulations in the 1957 Act: the Commons may not validate the position of a Member, as described above, if his position is subject to examination by an election court; conversely, no application to the Privy Council can succeed if the Commons have already decided that the disqualification in question shall be disregarded.

Social Experience

The predominant characteristic of Members of the Commons is that almost all of them are supporters either of the Conservative Party or the Labour Party. The single-member constituency system where victory goes to the candidate with the highest number of votes is unkind to the smaller parties. So the Liberals, in spite of significant support in the country as a whole, are left with a mere handful of Members: in 1970 Liberals secured 7·5% of the total vote but their six seats represented less than 1% of the membership of the Commons. Other minor groups, notably the Scottish and Welsh Nationalists, suffer in the same way. An independent candidate is in a hopeless plight since he cannot combat the strength of established political organisations when trying to win support from the 60,000 voters in a typical constituency. There was one remarkable Independent victory in 1970, Stephen Davies (Merthyr Tydfil); however, the conditions were exceptional as Davies had been the local Member since 1934 and, having been rejected by the local Labour Party on grounds of advanced age, was duly re-elected on the basis of his personal reputation. The dominance of the major parties is not so firm in Northern Ireland which in 1970 returned four Members of varying opinions who fall beyond normal party groupings. The only other Members elected in 1970 outside the two-party system were the Speaker[1] and the Scottish Nationalist who triumphed in the remote constituency of the Western Isles. Thus 617 out of the total 630 Members were either Labour or Conservative.

So the people who become Members are those who appear most suitable to local Conservative and Labour selection committees.[2] General practice is for a constituency party to re-adopt a retiring

---

[1] See p. 71 *infra*.

[2] Selection procedure has been fully analysed by Michael Rush, *The Selection of Parliamentary Candidates* (Nelson, 1969). See also Austin Ranney, *Pathways to Parliament* (Macmillan, 1965) and Peter Paterson, *The Selectorate* (MacGibbon and Kee, 1967).

Member.[1] Just occasionally this does not happen because of local dissatisfaction with a Member on personal or policy grounds. Of course, sometimes a Member will wish to retire or he may be defeated at the polls when there is a 'swing' against his party. It follows that the great majority of Members of a new House of Commons will have had previous parliamentary experience.

PARLIAMENTARY EXPERIENCE OF MEMBERS, 1970

	Conservative	Labour	Others
First elected 1970	83	64	3
Elected pre-1970	247	223	10
Elected pre-1960	166	116	4

The figures show that the Commons enjoy a high level of continuity. Indeed, the turnover of Members was higher in 1970 than at any election since 1945 because of the size of the movement of political opinion. So even in the least experienced House since the post-war election, nearly half the Members could claim ten years' service.

To select a candidate for a seat that a party hopes to win is obviously a more serious exercise than the choice of someone to fight a hopeless seat. But to fight a hopeless contest is regarded both as good experience and as evidence of true devotion to the Party cause: the candidate for a promising constituency is often someone who has stood and lost elsewhere. The 27 Conservative Members who retired in 1970 were replaced by 11 ex-Members, 11 previously unsuccessful candidates and 5 novices. Yet local Conservative Associations do not necessarily favour the candidate with the most political experience: defeated ex-Ministers can find it very difficult to find a fresh seat. An ex-Minister is obviously a potential future Minister and, as such, local selectors may fear that he will pay less attention to constituency problems. A similar tendency has been noticeable in the Labour Party.

The table overleaf shows the age distribution of Members analysed by party. It will be noticed that Labour has a higher proportion of Members above the age of 60: Labour Members are less willing to retire than Conservatives, no doubt because of less favourable financial circumstances.

The proportion of younger Members, those below 40, is very similar in the two main parties. When compared with previous Parliaments, the figures for the lowest age group, below 30, do show a major

---

[1] When constituency boundaries are re-drawn a Member loses his expectation of automatic renomination as more than one sitting Member may compete for selection by a new constituency. So a fresh electoral map is likely to interrupt or terminate many parliamentary careers.

change. It used to be the case that the youngest Members were Conservatives. After the 1959 Election the ten Members below 30 were all Conservatives. In 1970 the three youngest Conservatives, Winston Churchill (Stretford), Kenneth Clarke (Rushcliffe) and John Wilkinson (Bradford, West), were all within four months of their thirtieth birthdays; had the General Election been held in October 1970 it is probable that no Conservative Member would have been below the age of thirty. It seems that Conservative selectors now require some maturity and are unwilling to accept very young men from Eton and Oxbridge with strong family connections.

AGE OF MEMBERS, 1970

Age at 18.6.70	Conservative	Labour	Liberal	Others
21–29	3	5	—	2
30–39	60	53	3	—
40–49	121	87	2	3
50–59	106	78	1	—
60–69	38	59	—	1
Over 70	2	5	—	1
Totals	330	287	6	7

The number of female Members remains remarkably constant. In 1970 a total of 26 were elected, exactly the same as in 1966. There was, however, some change in the party composition of this group; the fifteen women Conservatives was an all-time record while the ten on the Labour side constituted the lowest figure since the war. As women form over half the electorate these very small numbers demand some comment. No evidence exists to show that voters discriminate against Conservative and Labour female candidates. It is impossible to show that selection committees discriminate against women because no information is available about the potential number of female parliamentary candidates. If few women wish to become Members then it is neither surprising nor unreasonable that there are few women Members. Meanwhile the total of female candidates rises slowly: Conservatives nominated 21 in 1966 and 27 in 1970 while Labour nominated 30 in 1966 and 29 in 1970. One factor to be noted is that local party selectors are unwilling to take the risk that their Member will become pregnant. It is unusual for a woman to be elected while she is in the age range when child-bearing is most common. Yet this generalisation is subject to a notable exception: the youngest Member of either sex elected in 1970 was Bernadette Devlin (Ind. Mid. Ulster).

The contrast between the social experiences of Conservative and Labour Members is best illustrated by a comparison of the educational and occupational backgrounds.[1] 77% of Conservative Members attended a public school; only 20% of Labour Members did so. No fewer than 59 Conservatives went to Eton—nearly 20% of male Tory Members. Old Etonians were also very successful at Conservative selection conferences for winnable seats: 69 Conservative candidates were old Etonians, so 85% were victorious. It used to be the case that the Conservatives had a higher proportion of Members with a university education but this gap is now narrowing; the percentages after the 1970 election were Conservatives 63%, Labour 53%. But far more Conservatives went to Oxbridge—82% of all Conservative graduates as compared with 46% of Labour graduates. At the other end of the educational scale the schooling of 20% of Labour Members was 'elementary', while only a single Conservative Member fits into this category.

Certain occupations are heavily represented in the House. In 1970 there were as many as 125 lawyers; 97 barristers and 28 solicitors spread across all parties including the Liberals. There were 66 teachers; all except ten were Labour Members. All but four of 84 company directors were Conservatives. The 58 publishers and journalists were spread across the parties. 31 of 32 farmers were Conservatives. Inevitably the 22 miners were solidly Labour. While 72 Labour Members could be described as 'workers' only 2 Conservatives fell into this grouping. These occupation figures can be misleading for they refer to a Member's means of livelihood prior to election: in some cases, but not in others, a Member has continued to earn money from this original calling. Thus some lawyers continue to practise after election to Westminster but teachers cannot continue to teach. Journalists can carry on with their writing and company directors with their directing but the worker from the shop floor leaves his old environment behind. Especially with Labour Members who have been in the House for several years, something of a gap can develop between their previous occupation and their contemporary situation.

The occupational background of Labour Members is affected substantially by the practice of sponsoring candidates. This means that a trade union makes a substantial contribution to the election expenses of a local party where a member of the union has been selected as the parliamentary candidate.[2] 112 Labour Members were sponsored in

---

[1] The information in this and the following paragraph is based on D. Butler and M. Pinto-Duschinsky, *The British General Election of 1970* (Macmillan, 1971), pp. 301–3.

[2] For fuller discussion of sponsoring see pp. 172–4 *infra*.

1970. A further 17 Labour Members were financially assisted at the election by the Co-operative Party, the political wing of the Co-operative Movement.

TRADE UNION CANDIDATES 1945–70

Year	Union candidates elected	Total of Labour Members	T.U. Members as % Labour Members
1945	120	394	30
1950	111	315	35
1951	105	295	36
1955	96	277	35
1959	92	258	35
1964	120	317	37
1966	132	363	36
1970	112	287	39

The table reveals two tendencies. Union influence has been stronger since 1964 and it also tends to be weaker when the political climate is favourable to Labour—this is because union assistance is centred on seats that are likely to be won. The system helps to maintain the link between the Parliamentary Labour Party and the shop floor although an increasing number of sponsored candidates are people with professional qualifications. In the past, sponsoring arrangements have also been criticised as being responsible for the poor quality of some Labour Members.

Many Members have served on a local authority. Selection committees seem to regard local government service as a positive merit since it means that a candidate has had experience of the welfare aspect of the work of an elected representative. This tendency is strongest in urban areas. In some large cities, especially Glasgow and Liverpool, Labour Members are almost always 'promoted' from the local council. The figures below show that it is the Labour Party which has the strongest link with local government.

MEMBERS WITH EXPERIENCE AS COUNCILLORS: 1970[1]

Labour	Conservative	Liberal	Others
99 (34%)	81 (25%)	0	1 (14%)

Information about the religious beliefs of Members is incomplete and possibly misleading. Some Members are not willing to publicise

---

Based on biographical material in *Dod's Parliamentary Companion* (1971).

the nature of their faith, perhaps because they have not got any. Another difficulty is that intensity of interest in religious questions will vary: some Members are active supporters of a particular church, while for others religious affiliation is nominal. So meaningful statistics on this subject cannot be produced. Even so, a few quite important generalisations can be made. The old tag that the Church of England is the Conservative Party at prayer is, of course, an over-simplification, yet support for the Established Church is stronger among Conservatives than among Labour Members. In the case of the non-conformist churches, the reverse is true. Roman Catholics are fairly evenly spread between both sides of the House. An overwhelming preponderance of Jewish Members used to be Labour, but this disproportion was reduced substantially in 1970 when the number of Conservative Jews rose from two to nine. Atheist or humanist Members are certainly more prominent on the Labour benches. In general, it seems that a candidate's religious belief, or lack of it, does not have much influence in the selection process, although there have been individual cases where religion has been all important.

The preceding information has tended to stress differences in the social experience of Members. There are, however, common characteristics that cannot be expressed in numerical terms. Members are all politicians, party enthusiasts, with a high level of involvement in public affairs. They are forceful, vigorous and largely extrovert people. They are successful and ambitious, at least when first elected. Another common characteristic is their experience of parliamentary life. A few dislike it and drop out of the political scene. The vast majority develop a deep affection for parliamentary institutions. Despite party strife, frustrations and disappointments, Members are keen to uphold the authority of the Commons. This common attachment to Parliament does much to minimise the effect of contrasting social and cultural backgrounds.

Members share another attribute. Before election almost all of them were nonentities, at least in national terms. Political reputations are made at Westminster and few men change over to politics after outstanding achievements in some other walk of life. There have been exceptions—notably trade unionists Ernest Bevin and Frank Cousins (Lab. Nuneaton 1965–67) and John Davies (Con. Knutsford) formerly Director-General of the C.B.I. The trade unionists had varied achievements as Ministers: neither were successful in the Commons. Perhaps this is another reflection of Members' belief in the importance of Parliament as an institution—a feeling that Parliament should create its own leadership which should not be imported from the world outside.

CHAPTER 2

CONDITIONS OF SERVICE

The conditions of parliamentary service affect not only the type of people who are willing to serve as Members of the Commons but also the ability of Members to perform their functions effectively. These matters have too often received scant attention in the literature on Parliament; no doubt the literature has reflected the general lack of understanding and concern. Inevitably, Members' pay is a prickly subject. Equally important is the question of what facilities should be provided at Westminster to enable Members to do constructive work. Recently the complaints of Members about inadequate provision have grown louder and improvements are being made, but in 1969 John Smith (Con. Cities of London and Westminster 1965–70)[1] announced that he would 'quit this archaic House' because of its inadequate facilities for working.

Members' Pay and Pensions

So that all classes could be present in the Commons, the Chartists demanded the payment of Members. This was the fifth of the six points incorporated in 'The People's Charter' of 1838. As with other Chartist policies there was a considerable passage of time before the idea was accepted. The Liberal administration of Sir Henry Campbell-Bannerman supported the principle of payment, but it was not until the eve of the second general election of 1910 that the succeeding Liberal Cabinet of Asquith gave a definite pledge on the subject. Accordingly, the proposal to pay Members £400 per annum was introduced in the Budget statement to the Committee of Ways and Means in 1911,[2] and was subsequently approved by the House by 256 votes to 158, the Conservatives opposing the resolution. Presenting the case for the Government, Lloyd George, Chancellor of the Exchequer, commented:

'When we offer £400 a year as payment of Members of Parliament it is not a recognition of the magnitude of the service, it is not a remuneration, it is not a recompense, it is not even a

---

[1] See article in *The Times*, July 7th 1969 'From club to workshop'.
[2] H.C. Deb., Vol. 25, cols. 1854–5.

salary, it is just an allowance, and I think the minimum allowance, to enable men to come here, men who would render incalculable service to the State . . . but who cannot be here because their means do not allow it.'[1]

The original figure of £400 p.a. has been adjusted upwards on a number of occasions to keep pace with the fall in value of the currency unit. In 1937 the amount became £600 and in 1946 £1,000. In 1954 the Commons approved the proposal of the Select Committee on Members' Expenses that the parliamentary salary be £1,500;[2] on a free vote the majority in favour was 280 to 166 with the Labour Opposition in favour and Conservative Members hopelessly divided. The Churchill Conservative Government refused to accept the idea of the £500 increase and, instead, introduced an attendance allowance of £2 a day from Monday to Thursday. For an average session this was worth about £280 and it was also tax free. The attendance allowance ended in 1957 when the salary level went up to £1,750. In 1964 the figure rose to £3,250 following the report of the Lawrence Committee[3] and in 1971 came the latest rise to £4,500 after a report from the new Review Body on Top Salaries sitting under the chairmanship of Lord Boyle.[4] Also in 1971 an attendance allowance of £750 p.a. was reintroduced for provincial Members to defray their accommodation costs in London while Parliament is sitting. The intention is to provide a realistic scale of expenses so that Members do not have to meet the inevitable additional costs of parliamentary life out of their salaries.

Members receive free facilities, the scope of which has widened greatly in recent years. Free first-class rail travel was provided between London and a Member's constituency in 1924; third-class sleeping berths were added in 1932; four years later first-class berths were allowed; in 1945 free travel to the constituency was extended to sea and air travel; since 1946 a car mileage allowance has been available in lieu of rail fare. After the Boyle Report in 1971 other travel costs within the United Kingdom connected with public business were reimbursed and Members' spouses had ten free return trips to Westminster. In addition, Members receive a subsistence allowance when travelling on official business, for example, when going abroad in a parliamentary delegation: the rate of expenses allowed is that applicable to civil servants of the rank of assistant secretary.[5] Accident insurance

---

[1] H.C. Deb., Vol. 29, col. 1361 *et seq.* In spite of the Chancellor's description, the payment has always been regarded as taxable remuneration.

[2] 1953–54 (72) vii.   [3] 1964–65 Cmnd. 2516 xix.

[4] 1971–72 Cmnd. 4836. Lord Boyle was formerly Conservative Member for Birmingham, Handsworth 1950–70.

[5] H.C. Deb., Written answer, 14.2.57.

for Members travelling on the business of the House was provided in 1957. Since 1911 Members have been entitled to some free stationery; the ration is now equal to an annual value of £25. A free photocopying service is also available. Since 1969 Members have enjoyed free postage and telephone calls on parliamentary business: the Leader of the House commented that 'what constitutes parliamentary business is best left to the good sense of individual Members' and would not say whether the definition extended to Christmas cards.[1] The provision of official papers for Members is considered below.[2] Finally, since January 1970 Members have obtained an allowance in recompense for secretarial expenses actually incurred. This concession followed a recommendation from the Services Committee that 'provision should be made at public expense for secretarial assistance, or an allowance to meet the cost, up to a maximum of one full-time secretary per Member'.[3] In turn the Services Committee had reacted to pressure from an informal all-party group of backbenchers who were urging a variety of improvements in Members' conditions.[4] It was estimated that the cost of a full-time secretary would be around £1,000 p.a., but the Labour Government felt that this scale of provision would be too costly. The Leader of the House circulated Members to canvass opinion on the most acceptable form of help, i.e. whether a typing pool should be established or whether Members wanted to make private arrangements. Not surprisingly, the latter alternative was preferred and the compromise of a £500 allowance emerged which allowed each Member to engage a part-time secretary.[5] As a result of the Boyle Report this allowance was raised to £1,000 p.a. and can now be used to cover general office expenses including the purchase of equipment. Up to £300 p.a. of this sum may be used to pay for research assistance.[6]

The very special conditions of work for an elected representative must involve much unavoidable expenditure. The harder a Member works on his public duties, the more he will spend. Representation of constituencies near London is normally less expensive, as there is no need to stay away from home while attending the Commons or when visiting the constituency. For a Member who already has a home in

---

[1] H.C. Deb., Vol. 791, col. 404.   [2] pp. 38–9.

[3] Services Committee, Sixth Report, 1968–69 (374) paras. 4 and 5. For the nature and origin of the Services Committee see pp. 35–6.   [4] *The Times*, May 7th 1969.

[5] Some Labour Members were very disappointed that the Services Committee proposal was not adopted in full. Two of them wrote to the Leader of the House and threatened to strike. The 'strike' was to consist of refusing to serve on Standing Committees. Since one of the two Members was not, at that time, serving on a Standing Committee, the threat was scarcely persuasive.

[6] 1971–72 Cmnd. 4836, para. 45.

the provinces, and who is elected to represent a distant—but not a Metropolitan—division, there is a choice of moving house or of much triangular travelling and consequent hotel bills. The expense allowances introduced in 1971 were an attempt to meet this situation. Hospitality is an item that is also flexible. Some Members spend considerable sums on entertaining constituents and those who come to discuss public affairs with them: other Members barely rise to a cup of tea.

Members can claim tax remission for their expenses and the Lawrence Committee enquired into the rules applied by the Inland Revenue to the expenses of Members. The general criterion is that expenditure on party activity—as opposed to parliamentary activity—is not free of tax. This line may be hard to define and, when defined, harder still to justify. No allowance is made for canvassing literature, election expenses, charitable and political donations, entertaining or expenses incurred by a spouse. Nothing is allowed for extra costs arising from late-night sittings. The Lawrence Committee concluded that 'by no means all the reasonable expenditure of a Member is deductable for tax purposes'.[1] Not surprisingly the Report showed that the average sum allowed to a Member representing a London constituency (£620) was roughly half that allowed a Member from a rural constituency (£1,220). Since 1964 the sums allowed have increased considerably. The table below shows the size of claims agreed in 1968–69 and 1969–70; the comparison is complicated by the introduction of the secretarial allowance in 1970.

TAX ALLOWANCE FOR MEMBERS' EXPENSES
(excluding Ministers)[2]
Number of Members

Expenses allowed £'s	1968–69	1969–70	
		Including secretarial allowance	*Net of secretarial allowance*
0–999	67	56	95
1,000–1,999	264	262	267
2,000–2,999	113	144	119
OVER 3,000	19	26	7

[1] 1964–65 Cmnd. 2516 xix; paras. 45–6. The same tendency is illustrated in the Boyle Report, p. 79.

[2] Source: H.C. Deb., Vol. 818, col. *212* written answer and Cmnd. 4836, p. 81. The figures are incomplete.

The previous chapter showed the wide range in the social background of Members and gave an indication of the great variation in their personal financial circumstances. For a few Members the parliamentary salary is but a minor addition to their resources; others are almost wholly dependent on it. Members, except for Ministers, are free to follow occupations which attract additional remuneration, but the alternative employment must not demand regular attendance at fixed hours. A miner, a factory worker or a teacher cannot continue his normal living. There are six main vocations which are compatible with the performance of parliamentary duties—the law, journalism, public relations, trade union organisation, company directorships and the management of private wealth. Although opportunities in journalism, public relations and company direction may arise as a consequence of election to Westminster, there is no doubt that many people, who could not slip easily into one or more of the categories noted above, are deterred from entering upon a political career. Professional men of high ability, who are keenly interested in public affairs, may well shrink from the economic risks of attempting to enter the Commons. Major party candidates no longer contribute to election expenses, but the cost of 'nursing' a constituency remains; if, as is normally the case, a candidate is unsuccessful at his first attempt, the nursing expenditure is wasted. And politics is a highly uncertain walk of life. The possibility of losing a seat is always present, and Members with an insubstantial financial position must fear the prospect of unemployment. The hardship suffered by some ex-Members is discussed below.

Ministers and other Members in receipt of official salaries only receive a part of the parliamentary pay. Since 1971 this portion has been £3,000 p.a. But all Ministers have to surrender any position or employment that has added to their earned income.[1] Some Members, especially Conservatives, have suffered financial loss when joining the Government in a minor post.

How much should Members be paid? Inevitably this issue arouses differences of opinion inside and outside Parliament. Conservative Members have greater private resources and, in the past, have been more strongly opposed to raising salaries. This difference has now virtually disappeared. Pay increases came from Conservative Governments in 1937, 1954, 1957 and 1971 and from Labour Governments in 1946 and 1964. One basis for the controversy was whether Members should be regarded as having a full-time occupation. It used to be widely held in Tory circles that Members gained great advantage from retaining occupational links outside Parliament and that the additional experience

---

[1] D. C. M. Platt, 'The Commercial and Industrial Interests of Ministers of the Crown', *Political Studies*, Vol. IX, pp. 267–99.

acquired was of inestimable benefit in carrying out duties in the legislature. The objection to this argument was that the extra experience was of particular kinds which might lead Members to a less balanced view of the problems of society; they might come to know more about the management of industry and commerce but less about the plight of unemployed constituents. However, this issue is dead. Almost all Members now accept that their representative duties constitute a full-time activity and should be remunerated accordingly.

Public opinion is not so convinced. Partly this is due to lack of knowledge. An attitude survey[1] conducted by the Office of Manpower Economics in 1971 showed some change of mind after respondents had been given a factual statement about Members' pay and expenses.

PUBLIC ATTITUDE TO MEMBERS' PAY
(*% responses*)

Members are	Before statement	After statement
Grossly overpaid	11	4
Rather overpaid	25	11
Paid about right	38	50
Rather underpaid	31	28
Grossly underpaid	1	5
Don't know/no reply	12	2

It was notable that marked differences of opinion existed as between social classes; higher social and income groups were more sympathetic to the need to raise the salary of our legislators. So Labour voters, rather than Conservative supporters, opposed higher pay in spite of the fact that Labour Members are the more in need of the money. Public reaction is coloured, at least in part, by a lack of appreciation of the expenses Members have to meet and to a feeling that a Member has something less than a full-time job.[2]

In fact, backbenchers claim to spend an average of 63 hours a week on parliamentary business; only 6% of backbenchers admit to spending less than 40 hours a week on these duties while 5% claim to spend over 90 hours a week.[3] These figures are a little misleading since they refer presumably to periods when the House is sitting and, of course, Parliament is normally in recess for one-third of the year. The survey of Members' finances conducted by the Boyle Committee also showed that on average a backbencher spent between 10 and 20 hours a week on other gainful occupations and that this produced additional earnings in the region of £2,000 p.a. However, these averages conceal

---

[1] 1971–72 Cmnd. 4836, pp. 64–5.   [2] *Ibid.*, p. 68.   [3] *Ibid.*, pp. 51–2.

such wide variations as to be meaningless; 11% of backbenchers earned less than £250 in addition to their official salary while 20% earned at least an extra £5,000 p.a.[1] Members spend larger amounts of time on parliamentary and political affairs for varied reasons. Some are more conscientious; some have stronger political motivations and ambitions; some are forced to spend more time on travelling to a distant constituency; some have few links with commerce or journalism; some have greater responsibilities at Westminster. The last category provides scope for further argument about parliamentary salaries. The Opposition Whips, the chairman of Select Committees and the members of the Speaker's Panel of chairmen all have special duties. Should they receive extra remuneration? The Boyle Report showed some sympathy for this idea of financial recognition[2] and proposed that two Opposition Whips, in addition to the Chief Opposition Whip, should receive an additional salary. But any further extension of this principle is fraught with danger; to pay the chairmen of Select Committees extra salary would increase the patronage of the Whips.

The next question is *who* should decide the level of Members' pay? Legally, the Cabinet must assume responsibility: should it act on its own volition or seek advice from elsewhere? Recently the tendency has been to take counsel from outside. In 1963 the problem was put to a small committee composed of Sir Geoffrey Lawrence, Q.C., chairman, Mr. H. S. Kirkaldy and Professor W. J. M. Mackenzie, who obtained advice on parliamentary matters from a panel consisting of two peers and five Members: they recommended an increase in Members' pay to £3,250. The Lawrence Committee also considered whether an automatic link should be formed between Members' pay and some point in the civil service pay structure. This notion was rejected for three reasons: no comparison was possible between the task of a civil servant and that of a Member; any such link might involve the civil service in political controversy; Members should not enjoy an in-built protection against price changes. These arguments were persuasive and so Members failed to obtain any salary review machinery. Nothing further happened until 1969 when the Labour Government announced that the question of Members' pay would be referred to the Prices and Incomes Board after the next election[3] but this intention was not carried out because the Conservatives won the election and disbanded the P.I.B. The next move came in December 1970 when Douglas Houghton (Lab. Sowerby) introduced a private member's Bill under the ballot procedure which sought to establish an independent body to make recommendations on Members' pay. He withdrew the Bill when the Leader of the House

---

[1] *Ibid.*, p. 57.   [2] *Ibid.*, footnote on p. 10.
[3] H.C. Deb., Vol. 787, col. *474* (written answer).

announced that it was the intention of the Government that the question of parliamentary salaries should be referred to a new organisation, the Review Body on Top Salaries, serviced by the Office of Manpower Economics, which would also consider salaries of other high-ranking people in the public service, the judiciary, senior civil servants, senior officers in the armed forces and members of boards of nationalised industries.[1]

Should parliamentary pay be assessed at irregular intervals by quasi-autonomous bodies? In the past the objection has been not so much to the nature of the machinery but to the likelihood that any fresh review would always be unreasonably delayed. Pressure against a pay increase will always be substantial. In periods of inflation or financial stringency there will be Treasury resistance to more public expenditure or to any action which can provide an inducement to higher pay claims elsewhere. The prospect was that Members' pay would always lag behind the rising cost of living. They might feel forced to seek additional sources of income and pay less attention to parliamentary business; in the extreme case there could be a threat to the probity of public life. These dangers are minimised by the new review system which forges a link between salary levels in Parliament and elsewhere in the public service and the probability is that salaries will be revised once during the lifetime of each Parliament.

The introduction of payment to Members in 1911 led, as was intended, to the entry into the Commons of men without private wealth who surrendered their normal means of livelihood at the commencement of their parliamentary service. When these Members left the Commons, having reached an age appropriate to retirement, they were faced with acute financial hardship. It is a cruel doctrine which insists that one who has spent many years directing our national affairs might end his days at a standard of living comparable to that of the most indigent of old age pensioners.

In 1939 the House of Commons Members' Fund was started as a very modest attempt to relieve hardship.[2] £1 was deducted each month from Members' salaries to finance benefits to those in dire need. The maximum pension given to an ex-Member was £150 p.a. and was to be granted only if the total income of the recipient did not exceed £225 p.a.: a lesser sum was payable to widows. To be eligible for benefit an ex-Member had to be sixty years of age, or be incapacitated and have served in the Commons for at least ten years. Until

---

[1] H.C. Deb., Vol. 807, cols. 1715–27.

[2] It was based on the recommendations of the Fisher Committee. Report, 1937–38 Cmd. 5624 xii.

1957 the Fund continued as a private benevolent fund. Some flexibility was introduced to the rules governing the distribution of funds and the rates of benefit were adjusted upwards to take some account of the fall in the value of money. But ex-Members still suffered real hardship while some Members stayed in the Commons although in failing health because of the financial consequences of retirement. Then in 1957 Members' contributions were doubled and the Government also subscribed to the resources of the Fund. The idea of a full pensions scheme for Members failed to win support because some Members were unable to afford the high rate of contributions needed to support a worthwhile scheme. The difficulty inherent in any superannuation scheme for elected representatives is that the average period of contributory service is far less than in other occupations due both to the high average age of entry and the rate of dismissal through political vicissitudes. However, the substantial pay rise in 1964 made possible the establishment of pension arrangements upon lines suggested by the Lawrence Committee,[1] by which every Member contributed £150 p.a. to the pension fund and public revenues added an equal amount. No benefit was payable unless an ex-Member had reached 65 and had served ten years in the Commons. For those who satisfied these two conditions the amount of pension was linked to length of service: in 1971 the rates were £72 p.a. for each of the first fifteen years and £28·80 p.a. for each year thereafter: widows and widowers received half these sums.[2]

The acceptance of the proposals in the Boyle Report produced a substantial extension of the pension rights of Members.[3] The qualifying period was reduced from ten years to four so that almost all ex-Members in future will receive a pension. The amount, payable at the age of 65, is one-sixtieth of terminal salary for each year of service in the Commons. If a Member chooses to retire at the age of 60 he can do so with a lower rate of pension. Members are to contribute approximately three-eighths of the cost of these pensions, the remainder to be met by a grant from the Exchequer. If a Member dies, a year's salary is paid to his dependents. And, as with other public service pensions, arrangements will be made to secure that pension rights are protected against a fall in the value of money.

The link between the duration of a parliamentary career and pension entitlement is unfortunate since it provides an incentive, however small, for Members with limited wealth to try to defer retirement even

---

[1] Report, paras. 70–82.

[2] Those who were already Members in 1964 were given full and free credit for parliamentary service already completed.

[3] paras. 53–74.

if they are ageing and ailing. Meanwhile, the Members' Fund still exists to assist Members who retired before the pensions scheme became effective: the government grant to the Fund is being reduced as demands upon it are falling.

These arrangements do achieve a great advance in the economic security available for Members. Nevertheless, some of those defeated at a general election may experience financial stress. Politicians have to accept the risks associated with their calling. The greatest penalty is now suffered by those who lose their seats after many years at Westminster but who are still below retiring age: the outstanding example in 1970 was M. K. Macmillan (Lab. Western Isles) who was defeated at the age of 57 having been a Member for almost thirty-two years. Up to 1971 the parliamentary salary ceased the day on which Parliament was dissolved. Ex-Members are classed as self-employed and so are not eligible for unemployment pay; in addition, as self-employed persons they must continue to purchase social security stamps until they find a job. An ex-Member is not necessarily an ideal employee for he may be tempted to concentrate on attempts to return to Westminster rather than on the interests of his employer. A former manual worker, after a spell as a Member, may be reluctant to return to his former occupation. In 1970 the difficulties were intensified because many of the defeated Labour Members were teachers and lecturers and by the date of the election, June 18th, most schools and colleges had already completed recruiting staff for the coming academic year. The hardships were lessened through the use of the Parliamentary Labour Party's private benevolent fund which distributed over £4,000 to defeated Members. Essentially this is a one-party problem because Conservative ex-Members have either substantial financial reserves or sufficient business connections to ensure their economic security.

Other employments provide safeguards against an instant termination of pay. Salaried positions allow for one or three months' notice. Industrial workers now get redundancy payments. Should not some similar comfort be offered to Members dismissed by their constituents? A public opinion survey conducted for the Boyle Committee showed that two-thirds of those questioned thought that some similar arrangements should be made for Members. Accordingly the Committee proposed that Members should continue to be paid during the period in which Parliament is dissolved and that those Members who lose their seats should be entitled to claim a terminal payment equivalent to three months salary.[1] Now these proposals have been adopted the financial stress suffered by some ex-Members in 1970 should not occur again.

---

[1] paras. 48–52.

Accommodation for Members

An immediate task for a newly-elected Member is to become acquainted with the buildings in which the Mother of Parliaments conducts her business. To the new arrival the Palace of Westminster may appear impressive but inconvenient. Experienced Members may display a high degree of reverence for our parliamentary institutions but still wish for greater facilities in their physical home. The main complaint is the lack of private rooms for backbenchers but this shortage does have the compensating benefit of forcing them more into communal surroundings which encourage the exchange of opinions and the moderation of tempers.

Most of the building is early Victorian. The great fire of October 16th 1834, destroyed the major part of the Palace of Westminster with the important exception of Westminster Hall. Designs for a new Palace were invited in a public competition: 97 sets of drawings were submitted and finally those of Charles Barry were selected. The first stone of the new buildings was laid in 1840 by the architect's wife, but not until 1847 were the House of Lords and its lobbies available for use and the Commons did not finally settle in their new chamber until 1852. The Palace is thus little more than a century old. It was built in the age of the Gothic Revival and the fashion of the period is responsible for its medieval characteristics. What would the Palace be like today had the great fire taken place a quarter of a century earlier? The chance of fate has bequeathed to us a great edifice born of antiquarian enthusiasm, which is a magnificent sight on the river frontage and from a distance. At closer quarters the Palace may seem less impressive, and the wealth of decoration—largely the work of Barry's assistant, Pugin—frequently commands respect rather than admiration. These are, of course, matters of taste. But it is certain that the Palace does not stand up well to the modern criterion of functional efficiency, for 22% of the building is occupied by two miles of corridors.

The Commons' Chamber was destroyed in an air raid on May 10th 1941,[1] and at the end of 1943 a Select Committee was appointed to consider arrangements for rebuilding. It decided that the traditional dimensions and the essential features of the Chamber should be retained, so that the sense of intimacy and the conversational form of debate they encouraged should be preserved.[2] The short walk from the Central Lobby of the Palace to the Commons' Chamber presents a remarkable contrast. The Central Lobby, in which strangers congregate when they come to see their Members, is an octagonal vaulted

---

[1] From then on till 1950 the Commons normally met in the Lords' Chamber, while the Lords used the Queen's Robing Room.

[2] Cf. Report: 1943–44 (109) (109–1) ii.

apartment, 60 ft. across and 75 ft. high; it is impersonal and daunting. A little more than a hundred feet away the home of the Commons manages to combine friendliness with great dignity. It is surprisingly small. The floor is 68 ft. by 45 ft. 6 in.—exactly the same as Barry's Chamber—but at gallery level the dimensions have been increased to provide more room for strangers and reporters. The modest size is achieved because seats never have been provided for all Members; they have 346 seats on the floor of the House and a further 91 in the side galleries. For important debates the House is always crammed to capacity and the crush accentuates the sense of importance of the occasion; in quiet moments the few Members present seem far less isolated than they would be if six hundred odd seats were provided on the floor. There are also no desks between the benches, making it difficult to write or read and, thereby, increasing the possibility that attention will be paid to the speeches. In the Committee rooms there are desks, and a Member sitting in an inconspicuous position may deal with his correspondence.

Sir Giles Gilbert Scott was the architect of the new Chamber. In keeping with the rest of the Palace, the style is late Gothic, although no attempt has been made to follow the details of Barry's design. The ecclesiastical form of window was abandoned in favour of a more modern domestic type: most of the windows do not open in order that the excellent system of air-conditioning shall remain unaffected by nature. The woodwork, Shropshire oak, has received iron sulphate treatment to produce a restful light grey. The benches and the carpet are a pleasant green. Under the carpet are metal panels which can be heated to warm the feet of Members. Acoustically the Chamber is not satisfactory, in spite of a discreet system of amplifiers. A decision to have a sloping roof was taken for aesthetic reasons, although it was realised that this shape reflected sound waves, and the greater sim-plicity of ornament in the new building is thought to diminish audibility.

The Palace of Westminster is a Royal Palace which until 1965 was in the charge of the Lord Great Chamberlain. When the Commons were sitting, control of that part of the Palace allocated to them was delegated by the Lord Great Chamberlain to the Serjeant at Arms acting on behalf of the Speaker. During each recess and at week-ends the Lord Great Chamberlain resumed responsibility. This cumbrous arrangement created administrative difficulties. So since April 26th 1965 Mr. Speaker has controlled the Commons' section of the Palace. Also since 1965 a Select Committee has been regularly appointed to make recommendations on the 'domestic' aspects of running a legisla-ture.[1] This committee, the Services Committee, has three sub-committees concerned with accommodation and administration, catering and the

---

[1] For the debate on the new arrangements see H.C. Deb., Vol. 718, cols. 878–957.

Library.[1] The Services Committee must report to the House at least once each session and its chairman and, if required, the sub-committee chairmen will answer questions in the House. The new system allows Members more direct influence over the physical environment in which they work and has stimulated improvement of their facilities. Nevertheless, there are major obstacles in the way of change. The existing building does not easily lend itself to modification. The national status of the site must always arouse fierce aesthetic argument over the architectural merit of any proposed extension. Above all, expenditure on parliamentary services has to be borne by the taxpayer and is subjected to the normal processes of Treasury scrutiny.

Communal rooms available to Members are not dissimilar to those found in an old established London Club. They include the Library (described fully below), the Smoking Room, the Chess Room, a Newspaper room, and the Members' Bar[2] and Dining Room. All these rooms and many others have a screen attached to an internal television system which shows the name of the Member speaking in the Chamber so that Members can assemble rapidly if it is thought an important speech is being made. In 1939 the first wireless set for Members was introduced. Now there are three rooms with colour television sets provided by a radio relay firm.[3] There are also a number of committee rooms of varying size which may be booked by Members when not required for an official committee meeting. Such bookings may not be for longer than two hours and the business transacted must be closely linked with the work of Parliament. Ten smaller rooms on the so-called interview floor capable of seating up to twenty people may also be reserved by Members for smaller gatherings including deputations. Lobbying on a larger scale may be accommodated in the Grand Committee Room in Westminster Hall which holds up to 170 people. It is also equipped to be used as a cinema. Especially in summer, Members bring parties of visitors to the Terrace for a close view of the Thames. Under St. Stephen's Hall is the Crypt which is used for the celebration of Holy Communion, and sometimes for the wedding of a Member or the baptism of his children. In 1924 a Member who did

---

[1] The Select Committee on Publications and Debates, the Kitchen Committee, and the Speaker's advisory committee on the Library were discontinued.

[2] The normal restrictions on hours of consumption imposed by the Licensing Acts do not apply to the Palace of Westminster. The Law Courts accept that parliamentary privilege prevents them from enquiring into anything, other than crime, that occurs in the Palace. It was ruled in *R. v. Graham-Campbell—ex parte Herbert* (1935) 1 K.B. 394 that the Kitchen Committee had committed no offence by selling liquor without a licence.

[3] No licence fee is payable on these sets. The relay system is used because of the difficulty of erecting aerials that do not spoil the appearance of the buildings.

not belong to the Established Church, arranged to have his child christened in the Crypt: an attempt was made to stop the proceedings but the Law Officers decided that the Crypt was under the sole authority of the Lord Great Chamberlain and, therefore, that no ecclesiastical jurisdiction existed in respect of the Crypt.

In common with some London Clubs, the Commons provides its male Members with the services of a hairdresser. The cost of a hair-cut in 1970 was half-a-crown. No parallel provision is made for lady Members.

The major issue in relation to accommodation is the shortage of private rooms for backbenchers. At present only a lucky minority have this facility and Members can still be seen working at seats at the side of corridors. Admittedly, the situation has slowly improved over the last twenty years. In 1970 there were a total of 164 single rooms available for Members but rather more than half of these were allocated to office holders, i.e. Ministers, Opposition frontbenchers, some Whips, Mr. Speaker and his two deputies, the Chairmen of Select Committees, the Liberal Leader and the Second Church Estates Commissioner. A further 100 Members shared 50 double rooms and 296 desks were available in multiple 'Desk-rooms': the latter, of course give no privacy. Further, not all this accommodation is within the Palace itself. Approximately a third of the rooms made available to backbenchers are 'across the road' the other side of Bridge Street. This is highly inconvenient and helps to segregate some Members from the main centre of parliamentary activities, although the need for political discussion and perhaps refreshment will always draw them back into the Palace. The allocation of single and double rooms is decided by Government and Opposition Whips. Seats in desk rooms are distributed by the Serjeant at Arms but for these there is much less competition. In addition, there are writing places in the Library and elsewhere not permanently allocated which are used on a casual basis. A Member may also apply to the Serjeant at Arms for a desk either for a secretary or a research assistant; as the number of desks available in this category is limited to 200, no Member may be allotted more than one. Lockers are provided for Members, perhaps to remind them of school-days. Some filing cabinets are available.

There is deep dissatisfaction among Members over the shortage of private rooms: this emerged clearly from a survey undertaken in 1967 to discover the requirements of Members. A report from the Services Committee in 1969[1] accordingly proposed that the accommodation in the new parliamentary building to be erected in Bridge Street should be so designed as to provide each Member with his own room

---

[1] *Accommodation in the New Parliamentary Building:* 1968–69 (295) xv.

together with an adjacent room for a secretary. 450 Members would be so housed in the new building; adaptations in the Palace would provide for the more fortunate 180. The new building will also provide much needed extra space for the staff of the House. The Services Committee also suggested it should include a Conference Hall which could be used for a variety of purposes connected with parliamentary business during the session and which could be made available for wider use during the recess. Other ideas were for the provision of interview rooms for both radio and television and the introduction of some recreational facilities for Members including a swimming bath and a gymnasium. These improvements, when they materialise, will be long overdue. It is vital that a Member should have a private room where he can read, write, dictate letters and interview constituents and others who come to see him. In a period when progressive employers increasingly provide amenities for their employees, the suggestions of the Services Committee amount to little more than what is essential if Members are to carry out their duties effectively.

Information Services

Easy access to a wide range of information is essential if Members are to play an effective part in the tasks of government. The ever widening scope and complexity of public administration combined with technological progress and the flood of publications on all aspects of human endeavour have produced an information explosion which tends to make everybody—scholars, librarians and certainly backbenchers—feel a sense of hopelessness. Specialisation on particular topics will help Members to keep abreast of current events. They also need special facilities to enable them to gather information of particular concern to them; the facilities provided have two main facets, the free provision of certain official publications and the resources of the House of Commons Library.

Official publications are made available to Members through the Vote Office which is situated in the Members' Lobby adjacent to the Chamber. Those living within three miles of the Palace of Westminster enjoy a free delivery service by special messenger. The Vote Office supplies Members with the daily Order Paper or agenda for the House, the verbatim record of its debates, *Hansard*, in the daily parts, weekly edition and the bound volumes. Also provided are copies of Bills and Acts and parliamentary papers of the current and two preceding sessions. Older papers will be supplied if available and if a Member needs them for his parliamentary duties. The Minister in charge of a debate is expected to notify the Library beforehand of official publications of relevance to the subject and Members can ask the Vote Office for any of these documents.[1] But not all official documents of relevance to public policy are made available automatically to Members. In 1921, as part of an economy drive, the distinction was originated between parliamentary and non-parliamentary papers: the latter category are available free to Members only upon request and the free supply does not extend to some of the more expensive cultural and scientific publications issued by the Stationery Office. The theory is that parliamentary papers are those most relevant to current parliamentary business, but the boundary line sometimes seems arbitrary. The reports of the regional economic planning councils are classed as non-parliamentary, but these are always of concern to Members who are expected to watch the interests of their constituencies. Another rule is that parliamentary papers must be of royal octavo size: since statistical publications include large tabulations they are excluded from this category for a physical reason. However, since Members can readily obtain non-parliamentary documents, the distinction is not of importance to them. What can be of concern is that in some fields the flow of information has been reduced. Pre-1939 official committees of enquiry often published the evidence submitted to them; now, save in the case of Royal Commissions, publication is unusual. Annual Reports from Government Departments are withering. The Report of the Ministry of Housing and Local Government, which used to be a valuable annual record of developments in local administration, no longer appears annually. Reports from the Ministries of Labour and Works—to use the old titles—have disappeared. Further, some Reports from public bodies required to be issued by Act of Parliament are not published by the Stationery Office, nor are they available through the Vote Office; they can, however, be seen in the Library. If a Member wishes to have a personal copy of one of these documents he has to apply directly to the body that issued it and has no right to a free copy.

The total volume of publications issued by the Vote Office to Members is substantial: it exceeds an average of a thousand documents per Member per year. What proportion of these publications are actually read by Members cannot be known. They tend to consist of factual records of past events. Especially in the field of foreign affairs the official publications commonly make little contribution to the understanding of current international problems.[2] On the other hand, in economic matters there has been some movement in recent years

---

[1] Before 1966 Ministers were expected to supply the Vote Office with stocks of the relevant documents. Some Ministers over-provided and the Vote Office accumulated papers that were not required. H.C. Deb., Vol. 725, vol. 34.

[2] Peter G. Richards, *Parliament and Foreign Affairs* (Allen and Unwin, 1970), pp. 50–1.

to provide Members with more statistical information and fore-casts of future public spending.[1] It is inevitable that Ministers will seek to prevent the dissemination of material that could prove embarrassing. If Ministers issue long-term forecasts of public expenditure they could be making a rod for their own backs; equally, if there is a change of Government leading to fresh policies, then the forecasts become less meaningful.

The need for a wider range of information is met through the House of Commons Library. First established in 1818 it developed a nineteenth-century atmosphere which remained until after 1945. Members used the Library to write letters, to read, to have a short nap. The splendid suite of rooms overlooking the river was peaceful and serene. Since the last war the scene has changed steadily. Today the Library is an information workshop: it is not merely a library but a vital service for Members. More accommodation has been acquired. The staff has expanded substantially: in 1946 two research staff were recruited to assist Members: in 1970 a separate Research Division in the Library had twelve graduates on its staff.[2]

The Library has a stock in the region of 120,000 volumes and, with some exceptions, mainly reference works, Members can borrow books for a month. It has a full collection of British parliamentary papers and tends to specialise in law and the social sciences. There is a fair stock of British and foreign classic literary works but little modern fiction. Occasionally the Library receives a number of requests from Members for a recently published novel: this will be because some-body (possibly a Member) has suggested it is obscene and should be the subject of prosecution. The Library collects publications from the United Nations, the Council of Europe, the European Economic Community and other international organisations. Many Government publications are obtained from the United States and from Common-wealth countries. It takes a wide range of periodicals and newspapers from a large number of countries. Thus there is a vast amount of material about contemporary events available for Members, but it is of equal importance that this wealth of material should be analysed and arranged so that Members can be readily directed to items that concern them. Clearly, this is an endless task. Yet within the limits of available resources, much is done to help Members. Since 1966 the

---

[1] Cf. *Public Expenditure: A New Presentation*, 1968–69 Cmnd. 4017 liii and *Information and the Public Interest*, 1968–69 Cmnd. 4098 liii.

[2] The development of the Library is described by A. Barker and M. Rush, *The Member of Parliament and his Information* (Allen and Unwin, 1970), Ch. VI. Further accounts of the Library have been given by members of the Library staff: D. Men-hennet in *Political Quarterly* (1965), pp. 323–32 and G. Lock, *The Commons in Transition* (Collins, 1970), Ch. 7.

Library has subscribed to *The Times* press cuttings service. Visible strip indexes are maintained for major topics which show references to recent parliamentary debates and official publications on each topic. The International Affairs desk deals with Members' queries on events abroad. Sometimes the staff show a Member where the information required can be found: sometimes the staff will search out the information.

The more complex queries from Members are dealt with by a separate Research Division. In a sense this section is misnamed for it is not concerned with research as an academic understands the word— i.e. pushing forward the frontiers of knowledge. Instead a dozen graduates, specialists in various fields, try to find answers to the type of enquiry that cannot be satisfied by a fairly quick reference in the main library. For the most part, the Research Division communicates with Members through correspondence. Obviously, the more time a Member allows for a reply, the better service from the research staff will he receive. The Division also prepares reference sheets on particular topics, e.g. the reform of local government, which extend to several pages of references to recent official reports, parliamentary proceedings, press comment and general literature on the chosen subject. Occasionally pamphlet-length articles, known as Background Papers, are issued on items of topical concern, e.g. pollution. And a fortnightly Science Digest is prepared which summarises important articles from the scientific and technical press.

Since Members can put down questions on the Order Paper to be answered by Ministers—why is a separate service needed from the Library? The right to question Ministers is hedged around by many restrictions.[1] The subject-matter must lie within the responsibility of the Minister: thus no information could be obtained about economic and social conditions abroad or about particular British firms. Parliamentary questions must not be historical or theoretical. Nor will they be accepted if the answer has already appeared in published form. None of these restrictions apply to the work of the Library. And since ministerial replies tend to be cautious, a Member will usually get a fuller and more helpful answer if he directs his enquiries to the Library staff.

Development of the information services of the Library has created some problems. It is the duty of the Library to help Members on matters relating to their parliamentary duties. But 'parliamentary duties' cannot be precisely defined. It is possible that some of the help received by Members will enable them to increase their income from non-parliamentary sources. Again, it is the task of the Library to seek

---

[1] For a fuller discussion of parliamentary questions see pp. 105–10 *infra*.

information in an objective fashion: there is a proper reluctance to write up material for a Member in a selective manner favourable to a particular viewpoint. It is also important for the Library to maintain a high standard of accuracy even when working under severe pressure of time, for a memorandum from the research staff containing the reply to a Member's query may, within a few hours, become the basis of a speech in the Chamber. Above all, now that the research service has been firmly established, there is the issue of how extensive it should be. The service is available to all Members but is naturally little used by Ministers who can call upon the assistance of their civil servants: however, Ministers do sometimes use the Library if they want information about the business of another Government Department. Making allowance for this factor, roughly 560 Members can call upon the research facilities of the Library. If the total of graduates on the research staff is taken as fourteen (including two on the International Affairs Desk) then the equivalent of one-fortieth of a research assistant is provided for each Member. This is scarcely generous or excessive. Yet any expansion in the research service must encounter difficulties, quite apart from cost. Any considerable expansion of staff would raise acute problems of accommodation. Even more important is how far Members need and would use extended facilities. Barker and Rush asked Members in 1967 how often they used the services of the Research Division: 81% of Members claimed that they did so. Of these a third stated that they submitted a question once a fortnight and another third said they used the service once a month.[1] One Labour Member did not know of the existence of the research services. In general, Labour Members were more frequent customers than Conservatives and the younger Members were more regular users than the older Members. Barker and Rush also showed that many Members restricted the use made of the research services because they felt that the staff were hard-pressed and that the whole system would break down if much more pressure were placed upon it.

Further opportunities to gain information and experience come from visits arranged in connection with parliamentary business. It is increasingly common for Select Committees to make journeys at home and abroad to collect evidence. Apart from Select Committee work, a strong delegation goes to Strasbourg each year to attend the Consultative Assembly of the Council of Europe. There is a stream of parliamentary delegations to other countries in connection with NATO, the Commonwealth Parliamentary Association and the Inter-Parliamentary Union. These official trips are pleasant for Members: not only are expenses paid but they allow Members to be absent from

---

[1] *The Member of Parliament and his Information,* p. 310.

Westminster when Parliament is sitting without incurring displeasure from the Whips. The delegations reflect party strength in the Commons but Peers can be included in such a way as to leave unaffected the Government majority in the Lower House.

Of course, Members enjoy a variety of assistance and invitations which come to them because of their status as Members—but which are not officially provided. Information will flow in from their con-stituencies and from various organisations. A Labour Member sponsored by a trade union will be kept informed of the views of the sponsoring body. A Member who is a Vice-President of one of the local authority associations will be fully briefed on the policy of his associa-tion. But unsolicited information is normally slanted to promote a particular cause: it should be treated with caution. Similarly, Members should beware of some invitations, notably those to go on journeys overseas, as these may be intended to arouse sympathy for a certain policy or national cause.[1] Members also get some information from the research staff at their own party's headquarters. Briefs are made available outlining Party policy in advance of major debates and weekly newsletters are issued to Members containing the sort of material that is suitable for week-end constituency speeches. The duties of party research staff vary depending on whether the party is in office or opposition. In opposition the Shadow Ministers have a prior claim on the party's research service; in office the party leaders are served by civil servants and more time should be available to help backbench Members. However, the research department at Transport House is weaker than the Conservative Research Department and it appears to be fairly unusual for a Labour backbencher to get much individual assistance from his Party headquarters. Barker and Rush discovered that Conservative Members were far more satisfied with the support received from Party headquarters than were Labour Members.[2] But it must be emphasised that material supplied by a party organisation tends to have a political bite or slant to it; the standards of objectivity maintained by the Commons' Library staff do not apply.

Some vital information about affairs of state is not available to Members. Cabinet business has always been shrouded in secrecy. An incoming Government is not allowed to see the policy files of their predecessors. Advice given by civil servants to Ministers is strictly confidential to preserve the anonymity and impartiality of permanent servants. Official papers are now protected by the Official Secrets Acts, originally intended to prevent espionage by foreign agents. Thus there are formidable barriers which hamper Members who wish to discover

---

[1] Peter G. Richards, *Parliament and Foreign Affairs*, pp. 55–6.

[2] pp. 233–64.

trends in future Government policy. In some cases secrecy is essential, e.g. over coming tax changes and certain defence matters. Elsewhere it is rather a convenience for Ministers. There are occasions when information about future policy is 'leaked' to journalists and this forms the basis for accurate press speculation. Members, especially those on the Government benches, will gather news confidentially from friends who are Ministers. There is no doubt that Members do from time to time come to possess information that is covered by the Official Secrets Acts. In 1938 Duncan Sandys (Con. Norwood 1933–45 and Streatham since 1950) submitted privately to the Secretary of State for War the draft of a parliamentary question based on confidential information about the nation's aircraft defences. Sandys subsequently complained to the Commons that pressure had been put upon him to reveal the source of the information. There followed an enquiry by a Select Committee which reported that Members were not entitled to solicit the disclosure of confidential material but that Members did sometimes get access to such information and that it would affect their parliamentary duties if they did not. The extent of a Member's immunity from the Official Secrets Acts has not been precisely defined and the 1939 Report recommended that the Acts should not be used to impede Members from carrying out their parliamentary duties.[1] A Member must not seek to derive financial benefit from passing on confidential information. In 1970 Will Owen (Lab. Morpeth 1954–70) was acquitted of charges under the Official Secrets Acts. Owen was not and never had been a Minister. The allegation was that confidential material had come to him as a member of the Estimates Committee and that he had passed on some of this material to a member of the staff at a foreign embassy. It is a tribute to the probity of our public life that allegations of this nature are very infrequent.

---

[1] *Official Secrets Acts*. Select Committee Report: 1938–39 (101) viii.

CHAPTER 3

MEMBERS AND PARTY

Party Meetings and Committees

Party represents the informal dimension of parliamentary life. It is not merely a unit to organise and discipline Members; above all, it provides a forum for argument and a springboard for action. Unofficial gatherings of Members in party groups or committees now occupy a considerable amount of time. These private meetings are more popular than the average debate in the Chamber; thus when the House is thinly attended it is probable that some committee rooms are full. The reason for this preference is not hard to appreciate. Discussion in private is more frank and rewarding, and opinions critical of the policy of a Member's own party can be voiced with less embarrassment. Plans may be laid to exert pressure on a Minister, or information may be gathered for use in subsequent parliamentary speeches. At meetings of Government backbenchers a Minister may be there in person to hear criticism or answer questions; failing a Minister, the appropriate private parliamentary secretary will be present to take notes and report back to his master. At Opposition meetings tactics will be determined for assaults on ministerial policy. It is certain that proceedings at these informal groups have an important effect on the pattern of parliamentary debate and form a major channel through which, by collective action, Members can exert influence. The normal rule is that a Member is permitted to attend meetings of any committee formed by his own party, and notice of these committee and sub-committee gatherings is given on the weekly party whip. In choosing which meetings to attend Members are guided by their interests and experience, and by the nature of the constituencies they represent. Thus, company directors tend to go along to a Trade and Industry Committee; ex-officers gravitate to meetings about the Services; Members from rural areas feel it important to be present at the Agriculture Committee to keep abreast of developments that may be of concern in their localities.

The extent of these party committees has grown steadily in recent years, and a point has been reached at which a number of meetings by Members of one party may be in progress at the same time. Thus a Member may wish to be at two meetings at once. Although party committees have reached a new scale of importance since the war they are not entirely a modern development; the Unionist Agricultural Committee was in existence before 1914. The general meeting of

Conservative Members, the 1922 Committee, dates itself, and after its
formation a number of specialised groups concerned with each of the
Armed Services, Finance, Foreign Affairs and Trade and Industry
came into existence.[1] As shown below, the energies of Conservative Members have now created 17 committees and a further 5 sub-committees.
In the Labour Party the present system of Subject committees commenced in 1944 when Labour Members set to work to consider the
many problems of post-war reconstruction. Before this time a number of
advisory committees of Labour Members had existed, especially in
the late nineteen-thirties, but these became more or less dormant for
much of the war. In addition to Subject Groups, Labour Members
also have Area Groups whose functions are considered later. In all,
it is clear that these party gatherings are an important and fairly new
feature of parliamentary life, and one which makes a major demand on
the time of Members.

Both parties also have general meetings of Members at least
once a week when the House is in session. The 1922 Committee is the
Conservative forum and may be attended by all Conservatives and
Ulster Unionists. It owes its name to the group of Conservatives,
newly-elected in 1922, who started to hold private meetings for the
discussion of policy in the belief that there was insufficient consultation
between backbenchers and the party leadership. Both Austen Chamberlain's fall in 1922 and Baldwin's unexpected and disastrous dissolution
in 1923 helped to strengthen this view. The 1922 Committee, originally
frowned on by Conservative leaders, now occupies a position of major
importance in the Party organisation. When the Conservatives are in
opposition, members of the 'Shadow Cabinet' may attend (but not the
leader of the Party—the potential Prime Minister) although they have
no special *locus standi* and are considered ineligible for election as
officers of the Committee. When the Party is in office Ministers attend
to discuss policies for which they are responsible, and the Prime
Minister may come to talk about the general political situation,
especially just before the House goes into recess. The 1922 Committee—
the Conservative Private Members' Committee is the formal title—
meets normally each Thursday at 6 p.m. and its executive committee of
16 meets for half an hour before the full assembly. A Conservative
Whip is present at the full meeting to outline parliamentary business
for the coming week, and any of the items which are matters of contention within the Party may be discussed. Problems brought forward by
one of the functional committees may also be considered.

The 1922 Committee is essentially a political discussion group.
Resolutions are not proposed and votes are not taken. The 'feeling of the

[1] Sir W. I. Jennings, *Parliament* (C.U.P., 1939), pp. 358–9.

meeting' is, however, of much importance and is reported back through the Whips' Office to the appropriate Ministers. If the dissatisfaction of a meeting with official policy is great, a deputation may wait upon a Minister, or the Chairman of the Committee might see the Prime Minister; usually the informal channels of communication are found to be adequate. These matters are conducted in confidence and, as the Conservatives are adept at keeping party secrets, it is difficult to estimate how much influence the Committee wields. No doubt, it varies from time to time between subject and subject. Opponents of the Conservatives frequently allege that the 1922 Committee is the 'core of Tory reaction'; the impression is created of a body dominated by more extreme sentiments. It is often true that privacy is not an aid to moderation. Yet as all backbench Conservatives can attend the 1922 Committee, it can claim to be fully representative of opinion in the Party. Should it urge a Conservative Government to follow a more extreme—or liberal—policy, it is arguable that Ministers are out of tune with the prevailing view among their supporters. The guiding principle in Conservative organisation is that the Leader of the Party has the right to determine party policy; the 1922 Committee does not question this principle, but the replacement of Austen Chamberlain by Bonar Law in 1922 shows that it is unwise for a Leader to become too far divorced from his followers. Lord Morrison has suggested that Conservatives have a theory that Ministers, although responsible to the Commons as a whole, should not 'live too closely' with their backbenchers, who, in turn, retain the right to pass critical judgements in private on the policies of their leaders.[1] That is certainly the way that Conservative Members act in practice.

The full range of Conservative committees existing in the session 1970–71 is set out overleaf. The pattern changes a little as the distribution of functions between Ministries is altered and the number of subcommittees is less than it was ten years earlier.

In addition, regional groups of Conservative Members have been formed for Greater London, Scotland, Ulster, (the Ulster Unionist Party), the West Country and Yorkshire. The party committees receive some assistance from the Conservative Research Department at the Party's Central Office. When in opposition, each committee chairman will be the Shadow Minister for its subject. When the Party is in power the chairmen will be backbenchers of varying seniority and experience. Some will be ex-Ministers. In 1970 two had previously held office in the Department corresponding to their committee's sphere of interest;

---

[1] *Government and Parliament* (O.U.P., 1954), p. 131. Morrison was Labour Member for Hackney, S., 1923–24, 1929–31 and 1935–45, Lewisham, E. 1945–50 and Lewisham, S. 1950–59.

they were James Ramsden (Harrogate), chairman of the Defence Committee and William Deedes (Ashford), chairman of the Home Affairs Committee. Occasionally, a contest for a committee office has some political significance. In 1967 a Monday Club supporter, Ronald Bell (South Buckinghamshire), defeated a progressive Tory, Richard Hornby (Tonbridge), in the election of vice-chairman of the Education

CONSERVATIVE AND UNIONIST PARTY COMMITTEES

Conservative and Unionist Private Members' Committee
(the 1922 Committee)
Agriculture, Fisheries and Food
   Sub-Committees: Fisheries
                 Food
                 Forestry
                 Horticulture
Arts and Amenities
Aviation Supply
Broadcasting and Communications
Defence
Education
Employment
Finance
Foreign and Commonwealth Affairs
Health and Social Security
Home Affairs
Housing and Construction
Industry
   Sub-Committee: Shipping
Legal
Local Government and Development
Trade
Transport Industries

Committee: this was widely interpreted as a rebuff for the Shadow Minister Edward Boyle.[1] Conservative theory is that these bodies should be thought of as 'sounding boards' and since they operate in private it is impossible to make any precise statement about their influence. The Agriculture Committee is reputed to be important. The Trade and Industry Committee, and especially its chairman John

---

[1] Birmingham, Handsworth 1950–70. Created a peer 1970. Now Vice Chancellor University of Leeds.

Vaughan-Morgan (Con. Reigate 1950–70), was active and not un-successful in securing changes in the Retail Price Maintenance Bill.[1] In opposition the Foreign Affairs and Defence Committees both helped to frame the Party's east of Suez policy and the Commonwealth Affairs Committee was a natural focus for discussion of the Rhodesian problem. The chairmen of six subject committees jointly sponsored in October 1970 a Commons motion objecting to any extension of metrication. There can be little doubt that backbench pressure can be exerted effectively through this network.

Other groups to which Conservative Members belong are non-official and outside the ambit of the 1922 Committee. One example is the '25 Club' which opposes British entry into Europe. The contrary view is expressed by the Conservative Group for Europe, a larger organisation which extends its membership outside Parliament.

A party in opposition has the opportunity to frame long-term policy in preparation for the happy day when it returns to power. From 1964 onwards the Conservatives formed over thirty policy groups in anticipation of their resumption of office. Not all these groups were equally productive, but the sum total of their work was certainly of assistance to the Party leaders after their victory in 1970.[2] A typical policy group consisted of about six parliamentarians, including Peers and Members, and six outside experts, businessmen or academics. The appropriate Shadow Minister was chairman and the groups had the assistance of the Conservative Research Department. The composition of the groups was not published. They were chosen by Edward Heath and an attempt was made to include opposing schools of thought. The Law Reform group consisted solely of parliamentarians. To a large extent the Members of the Commons on these groups tended to choose themselves as being the more active participants on the relevant backbenchers' committee. One might expect the long-term planning of party policy to be exciting and important to backbenchers. In fact, it seems that only a minority of Conservative Members were keenly interested. But those who did make a significant contribution to the task of policy formation no doubt had a better chance of being invited to join the 1970 Government.

To turn to the Labour Party—here the organisation differs substantially from the Conservative system. The Parliamentary Labour Party has a formal democratic constitution; resolutions on policy are proposed and decisions are made by vote. Both Labour Peers and Labour Members belong but the Peers play a limited role. During

---

[1] R. Butt, *The Power of Parliament* (Constable, 1967), pp. 262–7.

[2] For fuller discussion see David Butler and Michael Pinto-Duschinsky, *The British General Election of 1970* (Macmillan, 1971), Ch. III.

the session the P.L.P. meets each Thursday evening to consider parliamentary business for the coming week and additional meetings are held as required to discuss policy issues. The pattern of leadership depends on whether or not the Party is in office. When it is in office a Liaison Committee is elected, composed of a minority of Ministers and a majority of backbenchers to keep the Cabinet in touch with rank-and-file opinion. The chairman is a backbencher. Under the Wilson administration there were two chairmen—Emanuel Shinwell,[1] who resigned in April 1967, was followed by Douglas Houghton (Sowerby). Houghton increased substantially the authority and reputation of this office; as a spokesman for backbenchers he had a significant effect on the Cabinet's decision to abandon the projected Industrial Relations Bill. In opposition, Labour Members elect an Executive Committee of the P.L.P. which comprises the Chairman, the Leader, Deputy Leader, Chief Whip and twelve other Members together with three Peers making a total of nineteen. The Leader of the Party used also to be chairman but in November 1970 it was decided to separate the two functions. Houghton again became Chairman. This Executive Committee forms the Shadow Cabinet and takes decisions on Party tactics in Parliament; its members become the frontbench Party spokesmen.

Discussions at P.L.P. meetings are often vigorous and argumentative. In the atmosphere of a Party meeting Members are willing to express their views with great frankness. On occasion the intra-party conflict has been more bitter than the conflict with Conservatives. There are quarrels over policy and disputes about party discipline. Left-wingers are often restive, not least when the Party is in office. Party leaders have to come to P.L.P. meetings to defend their attitudes and perhaps appeal for unity. The rows provide exciting material for journalists and the element of secrecy at these meetings has vanished. Detailed reports of what has been said appear in the press; one or more Labour Members must have leaked information consistently.[2] To try and ensure that material published about these proceedings does represent a balanced account, the P.L.P. decided that its Chairman should make a statement to parliamentary journalists which would outline the various views expressed.

At Party meetings the leadership sit at one end of the room facing the main body of those present, an arrangement which symbolises an element of confrontation between leaders and led. During the period of the Wilson Government the impact made on policy by backbenchers increased. The formal procedures of the P.L.P. remained

---

[1] Now Lord Shinwell: Labour Member for Linlithgow 1922–24 and 1928–31, for Seaham 1935–50 and Easington 1950–70.

[2] For the Allighan case see p. 12n *infra*.

unaltered; the greater influence was due to the exertions of back-benchers. Even in a parliamentary setting the crucial factor is political behaviour rather than formal institutions. The bonds of discipline and loyalty have been created by Members and can be destroyed by firm enough collective action.

A vote at a Party meeting is, of course, a 'free' vote, subject to the conventions about the collective responsibility of Ministers or the Shadow Cabinet. When in power, the chances of the Labour leadership being defeated are remote. A block of approximately one hundred office holders can be expected to give solid support to the Cabinet—plus the corps of parliamentary private secretaries. Is it good tactics for critics to challenge votes on items of policy? Any vote may under-estimate the support enjoyed by the dissidents. Even in the freedom of a Party meeting some Members may hesitate to oppose their leaders and the latter also enjoy substantial advantages in debate. The Prime Minister—as Party Leader—is allowed a longer time to speak than any one of his critics. If the pattern of proceedings were altered so that the leadership were subjected to a form of interrogation, then issues might be clarified more sharply and voting figures might be affected. Pressure for a change in policy may be most effective when a vote is avoided—as in the Conservative Party. In this way an impression can be created of major, if unmeasured, dissatisfaction; the feeling may spread that something should be done to alleviate discontent. If a vote is taken and party leaders enjoy the moral support of a decisive majority, they may be satisfied that their critics can be fairly and safely disregarded.

Labour Members form committees to study areas of state action in the same way as Conservatives. In the Labour Party these are known as Subject Groups. In opposition, the chairman of a Group may or may not be the Shadow Cabinet spokesman on the subject: in office, the chairmen are backbenchers. A proposal from a Subject Group affecting Party policy has to be approved by a full P.L.P. meeting; this ensures that specialised enthusiasm is held in check. My impression is that these Groups have been rather less effective than the corresponding Con-servative committees. John Mackintosh (Lab. Berwick and East Lothian), commenting on his experience of four Groups, found no evidence of their influence, 'the meetings being irregular with no minutes kept, there is no fixed membership and no concerted conclusion or action.'[1]

In the nineteen-sixties the Groups were too numerous. It was perhaps too easy for a Member to get agreement that a new Group be established to consider his pet subject, e.g. consumer protection. The

---

[1] *Political Studies*, February 1968, Vol. XVI, p. 116.

Groups, unlike Conservative committees, have no research assistance from Party headquarters. Attendance at meetings has often been poor. Even with a better attendance the gathering can still be unrepresentative of the Party as a whole. The Transport Group is said to be dominated by railwaymen. The Foreign Affairs Group has steadily attracted the more extreme left-wing Members: tension between this Group and a Labour Foreign Secretary has become traditional. Of course, the Groups behave in different ways. When Labour was in office, the Agriculture Group felt it should be present in the Chamber to support the Minister when he had to make a speech or statement likely to be ill-received by the many representatives of farming constituencies on the benches opposite. On such occasions the leading Members of the Agriculture Group would have in advance some indication of what the Minister was likely to say. As Prime Minister, Harold Wilson recognised the existence of these Groups by having occasional meetings with their chairmen as a means of keeping in touch with backbenchers.

After the 1970 Election the pattern of Subject Groups was revised in an attempt to make them more effective and also to fit the structure of government departments in the Heath administration. Their number was reduced from 26 to 16.

LABOUR SUBJECT GROUPS: 1970

Foreign and Commonwealth
Overseas Aid
Europe
Defence
Trade and Industry
Aviation Supply
Power and Steel
Economic and Finance
Employment
Food and Agriculture
Health and Social Security
Education and Science
Environment
Home Office
Post Office
Parliamentary Affairs

At the start of the 1970 Parliament the Chief Whip circularised all his Members and asked them to name not more than three Groups on which they would like to serve. It was emphasised that to belong to a Group should be regarded as a real commitment, that anyone who joined was expected to make a real contribution to its work. Many

Members opted for only two groups. Membership of sub-groups is decided by the parent body: decisions of sub-groups have to be reported to and approved by the main group. 'Junior shadows', the Members asked by the Party Leader to support frontbench spokesmen in the Chamber, serve on the appropriate Group. Each of these bodies is expected to keep a sector of Government activity under review and, where appropriate, consult trade union opinion so that a Labour alternative to Government policy can be formulated for presentation in the House in general debates or in discussion of Conservative legislation. A Member who attends a Group concerned with X is likely to be appointed to any Standing Committee that is giving detailed examination to a Bill about X.

The Parliamentary Labour Party also has a full set of twelve regional groups. In the past these have been neither very active nor successful. They are likely to make greatest impact where regional consciousness is high, e.g. Scotland and Wales, or where there is strong pressure for regional development in areas of high unemployment, e.g. North-East England. As from 1970 the intention is that the regional groups should liaise with the Party's regional organiser as an attempt to improve Party organisation and strengthen its electoral machinery.

There are other groupings, official and otherwise, among Labour Members. At each general election a small group of candidates are jointly sponsored by the Labour Party and the Co-operative Party. This produces a small number of Lab.–Co-op Members who meet occasionally to consider matters of special interest to the co-operative movement. Many Labour candidates are sponsored by trade unions. 114 such candidates were elected in 1970 and they form a Trade Union Group of Members. The twenty Members sponsored by the National Union of Mineworkers also have their own Group. The more extreme left-wingers in the Party gather together for regular discussions in what is popularly known as the 'Tribune' Group.

It is fairly rare for the corresponding subject committees from each side of the House to co-operate with each other. However, the Arts and Amenities groups did act jointly to persuade the Government to purchase land at the side of the National Gallery to make possible its future extension.[1] Yet Members of all parties, including Liberals and also peers, do come together on a wholly unofficial basis to promote particular causes. The intention may be to focus attention on particular sectors of public policy or assist certain interests. To list these informal groups would be futile since they come and go with the changing interests of Members. A few examples will indicate the range of activity. One of the oldest and best known is the Parliamentary and Scientific Committee

---

[1] A. Barker and M. Rush, *The Member of Parliament and his Information* (Allen and Unwin, 1970), p. 280.

which exists to disseminate information on scientific matters that affect public policy: in a sense this body can claim to be the precursor of the Select Committee on Science and Technology. The New Towns Parliamentary Group considers the special problems of the new towns. The Tourists' and Resorts' Group is supported by Members whose constituencies are deeply concerned with the holiday trade. There is a Channel Tunnel Parliamentary Group, but its officers do not represent any part of Kent. Other collections of Members try to protect the interests of disabled drivers, inland waterways, fisheries and forestry. The Civil Liberties Parliamentary Group and the United Nations Group seek to gather support for their respective causes.

Non-party activity is important for it ensures that parliamentary life is not wholly dominated by party feeling. It helps Members to appreciate the qualities of their political opponents, and to establish yet more firmly an underlying consensus about the value of parliamentary institutions.

The Whips and Party Discipline

Unity is an essential condition for the success of a political party. Fissions and internal feuds are exploited by political opponents and do grave damage to the degree of public confidence that a party can command. In the Commons the Government must organise its supporters to secure a constant majority, and the Opposition must keep together if its ability to provide an alternative government is to be beyond question. The repeated inability of Liberal Members after 1916 to vote together in the same division lobby did much to accelerate the decline of their party: the strife within the Parliamentary Labour Party before the 1955 General Election cannot fail to have had some effect on the election results. But while politicians understand the need to restrict controversy in the interests of their party, the internal clashes within parties are severe; Conservatives must accommodate the Monday Club and Labour must tolerate the Tribune Group. When the rifts become too deep to be restrained by pleas for unity, some form of eruption must follow. 'Damn your principles and stick to your party' may be sound tactical advice but it not infrequently fails to appease rebellious spirits. In a Parliament dominated by two parties, the range of opinion within each must be wide. Members of the same party have a variety of interests, experience, social background and temperament which can but lead to conflict. They represent constituencies that are quite dissimilar in composition. From the nature of their calling it is inevitable that most Members possess unusual qualities of vigour and determination and are not easily amenable to the discipline demanded by teamwork. It is in this setting that the Whips of each party must try to promote harmony by smoothing tempers or, more rarely, by indicating pained displeasure at the waywardness of an erring soul in their flock.

The two major parties each have about one Whip for every thirty Members.[1] In the Conservative Party they are appointed by the Leader of the Party: the Parliamentary Labour Party elects its Chief Whip and he nominates his assistants. Whips of the party in office hold Government appointments: the Chief Whip—usually known as the Patronage Secretary—is the Parliamentary Secretary to the Treasury, five of his assistants are Lords Commissioners of the Treasury, three more hold positions in the Royal Household, as Treasurer, Controller and Vice-Chamberlain and a further three or four assistant Whips are appointed. The Chief Opposition Whip and two of his assistant Whips now receive an official salary in addition to normal Members' pay.

New Whips are often chosen from Members who have served in the House for about four years; many Whips have devoted by far the greater part of their parliamentary life to this function. Not all Members are suitable for the task. Only one woman has so far been chosen: Mrs. Harriet Slater (Lab. Stoke-on-Trent, North 1953–66) was a Government Whip in the 1964 Parliament. The younger intellectuals in the Labour Party tend to be avoided. Great reserves of passion and an overpowering sense of political mission are natural disqualifications. A Whip must be utterly loyal to his party; he must be discreet, tactful and approachable; he must also be a 'political animal' able to sense the tide of opinion. It does not matter if he is devoid of strong convictions if he can still guide backbenchers as the party wishes. Yet the popular conception of a Whip as a man who dragoons his flock is far too simple; he is in turn advocate, interpreter, lightning-conductor as well as sergeant major. The success of the Whips may be measured by the degree of party harmony and they accomplish more by persuasion than by threats.

Government Whips tend to lose their identity as individual Members. They never speak in the House, save to move procedural motions. As Junior Ministers they are not called on to serve on Select Committees. Constituency business they deal with by correspondence with Ministers. Their public speeches are careful, restrained and devoid of announcements of policy developments which may attract publicity to other Ministers. Opposition Whips are not so constrained in their political activities and their whipping duties are more limited. It is not for them to command the order of parliamentary business and try to avoid procedural hindrances.

---

[1] The original term, 'whipper-in' was drawn from the language of the hunting field where a whipper-in has the duty of preventing hounds from straying from the pack. Cf. I. Bulmer-Thomas, *The Party System in Great Britain* (Phoenix, 1953), p. 109.

Whips of each party have an office and these are the nerve-centres of party organisation in the House. From here are issued on Fridays the weekly 'documentary whips' which inform Members of forthcoming business and request their attendance. Additional whips may be sent during the week if it is thought to be necessary. The extent of the under-lining of the request to attend a debate indicates its degree of signifi-cance. A single underlining intimates that no division is anticipated: double underlining means that the business is of importance and that a division is expected: three line whips are issued when a vital vote is due to take place, and on these occasions no excuse for absence is acceptable, barring serious illness. Each Whip has special responsibility in relation to a group of supporters and Members are divided by geographical areas for this purpose: regional Labour groups have a Whip who represents a constituency within the area, but this practice is not followed by the Conservatives. The first task of a Whip is to interpret the somewhat formal contents of the documentary whip to his group by explaining party tactics and—in the case of the Opposi-tion—when a major assault on Government policy is planned. Attempts may be made to keep such information confidential and it is not thought suitable to commit to paper. A Whip must also see that his group are in the appropriate lobby for every division and, therefore, have a shrewd idea of where missing Members may be found. As Members hurry from all parts of the House when the division bells are rung they need guidance on which lobby to enter. The Whips act as tellers in divisions. Other Members are tellers only when there is a free vote and the Whips are off, or if they are leading a rebel group that has forced a vote in defiance of party policy.

Whips of both main parties have a roster to ensure that some are always present in the House, and they spend longer hours in the Palace of Westminster than most Members. One is always on duty on the Treasury bench. Government Whips must not only keep Ministers in office, they must also organise the work of the House so that govern-ment business proceeds successfully and without unexpected delay. It is, therefore, a part of their function to 'keep a House' by main-taining the presence of a quorum of 40 Members.[1] If a division is to be

---

[1] It used to be the case that if a Member drew the attention of the Chair to the fact that less than 40 Members were present in the Chamber, a 'count' was called. The division bells rang and if 40 Members did not assemble within four minutes the sitting came to an abrupt end. Since November 1971, 'counts' have been abolished. However, if fewer than 40 Members vote in any division, the business under consideration cannot proceed and the House passes on to the next item of business. This change does ease the task of the Whips and gives backbenchers—especially Government backbenchers—more freedom, because there is no need to maintain the attendance of 40 Members unless or until a division is to take place. Another effect of this reform is that it should now be a little easier to secure the passage of private members' Bills on Fridays when attendance at the Commons is often low.

challenged it is necessary to keep more supporters in the House than the Opposition can muster; even if the Opposition appear disinterested, and most of them go home, the Government still require an attendance of a hundred to move successfully the motion 'that the question now be put'. Failure to have this motion accepted might mean that the business would be 'talked out' and no decision reached. So long as Government business is under discussion the Government Whips must ensure that roughly 120 of their supporters are present to provide a safety margin. It is traditional to think of party discipline in terms of disputes over policy, but a more constant source of trouble to the Whips is absenteeism. Whips on each side keep a careful record of attendance at divisions. Except when a three-line whip is in operation many Members will be paired—i.e. individual Members of opposing parties will make agreements to be absent on a particular occasion. These arrangements have to be notified to the Whips.[1] Members absent but unpaired will be asked to explain their behaviour. Yet if a Member, usually an older Member or ex-Minister, fails to attend or pleads illness when the Whips suspect he is reasonably fit—what is to be done? Of course, a Member out of favour with the Whips is unlikely to get a Government post, but this will not weigh with Opposition Members or with older Government supporters who have no hope of political promotion. Recalcitrant Members can be excluded from overseas trips or excluded from official hospitality; but such sanctions are not very potent. An appeal can be made to a malingerer's conscience, to his sense of duty to his constituents or his loyalty to party colleagues. Should all this fail, the only recourse remaining is a quiet word with leading officials of the Member's local constituency party; this would damage his local reputation and raise the threat that he would not be adopted at the next election. Even such local pressure can be useless when a Member has decided he does not want re-election.[2] No Member has lost the whip for chronic absenteeism: in such cases publicity is avoided by all concerned. Obviously the problem will be greatest as a General Election approaches, but less than six months after the 1970 Election the Labour Chief Whip indicated to one of his backbenchers that a critical message would have to be sent to his constituency party unless his attendance improved.

A Whip should possess a good understanding of the opinions of Members, above all of those who are in his special charge: this enables the Whips' Offices to forecast reactions to any political situation. Both

---

[1] For fuller discussion of pairing see 82p.

[2] The prospect of a life peerage might encourage Members to give more satisfaction to the Whips. Were the number of life peerages to be increased, as implied by the abortive 1968 proposals on House of Lords reform, then the increased patronage available to the Prime Minister and the Leader of the Opposition could have had a significant impact on Members' behaviour.

major parties have a 'pairing' Whip to supervise pairs. A Whip will want to know if any of his group of Members leaves the country, if only for a single day. The Whips also control nominations to parliamentary committees: sometimes this will mean gathering unwilling volunteers but if the assignment is attractive the Whips have to choose between the competing claims of Members wishing to serve. They also nominate official parliamentary delegations and are the channel for invitations to Palace garden parties and other forms of Government hospitality. The Vice-Chamberlain of the Household is responsible for messages to and from the Queen. Another Government Whip is deputed to keep an eye on private members' Bills and motions. A Labour Member who wishes to table a motion must first consult his Chief Whip; the latter, however, has no veto power. Except for the Chief Whip, his Deputy, the pairing Whip and the Vice-Chamberlain, Conservative Whips are allocated a range of Government business, covering one or more Ministries,[1] in which they are required to take a particular interest. They attend all relevant backbench committees and have to report daily to the Chief Whip on the trend of the discussions, and on the views of Members as a whole, on topics within their range. The Conservative Leader, and now the Prime Minister, will receive a summary of this information at the end of each parliamentary day. In some measure the work of Government Whips overlaps with that of parliamentary private secretaries[2] and they must be well informed on policy developments so, if necessary, uneasy Members can be persuaded of the merits of the official attitude. When a group of Conservative Members are critical of Goverment policy the Whips may arrange for them to see the appropriate Minister in the hope that personal discussion may minimise discontent. Conservative Whips communicate to their Chief Whip any significant private information they may collect in the House on a form known as a 'Dirt'. One such Dirt recorded the behaviour of a Conservative Member who, while drunk in the Members' Bar, had described the then Conservative Prime Minister as a 'bloody fool'.[3] One of the more terrifying aspects of Parliament is that indiscretions are carefully recorded and are not forgotten for some considerable time. Such is the efficiency of Conservative whipping it is surprising that the activities of John Profumo did not receive closer scrutiny. One has the impression that the Conservative Whips' Office

---

[1] In 1970 there was an eight-part division: Foreign and Commonwealth affairs; Scotland; Trade, industry and legal questions; Defence and home affairs; Agriculture, broadcasting and communications; Health, social security, finance and aviation; Employment, education and the arts; Environment, including housing, local government, planning and transport.

[2] For the work of P.P.S.s see pp. 208–9.

[3] Robert J. Jackson, *Rebels and Whips* (Macmillan, 1968), p. 42.

is run on the lines of a military staff headquarters in which liaison duties are carefully distributed to each individual in the organisation.

In the Labour Party the policy that Whips have to urge on the recalcitrant has usually been decided at a meeting of the Parliamentary Labour Party, and the issue tends to be one of obedience to party decisions. Conservatives do not decide policy in such a formal manner and for them discipline is a matter of loyalty rather than obedience. This helps to explain why expulsions—the withdrawal of the whip— have been far more common in the Labour Party, but Labour rebels have often regained the whip as an election approaches. Before the 1955 Election the whip was hastily restored to eight rebels: Aneurin Bevan (Ebbw Vale 1929–60), G. Craddock (Bradford, S. 1949–70), S. O. Davies (Merthyr Tydfil), E. Fernyhough (Jarrow), E. Hughes (S. Ayrshire 1946–69), J. McGovern (Glasgow, Shettleston 1930–59), S. Silverman (Nelson and Colne 1935–68) and V. Yates (Birmingham, Ladywood 1945–69). In 1963 the whip was restored to five Members who had been excluded from the Parliamentary Labour Party in 1961 for ignoring a decision not to oppose the service estimates; the five were Messrs. Davies, Hughes and Silverman again, together with Michael Foot (Ebbw Vale) and William Baxter (West Stirling). With-drawal of the whip is an extreme measure and does not normally follow isolated acts of rebellion: more frequently rebels are reprimanded by the Chief Whip and warned to be of better behaviour in future. And ambitious young men know well that excessive independence of spirit will not ingratiate them with their leaders.

The Parliamentary Labour Party is acutely aware of disciplinary problems and has a set of Standing Orders which embody the duty of Members to support party decisions. The existence of these Standing Orders, however, has not prevented overt disagreements in the Parlia-mentary Party. In 1946 the Standing Orders were suspended as an experiment, it being hoped that this action would help to foster good fellowship and co-operation between Ministers and their backbench supporters. The right to withdraw the whip was retained as an ultimate sanction. In spite of a number of large-scale rebellions these Standing Orders remained in abeyance until March 1952, when 57 Labour Members defied a three-line whip in a division on defence. Standing Orders were thereupon revised and reinstated but were powerless to prevent friction between the party leadership and the 'Bevanite' group of Members who believed that British foreign and defence policy should be less tightly linked to that of the United States. In a defence debate on March 2nd 1955 Bevan challenged the party Leader, Clement Attlee, on policy relating to thermo-nuclear weapons[1] and 62 Members

---

[1] H.C. Deb., Vol. 537, col. 2176.

failed to support the Party in the division lobby. The P.L.P. decided by 132 votes to 72 to withdraw the whip from Bevan. However, he received a great deal of support from constituency organisations and the whip was hastily restored just before the 1955 Election.

Standing Orders were again rescinded after the 1959 General Election, but were reimposed in 1961. At this period the Labour Party was consumed by a major controversy over its attitude to unilateral nuclear disarmament. 72 Labour Members with unilateralist or pacifist convictions abstained from voting in defiance of a three-line whip at the end of a defence debate in December 1960. Three months later, as noted above, five Members lost the whip for voting against the air estimates. But the argument about defence policy was carried not merely in the Parliamentary Party but in the Labour movement as a whole. About 80 Labour Members were opposed to the moderate policies of Hugh Gaitskell in respect of nationalisation and defence and this cleavage weakened the effectiveness of the Labour Party as a parliamentary opposition. Yet few dramatic clashes developed in the Commons. The tactical reasons for this are plain: left-wing policies were more likely to achieve success through winning votes at the Party Conference than by rows in Parliament.

The 1961 version of Standing Orders commenced as follows:[1]

'1. If the Party is to be an effective force politically, its activities must be co-ordinated and effective decisions taken. The privilege of membership of the Parliamentary Labour Party involves the acceptance of these decisions.

2. The Party recognises the right of Members to abstain from voting in the House on matters of deeply held personal conviction, but this does not entitle Members to cast votes contrary to the decision of the Party Meeting.'

No limit was specified to the range of issues on which Members might have 'deeply held personal conviction', so a Labour dissentient could summon conscientious scruples to his aid whenever he disagreed profoundly with a Party decision. Nor were restrictions placed on making speeches which attacked Party decisions, and Labour left-wingers rarely have a reputation for silence. Earl Attlee, when still Leader of the Opposition, was constrained to remark that 'conscience is a still, small voice, not a loud-speaker'. Other Standing Orders authorised the withdrawal of the whip by the Parliamentary Party and laid down procedures to deal with breaches of discipline.

The relative peace that followed had little to do with the existence of these rules. Harold Wilson's election as Leader in 1963, combined

---

[1] The various editions of the Standing Orders of the Parliamentary Labour Party are reproduced in Jackson, *Rebels and Whips*, Appendix III.

with a growing prospect of victory at the polls, served to diminish disputes. The tight-rope result in 1964 required full support for the Wilson Government in face of the constant threat that Ministers would be defeated in the Commons. Disciplinary problems revived with the secure Labour majority achieved in 1966, but the Government Chief Whip, John Silkin (Deptford), was determined to follow a liberal policy with rebellious backbenchers; indeed his policy was too lenient to please some 'loyal' Members who protested that the 'rebels' avoided the odium of voting for unpopular Government measures and escaped without any penalty for their conduct. In November 1966, the Parliamentary Labour Party established a new code of conduct which condemned personal attacks on other Labour Members and required any organised groups of Members to be registered with the Chief Whip: in return for these restrictions it was agreed that a broader interpretation be placed on the traditional conscience clause. This new and undefined freedom soon produced sharp conflict. 37 Labour Members voted against the Government's attempt to enter the Common Market while a further 50 abstained. Silkin then notified the rebels that the right to abstain on a matter of conscience did not extend to voting against the Government on an issue of confidence supported by a three-line whip. Almost immediately afterwards another revolt took place on prices and incomes legislation. In January 1968, 25 Labour Members abstained on a vote of confidence relating to cuts in government expenditure. The Chief Whip thereupon suspended the 25 from Party meetings but subsequently rescinded this decision after the backbench officers of the Parliamentary Labour Party complained that the Chief Whip had no power of suspension. Subsequently the P.L.P. agreed that the rebels be banned from Party meetings for one month. Shortly afterwards the P.L.P. adopted a new code of discipline by 116 votes to 18: the vital clause reads 'while the Party recognises the right of Members to abstain from voting in the House on matters of deeply held personal conviction, this does not entitle Members to vote contrary to the decision of a party meeting or to abstain from voting on a vote of confidence in a Labour Government'. Although the Chief Whip could reprimand Members, the power of suspension was to be exercised through the Liaison Committee of the P.L.P., a body elected by Labour Members which encompassed most shades of opinion with the Party. However, the lenient policy continued and Labour Members enjoyed *de facto* a greater freedom than ever before. Disputes and rebellions became a common occurrence. Major issues included prices and incomes legislation, the Parliament Bill, industrial relations and the increase in selective employment tax in the 1969 Budget. Normally the protests took the form of abstention but in May 1968 one Labour Member, Peter Jackson (High Peak 1966–70), voted with the Conservatives against the Prices and Incomes Bill. The Liaison Committee refused to allow Jackson to be suspended from Party meetings; instead he was severely reprimanded. 27 Labour Members voted against the Parliament Bill in February 1969 and a month later no fewer than 53 opposed the policy set out in a White Paper, *In Place of Strife*, designed to modify trade union law. In April, Silkin was replaced as Chief Whip by Robert Mellish (Bermondsey). It seems that the Prime Minister believed that the policy of flexible discipline was putting in jeopardy the Government's legislative programme and overall credibility. The change at the Whips' Office was followed by a reduction in back-bench revolts. However, this was largely due to changes in Government policy. The Parliament Bill was dropped, the prices and incomes policy faded away and the legislation on industrial relations was abandoned before the Commons came to discuss it. In session 1969–70 back-bench rebellion centred on foreign affairs, Vietnam, Cambodia and the supply of arms to Nigeria during the civil war; from the viewpoint of domestic politics this was far less divisive and more comfortable for the Government.

After Labour returned to Opposition in 1970, there developed a major difference of opinion over the Party's attitude to Europe. The Wilson Government had been in favour of entry 'if the terms were right'. Many Labour Members felt strongly that the terms negotiated by the Heath Government were as good as could be expected and should be supported. They claimed that the issue was not one of principle but of a price. However, the Labour Annual Conference in 1971 voted overwhelmingly against acceptance of the terms and so did the P.L.P. by 159 votes to 89. The pro-Marketeers resisted the trend in Party sentiment as 69 defied the Whip and supported entry to the Common Market in the division lobby.[1] This revolt was unique, not because of its size, but because of the status of those involved: they included the P.L.P. Chairman, Douglas Houghton (Sowerby), the Deputy Leader, Roy Jenkins (Birmingham, Stechford) and other senior ex-Ministers. No penalties were imposed on the rebels. Jenkins later held his position as Deputy Leader in the annual election. This whole episode, like the Bevan case in 1955, demonstrates the limitation of party discipline. If the split is deep, the Whips are seen to be men of straw. Discipline depends on loyalty as much as sanctions. While it can eliminate from the Commons individuals who consistently reject party policy, it is impotent when a party falls into opposing groups.

Certainly, the Labour Party at Westminster now has a more re-laxed attitude to discipline than in earlier years. No Member has had the whip withdrawn since 1963. Even Desmond Donnelly (Pembroke 1951–70), who developed strong right-wing tendencies, remained

---

[1] H.C. Deb., Vol. 823, cols. 2212–18.

undisciplined until he resigned the Labour whip himself in 1968. The parliamentary private secretaries who failed to support the recommencement of negotiations to join the Common Market in 1967 were dismissed; with one exception, they continued to operate unofficially and were subsequently re-appointed.[1] Why has the change occurred? In the Wilson period, as compared with the Attlee period, Labour backbenchers have tended to be younger, better educated and more vigorous. Independence of thought and action is more respected. In this climate of opinion it becomes difficult to impose sanctions on rebels. A Member who is disciplined tends to reach for a martyr's crown. The incident is widely noticed in the Press and damages the overall image of the Party by stressing and inflating the amount of internal dissension. And since the handful of professional rebels have little influence in the Party, disciplinary action serves to increase their importance.

The Conservative Party also has disciplinary problems but they are less severe than those of the Labour Party. In the nineteen-fifties the storm centre for Conservatives was the Suez Canal. In July 1954 the 'Suez Group' mustered 28 Members to oppose the Government motion approving the agreement with Egypt over the future of the British base in the Canal zone. Military action against Egypt in 1956 caused rebellion on both wings of the Party; initially a few left-wingers opposed the use of force and when the decision to withdraw from Port Said was announced fifteen Members in the Suez Group abstained on a vote of confidence. Such moments of great tension cause Conservative Whips to exercise their art of persuasion to the limit. P. Maitland, one of the fifteen Suez rebels mentioned above, subsequently spoke of the 'Westminster machine' using 'extraordinary and unexampled pressures, some of them altogether underhand, to force the Tories into line'.[2] Under the Macmillan administration there were a number of Conservative backbench protests against Government policy. These included the deportation of Chief Enaharo, the Wedgwood Benn peerage case,[3] the desire to abolish Schedule A income tax and the Commonwealth

---

[1] They were Alex Eadie (Midlothian), Michael English (Nottingham, West), Raymond Fletcher (Ilkeston), David Kerr (Wandsworth, Central 1964–70), Alfred Morris (Manchester, Wythenshawe), Laurie Pavitt (Willesden, West), Tudor Watkins (Brecon and Radnor).

[2] Reported in *The Times*, December 8th 1956. Col. Wigg (Lab. Dudley 1945–67) tried to use this statement as the basis of a complaint of breach of privilege. The attempt failed because only Maitland could initiate a complaint about the nature of the pressures to which he had been subjected. That the activities of Whips might constitute a breach of privilege is a novel and stimulating doctrine; if ever it were accepted, the effects on the character of the House of Commons could not fail to be profound! (Cf. H.C. Deb., Vol. 561, cols. 32–4 and 227–30.) Maitland was Member for Lanark 1951–59.

[3] pp. 15–16 *supra*.

Immigrants Act, 1962. But the major revolt came over the Profumo incident: John Profumo, then Secretary of State for War, resigned office after admitting that a personal statement he had made to the House was untrue.[1] 27 Conservatives abstained on a motion which criticised the manner in which the Government, and especially the Prime Minister, had handled the matter. This debate is memorable for a searing attack on the Prime Minister by Nigel Birch.[2] A few months later the Prime Minister did resign through ill-health. The biggest revolt against the Douglas-Home administration came in 1964 over the Resale Price Maintenance Bill. This Bill was in the special care of Edward Heath, then Secretary of State for Industry, Trade and Regional Development. 21 Conservatives voted against the second reading and others abstained.[3] After negotiations with the objectors, a compromise was reached. But even after these concessions, a clause to exempt drugs and medicine from the Bill was defeated by a single vote since 31 Conservatives voted against the Government and others abstained. The following year when in Opposition, the Conservatives were deeply divided over their attitude to the Rhodesian situation. In December 1965 when the Commons voted on the imposition of oil sanctions, the advice of the Tory leadership was to abstain, but 50 right-wingers voted against sanctions while 31 Conservatives supported the Labour policy of imposing them. This example is not so much one of rebellion against party policy, but one of an absence of policy. The Conservatives subsequently papered over the rift by urging more 'talks' with the Smith regime. After the Conservatives returned to power and before fresh talks could be arranged, the Government proposed to continue the sanctions against Rhodesia; this led to a backbench revolt with 23 Conservatives voting against their leaders while another 130 failed to attend the division.

Yet the number and size of Conservative rebellions is less than that on the Labour benches. Partly this is because of the Tory tradition that intra-party disputes should be conducted in private as far as

---

[1] Profumo had claimed untruthfully that his friendship with a Miss Christine Keeler was platonic. Since Miss Keeler also had an association with a member of the staff of the Soviet Embassy, the matter had wider implications. Profumo was Member for Kettering 1940–45 and Stratford 1950–63.

[2] H.C. Deb., Vol. 679, col. 99. Birch quoted Browning's poem *The Lost Leader*

> '. . . let him never come back to us!
> There would be doubt, hesitation and pain,
> Forced praise on our part—the glimmer of twilight,
> Never glad confident morning again!'

Birch, a former Junior Minister, was Conservative Member for Flint 1945–70.

[3] H.C. Deb., Vol. 691, cols. 377–80. It is never possible to give a precise figure for abstentions because Members may be absent from a division for a number of reasons other than as a protest.

possible—for example, the left-wing Conservative pressure in 1971 that arms sales to South Africa should be restricted to a minimum. One would also expect less agitation in a party that wishes to conserve rather than change. The Tories are not so wedded to formal procedures; their theory is that policy should evolve empirically in response to a changing situation. Ultimate authority rests with the Leader, not in a Party meeting as with Labour.

With the Conservatives a decision to withdraw the whip is a matter for the Leader and is less likely to cause controversy than a similar decision in the Labour Party. In fact, no Conservative Member has lost the whip since 1942.[1] It seems that Sir Martin Redmayne, Government Chief Whip from 1959 to 1964, did sometimes wish to withdraw the whip from persistent rebels but that Prime Minister Harold Macmillan always objected.[2] A Conservative Member who votes in the wrong division lobby will certainly have a difficult interview with the Whips, but his political career is more likely to be terminated by action in his constituency than by action in Westminster. Persistent rebels are unlikely to gain ministerial office although occasional unorthodoxy by Members of clear ability is forgiven. But the prospect of office is not always a strong inducement to good behaviour because the level of ministerial salaries is such as to be a positive disincentive for some Conservatives. Another aspect of patronage is the distribution of honours. In the past the Conservatives, when in office, made a regular distribution of titles to their backbenchers, but under the Heath administration these awards have been greatly diminished. The stronger buttress to Tory discipline is the appeal for loyalty. Potential rebels will be urged not to 'let the side down' or to give encouragement to opponents. This is well illustrated by evidence to the 1963 Select Committee on Procedure:

> 'Sir Kenneth Pickthorn. "You are really saying to everybody 'Do not be a cad, old boy'?" Mr. Martin Redmayne (Government Chief Whip). "Well I spend my life saying that." '[3]

In contrast, a dissident Labour Member will be told that he should obey the decision of a Party meeting, that as a good democrat he should accept the majority view. The right to express an opinion at a Party meeting is felt to be justification to impose restriction on public protest.

---

[1] This was Captain Cunningham-Reid, Member for Warrington 1922–23, 1924–29 and St. Marylebone 1932–45. In 1940 the Captain had refused a request from his local association to resign.

[2] R. J. Jackson, pp. 302–3.

[3] 1962–63 (190) vi Q. 14. Sir Kenneth Pickthorn was Conservative Member for Cambridge University 1935–50 and Carlton 1950–66.

There is a distinct difference in the approach to whipping as between the two major parties. Labour discipline is more obvious and publicised. It is more concerned with disputes between groups within the Party and more disposed to impose penalties not merely for defying the Party line but also for absence. A Labour Member who fails to attend a division without good reason may find that he is refused permission to pair for a while. Conservatives avoid penalties. Pressure on the recalcitrant is much more on an 'old boy' basis. And there is much greater emphasis on intelligence in the military sense of the word. Conservative Whips take careful note of what their Members say in private, both to keep a check on the state of opinion and so the discontented may be dissuaded from making unhelpful speeches in public. Compared with Labour, the Conservative technique is less formal, more sophisticated but no less effective. Indeed, the lack of public comment about Conservative whipping is a measure of its success.

During the nineteen-sixties Government backbenchers were more rebellious than Opposition Members—save during the 1964–66 Parliament when the Labour majority was so tiny that any left-wing defections would have invited defeat and the Conservatives were divided over Rhodesia. Why are Government supporters more irascible? One cause is that they feel some responsibility for ministerial actions; Ministers are their leaders; they maintain Ministers in office. There is always the prospect that a little waywardness in the division lobbies will induce desired changes in policy. Moreover, active party supporters in the constituencies will complain about the shortcomings of their 'own' Government and press Government backbenchers to exert influence. Opposition Members have less hope that Ministers will accept their views: they feel no responsibility for the Government and are not expected to have any. Constituency dissatisfaction can be met by blaming Ministers for whatever is felt to be wrong. Arguments within an Opposition can have no practical effect so, unless high principles and great passions are evoked, they are less worth pursuing to extremes. Further, it is easier for Opposition leaders faced with backbench dissent to find a fresh policy formula that will lower tempers: Ministers in the same situation have less room for manoeuvre since, for them, a fresh policy has immediate consequences. And if patronage—the hope of gaining ministerial status—is a major support for party discipline, it does not always work for the greater advantage of the Government. When an Opposition has high expectations of gaining power, the potential patronage attributed to the Leader of the Opposition is much greater than the actual patronage available to the Prime Minister. A change of Government provides at least 70 jobs but once a Government is formed there is only a trickle of ministerial vacancies to be filled through deaths, resignations and shuffles.

So far this discussion of discipline has been in terms of failure to vote in support of party policy in the Commons. Of course, there are other ways in which Members can be awkward. They may threaten to rebel in advance; if the threat is successful, then there is no critical vote. Labour plans to nationalise steel in 1965 had to be postponed because of opposition from Desmond Donnelly, George Strauss (Vauxhall) and Woodrow Wyatt (Birmingham, Aston 1945–55 and Bosworth 1959–70). The Industrial Relations Bill, 1969, was withdrawn by the Labour Government in anticipation of the extent of backbench defection it would have caused. Members commonly give expression to their opinions by signing motions which appear on the Commons' Order Paper; these motions can be critical of official party policy and warn the Whips of forthcoming trouble. Members also have many opportunities to express their views outside Parliament and, if they are sufficiently controversial, the mass media will provide wide publicity. Opinions on racial questions expressed by Enoch Powell (Con. Wolverhampton S.W.), which caused much concern among the Conservative leadership, have been voiced on public platforms rather than in Parliament. Outside Parliament a Member can support an organisation that is hostile to his own Party's policy. Some Labour Members joined the Campaign for Nuclear Disarmament: Conservative Members joined groups opposed to Britain's entry into the Common Market. Opportunities to criticise are unlimited and the activities outlined in this paragraph, while not normally involving a breach of discipline may well do more damage to party harmony than an adverse vote in the division lobbies.

Occasionally a Member will resign the whip in protest against some aspect of party policy. Such action is tantamount to ending a parliamentary career unless he recants and asks to have the whip restored. The sole exception to this rule in recent times was Sir David Robertson who forsook the Conservatives in 1959 over their policy towards the Highlands and held his seat in the 1959 Election as an Independent.[1] Other Conservatives to resign the whip have been Sir William Duthie (Banff 1945–64), Dr. Donald Johnson (Carlisle 1955–64) and Geoffrey Hirst (Shipley 1950–70). This behaviour is less common with Labour Members although Reginald Paget (Northampton) did resign the whip in 1966 over Government policy on Rhodesia; subsequently he agreed to return to the Labour fold.

Members are sometimes permitted the luxury of a 'free' vote when the Whips are off. This has become traditional on issues of conscience involving religious and moral questions.[2] Measures concerning the

---

[1] Sir David was Member for Streatham 1939–50 and Caithness 1950–64.

[2] For fuller discussion see Peter G. Richards, *Parliament and Conscience* (Allen and Unwin, 1970).

Established Church are always decided on a free vote and the Commons rejected a revised version of the Prayer Book in 1927 and 1928 with Ministers voting in opposite lobbies. Free voting is normal in private members' time although the Government will always secure the defeat of a Bill or motion to which it objects strongly. Very occasionally an issue arises in Government time which is not thought to have any party significance: the decision in December 1970 to return to Greenwich Mean Time in the winter months was the result of a free vote. Ministers will not allow freedom to their supporters whenever there is a clear Government policy unless quite special political difficulties are involved, for to do so is to invite defeat especially when the Opposition is hostile. Both the Attlee and Eden Governments created grave embarrassment for themselves by allowing free votes on the capital punishment issue.[1] Normally the Opposition can more easily remove the Whips for it has no responsibility for implementing whatever the House may decide.

However, the most dramatic of all free votes was that allowed by the Heath Government in October 1971 on the principle of entry to the Common Market. There is no precedent for a Government to allow a free vote on the cardinal item of its whole programme. One may be sure that the move was a product of careful calculation. Many Conservative Members would have defied the whip had it been imposed: to remove the whip was not to cost Ministers many votes. The grant of a free vote opened the prospect that the Labour Opposition would feel compelled to follow the same course; even if this did not happen, the Conservative free vote was designed to make it easier for Labour pro-Marketeers to support the Government motion. The Parliamentary Labour Party rejected the idea of a free vote on the Common Market issue by 140 votes to 111. Even so, the Conservative tactics were successful for no fewer than 69 Labour Members supported entry into Europe in the division lobbies and helped to produce the majority of 112 for the crucial motion. The six-day debate that preceded this decision was the major parliamentary event of recent times; the drama of the occasion was augmented by the Conservative free vote which created additional uncertainty about the size of the pro-European majority.

---

[1] *Ibid.*, Ch. 3.

CHAPTER 4

THE FRAMEWORK OF PARLIAMENTARY BUSINESS

The Speaker and Chairmen

The first business of a newly-elected House of Commons is to choose a Speaker to preside over its debates. The Speaker embodies the authority of the House, enforces its rules of procedure and interprets them whenever necessary. He is the First Commoner in the Realm and in the table of precedence comes immediately behind the Prime Minister and the Lord President of the Council. He receives a salary of £13,000 per anum and has a residence in the north-east corner of the Palace of Westminster. Traditionally it has been the task of the Speaker to represent the views of the Commons to the Crown and to uphold the rights and privileges of individual Members: in modern times he has ensured a fair hearing for minority opinion in the Commons. The office of Speaker is deeply respected by Members, for it is recognised as being a guardian of their own status. The Speaker has no gavel with which to call for order, but when he rises in the Chair calm falls on the most excited debate. No doubt this ascendancy is assisted psychologically by the robes of office, but the Speaker himself may seem to be a lonely figure, isolated in the Chair from the cut and thrust of party warfare. It has been well said that the moral authority of the Speaker is far greater than his power, for any motion passed by the House relating to the conduct of its business must be accepted and enforced by him. An action of the Speaker may not be criticised inferentially during the course of a speech: his conduct is open to challenge solely on a specific motion to that effect.

When called to the Chair a Speaker abandons all his political connections and since 1870 has not spoken in the House save on procedural questions. Since 1835 he has been re-elected by successive Parliaments irrespective of any change in the political complexion of the House. If a vacancy occurs through death or retirement a new Speaker is chosen from the majority party; the selection is made by the Cabinet but it is the custom for the election to be moved and seconded by backbenchers. There are no clear conventions governing the choice. At the end of the nineteenth century it was generally accepted that Ministers were ineligible and that the traditions of the office made it appropriate to select a backbencher who had not been over-active in party controversy. Sometimes the man appointed was relatively unknown.

But in this century the practice developed of promoting either the Chairman of Ways and Means or the Deputy Chairman—these are the only two Members who may deputise for the Speaker.

The election of Speaker W. S. Morrison (Cirencester 1929–59) in 1951 failed to conform to pattern in three respects. For the first time since 1872 a Speaker with ministerial experience was chosen: for the first time since 1895 neither the Chairman of Ways and Means nor the Deputy Chairman was chosen: for the first time since 1895 the election of the Speaker was contested and forced to a division.[1] There was no explanation why the obvious candidate, Sir Charles MacAndrew,[2] was passed over. In 1959 the Solicitor-General, Sir Harry Hylton-Foster (Con. York 1950–59, Cities of London and Westminster 1959–65), was chosen without a division to succeed Speaker Morrison. Partly to offset the ill-will caused in 1951 the Conservative Government had been prepared to suggest Sir Frank Soskice, a former Labour Law Officer; but Sir Frank declined.[3] On the death of Speaker Hylton-Foster in 1965, Dr. Horace King[4] became the first Labour Speaker. As Dr. King was then the Chairman of Ways and Means his selection was a return to the pattern established in the first half of the century. In 1971, Speaker King was succeeded by Selwyn Lloyd (Con. Wirral). Speaker Lloyd had held high ministerial office yet his case was not on a par with Speaker Morrison since he had firmly established himself since leaving the Cabinet as a 'good House of Commons man', especially through his work on the House of Commons Services Committee—the 'house-keeping' committee concerned with Members' facilities and accommodation.

Since the historic duty of the Speaker is to protect the rights of private Members, it is arguable that a man with a ministerial background should not be chosen. Certainly no one should ever move directly from the Government to the Speaker's chair. Exactly how the Speaker should be chosen has often been a bone of contention, not least in 1971. The election in the Commons is merely a formal ratification of what has been decided elsewhere. In 1965 and 1971 the choice was agreed between opposing front benches; on both occasions the Shadow Cabinet had a large part in the decision. In 1971 backbenchers on both sides of the House were irritated because they had been ignored

---

[1] H.C. Deb., Vol. 493, cols. 2–24.

[2] Conservative Member for Kilmarnock 1924–29, Glasgow, Partick 1931–35 and Bute and North Ayrshire 1935–59. Sir Charles was Deputy Chairman of Ways and Means in 1945 and 1950–51, and Chairman of Ways and Means 1951–59.

[3] H.C. Deb., Vol. 612, cols. 6–14. Sir Frank Soskice was Labour Member for Birkenhead, East, 1945–50, Sheffield, Neepsend 1950–55 and Newport (Mon.) 1956–66.

[4] Member for Southampton, Test 1950–55, Southampton, Itchen 1955–71.

and 55 Members voted against the election of Speaker Lloyd not on personal grounds but as a protest against the procedure that had been followed. There was a strong body of opinion that some fresh method of selection should be found.[1] Clearly it is desirable that all parliamentary opinion should be heard. Yet if a Speaker retires at a dissolution, as in 1951 and 1959, there must be special difficulties in the way of choosing a successor. In this situation if some type of informal ballot were arranged it might seem reasonable to exclude new Members with no parliamentary experience.

Because the Speaker must maintain a position of strict political neutrality, he is in difficulty when forced to defend his seat at a general election. It would be unfitting for him to praise or criticise the Government and, therefore, to campaign in the normal fashion. Until 1935 the Speaker was usually re-elected unopposed, but since then he has been opposed regularly by minor party or independent candidates. If the Speaker did not represent a fairly safe 'seat', his presence in the Commons after an election could not be guaranteed. Another unsatisfactory aspect of this situation is that the Speaker's constituency is virtually disenfranchised, for its Member is not able to represent local interests as other Members do. A Select Committee was appointed in 1938 to examine these problems, but would not accept any of the innovations proposed to it. The best suggestion was that the Speaker should represent a special constituency, St. Stephen's, for which the only electors would be Honourable Members: this would both eliminate any disadvantages the Speaker's constituents may be thought to suffer and isolate his election from political controversy. The Select Committee rejected this idea for the peculiar reason that the Speaker would be left without a seat in the House should the House itself decide not to re-elect him.[2] As the Commons have not refused to re-elect the Speaker since 1835, this contingency seems more unlikely than the possibility of a Speaker losing his seat if he continues to represent an ordinary constituency.

The offices of Chairman of Ways and Means and two Deputy Chairmen[3] are political prizes in the sense that they change hands when the party in power is replaced by another. Normally Government supporters, backbenchers with considerable parliamentary experience, are chosen. These Members act as Deputy Speakers: unlike Mr. Speaker they retain party allegiance but, like him, they never vote or

---

[1] H.C. Deb., Vol. 809, cols. 1–26.

[2] Cf. Parliamentary Elections (Mr. Speaker's Seat). Select Committee Report, 1938–39 (98) viii. In 1963 the House of Commons rejected the idea of a St. Stephen's constituency by 76 votes to 68.

[3] A second Deputy Chairman—and third Deputy Speaker—was appointed for the first time in 1971. He was E. L. Mallalieu (Lab. Brigg).

contribute to debates. When a Government had a narrow majority as in 1950, 1951 and 1964, it was unwilling to 'waste' two supporters in these posts: on such occasions one or two Opposition Members have been chosen. In 1970 came the first woman Deputy Speaker with the appointment of Miss Harvie Anderson (Con. Renfrew East).

Independence and impartiality of the Chair are crucial to the separate status of the House of Commons. The price now paid for the valuable tradition is that, in some senses, four constituencies are disenfranchised. This is noticed less by the constituents of Deputy Speakers since their Members continue to contest elections in the normal party manner. One suspects that there would be greater public protest if the limitations placed upon Deputy Speakers were more widely appreciated. It is possible that acceptance of this office by Roderick Bowen (Lib. Cardigan 1945–66) may have contributed to his defeat in a highly marginal constituency.

The Chairman of Ways and Means has a salary of £6,750 per annum; his assistants, the Deputy Chairmen of Ways and Means, have a salary of £5,500 per annum. These Members can take the Chair when the House is in Committee and the Speaker may not be present. The Chairman of Ways and Means has the delicate task of deciding which amendments shall be selected for discussion when a Bill goes to a Committee of the Whole House. He is also responsible for the supervision of Private and Personal Bills and for seeing, when necessary, that an opportunity is found to debate them. When the House is in Committee the Chair may also be taken by a Temporary Chairman who is on the Speaker's Panel. In 1948, Mrs. F. Paton (Lab. Rushcliffe 1945–50) became the first woman to preside over the Whole House as Temporary Chairman.

The Speaker's Panel is a body of about eighteen Members chosen by the Speaker who act as Chairmen of the Standing Committees. They are unpaid for these services and come from both sides of the House. Members on the Panel do not abstain from Party warfare, except when in the Chair, but Members with violent and extreme opinions are probably not selected by the Speaker for this purpose. The Panel meets occasionally to discuss difficult points of procedure that may arise in Committee. A Chairman may be called on to decide whether an amendment to a Bill is outside the terms of the financial resolution passed by the whole House, or if a starred amendment— one that appears on the Order Paper for the first time—should be rejected because there has been inadequate time for prior consideration. It is generally agreed that the Chairmen reach a high standard of impartiality and their judgement is accepted without question. Thus an Opposition supporter, occupying the Chair, may rule out of order a motion or a speech by a Minister, and this is indicative of the atmosphere in which parliamentary business proceeds. The Chairman and

)eputy Chairmen of Ways and Means are often chosen from Members
vho have obtained appropriate experience through service on the Panel.

The procedure of the Commons is admittedly complex. New Mem-
)ers returned at a general election are invited to attend lectures by the
:lerk of the House to help them to master it. Intricacy arises because of
ittempts to achieve a compromise between conflicting requirements—
he need for a Government to complete its business and the need for
Members to have reasonable opportunity to voice opinions and grie-
/ances. The present volume does not describe the details of procedure,
)ut some aspects will emerge in the following pages which sketch
he parliamentary scene and the pattern of parliamentary endeavour.

The Pattern of Parliamentary Behaviour

The Commons' Chamber is rectangular in shape and is divided length-
wise by a wide central aisle which separates the parallel benches facing
each other. Thus is symbolized the division of the House between
Government and Opposition. At one end of the aisle is placed the
Speaker's chair, below it sit the Clerks of the House and in front again
are the two dispatch-boxes used by frontbench spokesmen when making
a major contribution to the debate. At the other end is the bar of the
House, where those who have offended against the dignity or authority
of the Commons may be brought for judgement. Immediately behind
the bar is the seat of the Serjeant-at-Arms. The benches contain room
for 346 Members and a further 91 can be accommodated in the side
galleries; Members may address the House from the galleries, although
this is inconvenient and never done, but they cannot speak from seats
on the floor of the Chamber which are 'below the bar' and, therefore,
farthest from the Speaker. In the middle of the Chamber, at right
angles to the central aisle, a gangway runs up between the benches
on both sides. The allocation of seating in the House is governed by
ancient convention. The Treasury Bench, the front bench above the
gangway on the Speaker's right hand, is occupied by Ministers: on
major parliamentary occasions Junior Ministers may be crowded off
and they retire to the bench immediately behind. On the front bench to
the Speaker's left sit the leading Members of the Opposition—Privy
Councillors, the 'Shadow Cabinet' and any Members who may have
been invited to make a major speech for the Opposition on that particular day. No permanent reservation of seats is allowed, but as a matter
of courtesy a few eminent backbenchers will always be allowed to
occupy the place of their choice. A Member who intends to be present at
prayers at the start of a sitting can place a 'prayer card' on a bench;
this card has to be obtained personally from an attendant at the House
at any time after eight a.m. on the same day.

After the election of the Speaker a new House of Commons proceeds to take the oath of allegiance. Since 1888 Members have been allowed to make an affirmation in lieu of an oath if the oath is contrary to their beliefs. A Member need not take the oath at the commencement of a Parliament, but he may take no part in business until he has done so. The House as such no longer attempts to compel the attendance of Members, for this function is undertaken by the Whips. At the opening of a Parliament those returned for the first time take the oath in the same way as other Members, but Members returned at by-elections are introduced at the end of question-time by two sponsors: in 1945 Dr. MacIntyre[1] attempted to take the oath without sponsors but the House, on a division, refused to agree.

A new Parliament meets after a general election and, therefore, may be summoned at any time of the year; it continues to sit, apart from adjournments for the recognised holiday periods, until the prorogation. Prorogation is normally in the autumn and takes place only a short time before a new session is convened. Pressure of business means that the hours of labour for Members are much longer than in the nineteenth century when it was common for the session to open in February and end in July or August. In modern times the House sits on average for 35 weeks in a session, and the burden of committee work is far greater. From Mondays to Thursdays the House meets from 2.30 p.m. to 10.30 p.m., unless the closing time is postponed for one of a number of possible reasons: on Fridays the sitting lasts usually from 11 a.m. to 4.30 p.m. Thus in a normal week the House will be in session for $37\frac{1}{2}$ hours. But few weeks are normal. The House may agree to sit later than 10.30 p.m.; more rarely it will rise early if a debate collapses through lack of interest. Occasionally, morning sittings are held. As a result the length of the parliamentary day tends to grow and is certainly longer than it was in the nineteen-fifties. In 1968–69 the average parliamentary day was nearly $9\frac{1}{2}$ hours.[2] This must mean that Members are working harder and have more opportunity to participate in debates.

Each sitting commences with prayers. Then follow items of uncontentious business which may include a reply to an address to the Crown delivered by the Vice-Chamberlain of the Household;[3] communications to the Speaker; the announcement of the death of a Member; motions for writs for by-elections[4] and unopposed private business.

---

[1] Scottish Nationalist Member for Motherwell for two months.

[2] In 1957–58 the House sat for 1234 hours on 156 days; 53 hours were outside 'normal' hours. In 1968–69 the House sat for $1547\frac{1}{2}$ hours on 164 days; 413 hours were outside 'normal' hours. The average duration of the parliamentary day rose from $7\frac{1}{2}$ hours to almost $9\frac{1}{2}$ hours.

[3] A Member who acts also as a Government Whip.

[4] If a writ is opposed, consideration of it is deferred until after questions.

These items occupy but a few minutes and the remaining time until 3.30 p.m. on Monday to Thursday is devoted to questions.[1] (There is no question hour on Fridays.) The main business of the day due to start at 3.30 p.m. may be preceded by any of the following matters, each of which has priority. New Members are introduced to take the oath. Any Member may seek to move an emergency adjournment of the House.[2] The result is announced of the ballot to determine which Members shall move motions in private Members' time.[3] Ministerial statements explaining the policy of the Government may be made. A Member may give a personal explanation or apology arising from a previous speech in the Chamber. This is also the time for raising matters of privilege,[4] the formal introduction of public bills and for a back-bencher to bring in a bill under the Ten-Minute Rule.[5] Finally, Government motions relating to the business or the sittings of the House may be moved; a common form of such a motion is to postpone the termination of the main business of the day from ten o'clock to eleven o'clock.

When all these items have been completed, the House proceeds to the main business—the Orders of the Day. On the majority of sitting days only one or two matters arise in the categories described in the paragraph above, and it is unusual for the House to fail to reach its main business by 4 p.m. Most time is consumed by the passage of legislation[6] and the consideration of Opposition criticisms of the Government on Supply Days.[7] The normal closure at ten o'clock may be postponed— as already noted—by resolution of the House, and does not apply when business exempt from the ten o'clock rule is under discussion. The chief forms of 'exempted business' are the annual Finance Bills and proceedings pursuant to an Act of Parliament, which covers parliamentary examination of Statutory Instruments.[8] In addition, when ordinary business is interrupted for an emergency adjournment debate, the ten o'clock closure is postponed for a period equal to that of the interruption. And however late the hour at which other business ends, the motion 'that the House do now adjourn' can be discussed for thirty minutes by a backbencher who raises a topic of which notice has been given.[9]

The whole of the time of the House is now controlled by the Government, apart from the 29 Supply Days when the Opposition chooses the subjects for debate, and the 24 occasions still permitted for private members' bills and motions. It is the responsibility of the Leader of the

---

[1] For a description of question-time, see pp. 105–10.

[2] See pp. 110–11.   [3] See p. 114.   [4] See pp. 185–97.

[5] See pp. 143–4.   [6] See pp. 97–104.   [7] See p. 95.

[8] See pp. 104–5.   [9] See pp. 111–13.

House and the Government Chief Whip to plan the parliamentary timetable so that time is available for Government legislation and for the discussion of the most urgent matters of public policy. The Leader of the House announces the business for the coming week on a Thursday afternoon in reply to a question from the Leader of the Opposition. The content of the business statement is made known to the Opposition Chief Whip on Tuesday evening. This provides an opportunity for confidential negotiations between the Chief Whips of the main parties, commonly known as the 'usual channels', if the Opposition wish to have the pattern of business adjusted. The Labour Party likes to avoid controversial debates that lead to divisions on Thursday evenings: the reason is that if Members from Scotland, Wales and the provinces can leave early on Thursdays, their London hotel-bills are reduced. There is a great deal of flexibility in the parliamentary timetable and when the usual channels are working smoothly adjustments are readily made to minimise inconvenience to Members. If the Opposition wish to discuss a topic for which the Government can find no time, the Opposition may agree to cut short the debate on a Government bill and use the time thus saved to their own desires. Such arrangements originating in the usual channels are made known to Members by the Whips and constitute an unofficial timetable for the day's proceedings; they would tend to become inoperable if there were any considerable number of independent Members in the Chamber. An individual Member has little influence over the pattern of parliamentary activity, but if there is evidence of a widespread desire to debate a particular topic the Government does its best to be accommodating so far as the limited time available permits. At times of high political tension the normal friendly relations between the usual channels may deteriorate. Government and Opposition will cease to co-operate. Parliamentary life will become rougher. The Leader of the House will be less able to steer its business smoothly until a sweeter atmosphere returns. Management of the parliamentary programme is a delicate art, and the temper and quality of debate depends to a great extent on the skill with which the programme is stage-managed.

The shortage of parliamentary time also limits severely the period for which any single Member can expect to be able to claim the attention of the House. Choice of those who are called to participate in debates rests entirely upon the discretion of the Speaker, but is also conditioned by convention. A major debate is opened by a speech from each of the front benches, and is ended in the same fashion: the normal maximum debating time for the main business of the day is $6\frac{1}{2}$ hours of which at least two will be used by front-bench speeches. It follows that backbenchers do not usually command the ear of the House for more than $4\frac{1}{2}$ hours a day or, allowing 4 hours on a Friday, for more than roughly 22 hours a week, excluding question-time and the adjournment periods. This calculation can be made only in very general terms. A plethora of ministerial statements or verbosity from opening speakers will curtail the opportunities of backbenchers, but any postponement of the ten o'clock closure will increase them. On the basis that there are about 35 weeks in a session, there is an average of less than two hours of debating time per backbencher each session. Most Members do not obtain even this meagre ration, for backbench Privy Councillors—ex-Ministers—have precedence over their less distinguished fellows.

Members who wish to address the House rise in their places when a speech is concluded.[1] Those who are wise will have mentioned their desire to the Whips or will have written to the Speaker. The Whips advise the Speaker informally of the names of their supporters who hope to join in a debate, but they have no control whatsoever over the Speaker's choice. Whips may also ask a Member to be prepared to speak if it is felt that he could make a useful contribution, or if a debate seems in danger of dying inconveniently. The Speaker attempts to distribute the time available in such a way as to produce the most varied discussion and Members tend to be called from alternate sides of the House. Holders of less orthodox opinions often find it easier 'to catch the Speaker's eye'. Independents and Members belonging to minor groups enjoy a generous proportion of the attention of the House. The Speaker, being human, is more likely to favour Members known to be lively and witty debaters than those with the reputation of being tedious bores. Members who seldom wish to speak are also less likely to go to bed with their speeches unrecorded. But after most important debates there must be a number of frustrated Members who have sat through many speeches in the unrealised ambition of being asked to address the House themselves.

A verbatim record of everything said aloud in the Chamber is printed in *Hansard*, which is a daily publication when the House is sitting. There are strict rules about maintaining the accuracy of the parliamentary reports. Members frequently examine the official transcripts of their speeches and may make corrections which improve the grammar or clarity. 'But let there be no mistake about the rule of the House in these matters. It is not permissible to make alterations in the transcript which materially alter the sense of what was said.'[2]

Hansard is an invaluable source of information regarding the interests and energies of Members, but there is no satisfactory method

---

[1] There is one exception to this rule: a Member who wishes to raise a point of order while a division is in progress must sit down and put on a hat. This is the most effective method of becoming conspicuous when other Members are moving around in the Chamber.   [2] Mr. Speaker's ruling: H.C. Deb., Vol. 536, cols. 1275-7.

of measuring the extent to which Members participate in parliamentary business. The table opposite is an attempt to show variations in the amount of activity, by using the length of the entry under the name of each Member in the Index volume to *Hansard* for the session 1968–69. Members who belonged to the Commons for only a short part of the session are excluded, as are the Speaker, the Chairman, and the Deputy Chairman of Ways and Means, all of whom take no part in debates except from the Chair. Before commenting on the table it is important to stress its limitations. At best, the figures are but a rough guide to the frequency with which individuals were active in the parliamentary scene; there are roughly six entries per column inch in the *Hansard* index. But the size of his entry is no indication of the importance of a Member's work. The putting down of a large number of questions—which may be relatively trivial—will produce a lengthy entry in the *Hansard* index, while a dozen thoughtful contributions to major debates will score but two inches. Nor can *Hansard* record attendance at committee meetings, either unofficial party gatherings or the Select or Standing Committees. Of course a Member active in committees is more likely to intervene in the Chamber when topics relevant to his committee work are under discussion, but there is no necessary correlation between activity in committee work and in the Chamber, for Members who seek publicity will concentrate on the latter. Parliamentary private secretaries, many of whom devote much energy to their duties, tend to be restrained in their comments in the House and make, therefore, a slim showing in the index.

These qualifications do not detract from the central message of the table—that Members command very uneven shares of parliamentary time. In 1968–69 it will be seen that eight Members did not detain the House at all, and that over 30 made a negligible contribution to the discussions. Ministers are, of necessity, the most heavily engaged since every question demands a ministerial reply and most debates contain at least two ministerial contributions. Opposition Members are more active than government supporters, but on this matter the figures are again a little deceptive. They do not distinguish between the front-benchers and the rank and file on the Opposition side, where it is impossible to draw the sharp distinction that exists between Ministers and their supporters. The Conservative Members with the biggest entries in the index were not the Shadow Cabinet: the most active Tory was Edward Taylor (Glasgow, Cathcart) with 58 column inches and he was easily beaten by another Member on the opposition benches, Mrs. Winifred Ewing (Scot. Nat., Hamilton 1967–70) with 86 column inches. Top of the backbenchers was Arthur Lewis (Lab. West Ham, North) with nearly 100 inches. The longest entry of all was for the Secretary of State for Scotland with 153 inches. The index also gives an indication of the different tactics adopted by Members. Some rarely or

never ask a question; some ask questions only on policy matters and
not on personal cases; some restrict themselves to debates on a few
topics and others seem willing to speak on everything. These characteristics are widely understood in the House and one of the hardest
things for a Member to achieve is to surprise his friends.

PARLIAMENTARY ACTIVITY MEASURED FROM THE INDEX TO HANSARD: SESSION 1968–69

Length of entry (column inches to nearest inch)	*Ministers*	*Government Supporters*	*Opposition*[1] *Members*
No entry	1[2]	6	1
Less than $\frac{1}{2}$	7[2]	12	5
1–3	3	64	57
4–6	6	52	53
7–9	2	39	42
10–12	2	19	31
13–15	10	15	28
16–22	10	22	40
23–30	14	14	7
31–40	11	6	7
41–50	9	3	4
51–60	5	0	1
61+	10	2	1
Total	90[3]	254[3]	277[3]

Voting figures at divisions in the House are a good indication of
the level of attendance of Members in the Palace of Westminster. When
a question is put in the Chamber the Speaker or his Deputy proceeds to
'collect the voices'. If his verdict on the relative volumes of sound produced by the 'Ayes' and the 'Noes' is disputed, the order is given for the
division lobbies to be cleared and the exit doors are locked. Division
bells are rung all over the Palace,[4] and policemen shout 'Division' in

---

[1] Includes Liberals and Independents.

[2] Whips.

[3] The total for Ministers contains some double counting due to government
changes during the session; the other figures do not include Members who left during
the session *without* speaking or new Members.

[4] It has not been unknown for Members living nearby to have had division bells,
attached to the House circuit, installed in their homes.

the corridors. Immediately the bells ring, committee meetings, meals, interviews and a wide variety of other activities are interrupted. Members have six minutes in which to assemble before the entrances to the division lobbies are locked. Extreme measures have sometimes been taken to vote; on one occasion a Member having a bath in the Palace arrived in the lobby with a large towel swathed round his person. The names of Members voting in each lobby are recorded by clerks at the entrance of each division lobby, and Members are counted at the lobby exits by tellers: the names of tellers are announced by the Speaker who is advised by the Whips. For most divisions party discipline is invoked; the 'Whips are on' and two Whips on each side act as tellers. This system of voting does, of course, take time, on average about ten minutes. But it is widely urged that the tramp through the division lobbies helps to cool the passions of debate, and the Select Committee on Procedure[1] decided against any change in the present system. The use of time in this way would become serious if the number of divisions were as large as in 1909 when 895 were recorded; the average number in the nineteen-sixties was little more than a third of the 1909 figure.[2]

The table opposite analyses the voting records of four parliamentary sessions. Two sessions, 1950 and 1964–65, were selected because of the narrowness of the Government majority. The other two, 1956–57 and 1968–69, represent respectively periods with firm Conservative and Labour majorities. The figures have two clear messages: attendance at divisions was lower in the nineteen-sixties than the nineteen-fifties and within that overriding conclusion it emerges that attendance is higher when the Government majority is low. The lower figures for the nineteen-sixties may be a little surprising since it is generally assumed that we are moving towards a House of Commons whose Members have fewer outside interests, and that the species of full-time professional politician is growing. But the figures simply relate to presence at divisions, not to total time spent in the Palace of Westminster and could be misleading. One Member might drop in to the Commons for half-an-hour to vote at the ten o'clock division while another might spend the whole day there on constituency and committee business and then get a 'pair' in the evening to go and speak at a political meeting. In the fifties there were fewer divisions; each assumed a rather greater significance, especially in 1950 when the whipping was of unprecedented severity. When the Government majority is low, three-line Whips, which insist on the attendance of party supporters, must be more

---

[1] 1958–59 (92) vi.

[2] There was a sharp rise in the number of divisions in session 1970–71 largely caused by the tension aroused by the Industrial Relations Bill. During the 21-hour sitting to conclude the report stage that commenced on March 23rd 1971 there were 58 divisions—a record; the previous highest number, 44, occurred in 1907.

common. On occasions of less urgency a two-line Whip is issued that allows Members of opposing parties to come to a mutual agreement to absent themselves. In 1964–65 the average attendance at 'whipped' divisions was lowered by the poorer turnout at night-time divisions on the Finance Bill. In the same session the 'unwhipped' figures were raised by the high level of interest shown in the many divisions relating to capital punishment. When, as in 1956–57 and 1968–69, the position of the Cabinet is secure, the Government Whips can allow more latitude.

MEMBERS' ATTENDANCE AT DIVISIONS

Session	1950	1956–57	1964–65	1968–69
Number of Members[1]	622	627	627	627
Number of Divisions	65	180	276	353
Average of Members voting in all divisions	507	420	401	320
Average of Members voting when main parties used Whips	566	434	425	390
Average of Members voting in other divisions	293	224	291	205
Government majority over all other parties	8	63	6	75[2]
Average Government majority when main parties used Whips	17	49	17	51

The relatively low majorities recorded in 1968–69 were also partly due to left-wing dissatisfaction with the policies of the Wilson administration which led to a significant number of abstentions. One other notable feature of the table is that when Ministers have a bare majority in the House their support in the division lobbies improves to a point of relative safety.[3] Two factors combine to produce this result. Both in 1950 and 1964–65 the Government was Labour so Liberal Members sometimes sided with Labour against Conservatives. Opposition Whips may also co-operate to avoid imposing a defeat on Ministers if they

---

[1] Excluding the Speaker, Deputy Speakers and ignoring casual vacancies.

[2] Fell to 71 during the session.

[3] However, in both 1950 and 1964–65 there was one occasion when a division resulted in a tie: when this happens the casting vote of the Chair must be used to allow the question to be reconsidered which normally implies a vote in support of the Government.

fear that the Prime Minister might use a defeat as a justification for an election: whether the Opposition would use such tactics will depend on their view of the contemporary state of public opinion.

As noted above, a Member who wishes to be away from the House may arrange a 'pair' with a Member of the opposing party. A 'pair' reduces the numbers voting but leaves the size of the Government majority unaffected. Pairing arrangements are made known to the Whips, who see that they are honoured, and are very convenient for Members who have important engagements away from Westminster or who are uninterested in the day's business. Except when a three-line Whip is in operation, pairing is very common: many Members, especially those in the legal profession, have a regular 'pair' with someone on the other side of the House. Pairing arrangements are also made for those abroad on official business and for those who are ill. The system adds to the flexibility of parliamentary life and enables Members to travel and pursue a wider range of interests. When there is exceptional ill-feeling between the main parties, the Opposition may refuse to operate 'pairs'; this occurred in 1971 over the Industrial Relations Bill.

Proxy voting is not allowed. Its introduction was seriously mooted in 1965 when some Labour Members had to be brought to the House by ambulance to maintain the Government's majority in critical divisions. One sick Member, James Hill (Midlothian 1959–66), had to be brought from Edinburgh to vote. *The Times* reported[1] that beds for invalids were being installed in Ministers' rooms. The inhumanity of these necessities led to the suggestion that Members certified to be ill should be allowed to register a vote in their absence: a Cabinet committee was said to favour the proposal.[2] The Select Committee on Procedure obviously disliked the idea but agreed that 'such a system should be introduced, unless the usual channels can agree upon an alternative acceptable method'.[3] Proxy votes would undermine the basic concept of parliamentary government—that Members listen to arguments put forward in debate and pass judgement on the arguments by their votes. Everyone knows that this is a myth, with occasional exceptions, because the votes of Members are foresworn by party loyalty and party discipline. But the myth is of value if only for the constant possibility that it will become a reality. The Conservative Chief Whip in 1965, William Whitelaw (Penrith), was strongly opposed to proxy voting so the 'usual channels', the Whips of the major parties, reached an understanding that 'pairs' would be provided for ailing Members.

Those present in the Chamber itself are frequently but a small part of the numbers who will suddenly appear when division bells

---

[1] July 30th 1965.   [2] *Ibid.*, October 22nd 1965.
[3] Fifth Report, para. 3; 1964–65 (361) viii.

ring. A visitor in the public galleries may see but a thin sprinkling of Members on each side of the House if the debate is on an unexciting topic. Attendance also varies with the time of day. The Chamber is usually well filled for question-time and to hear the opening speeches in the main debate; by tea-time backbenchers are addressing the House and many of those left in the Chamber will be hoping for a chance to speak. Yet the news travels fast if a contribution of unusual interest is being made. Towards ten o'clock the Chamber will fill again to hear the closing frontbench speeches, especially if a division is anticipated. Ten o'clock is the most usual time for divisions, but voting on procedural motions takes place after question-time about 3.30 p.m. If the main business of the day is split into two, the second topic will be due to commence at 7 p.m., when a division may also be challenged on the first item of business. On the Committee or Report stages of a Bill, divisions can be more frequent and occur at any time: it is traditional that some sittings on the Committee stage of the Finance Bill go on through the night and some divisions then take place in the small hours.

The House of Commons is not an easy audience to address, and Members soon realise that the conditions are very different from those of the public platform or the lecture theatre. Unless a Member speaks from the rearmost bench at least a part of his audience will be behind him. The effect of this is lessened in so far as those behind are party colleagues; but a Member, or a Minister, who makes comments that are unwelcome to his own side, is not made more comfortable by the sense of disapproval at his back. Another distracting feature is that Members do not sit still. There is continuous movement in and out of the Chamber as Members leave to attend to other business or return from a meal, a committee or an interview with a constituent. The backbencher who speaks immediately after a Minister must expect his hearers to dwindle at the start of his speech. Attendance in the Chamber has fallen substantially since 1939. Members feel that their time is spent more usefully elsewhere in the parliament buildings—perhaps in private rooms dealing with constituency and other business or perhaps at committee meetings, formal or informal. It is difficult to find a clear-cut example of a backbench speech which had a major impact on public policy but Members may hope that their efforts for their constituents or at committees will have more positive results. Increasingly what takes place in the Chamber is regarded as unimportant.[1] Much is merely 'for the record'.[2] The element of spontaneity is

---

[1] Barker and Rush showed that little more than half the Members feel that the Chamber is of value as a source of information. Newer Members are even less enamoured of debates than their longer-serving colleagues: *The Member of Parliament and his Information*, p. 138.

[2] 'The record' is still very important.

low. If a Member intends to raise a serious point of order about procedure, he will often give the Speaker prior notice. Shadow Ministers have prior (albeit brief) notice of the contents of ministerial statements. Frontbench spokesmen may know in advance the line their opponents will follow in debate; this is especially probable on less controversial items. If backbench speeches are sometimes less predictable they are also less important. When the House is allowed a free vote, normally on private members' business, the element of uncertainty does generate added interest for there is a possibility that the course of debate will effect the outcome.

The atmosphere of debate depends upon the nature of the business. There are a few big occasions, e.g. Budget Day, when the House is crammed to capacity and is the centre of national attention. At the other extreme, when the House is engaged on the Report stage of a technical but mildly controversial Bill, the Chamber will be virtually unoccupied. A Minister's explanation of an important Bill on Second Reading will command much publicity but most debates are attended only by specialists in the particular subject. When Government policy is being subjected to major challenge, a debate can get noisy, notably in the evening; speeches are interrupted, spurious points of order arise and a political slanging match can develop. The temper of the House can change rapidly, especially if a frontbench speaker chooses to turn from detailed reasoning to partisan argument. Temptation to engage in political jousting is greatest when a general election is anticipated or desired. Trivial invective may attract newspaper headlines and be good for party morale but enshrined in the sober columns of *Hansard* it makes drab reading. This variety of manners ensures that there is no really distinctive House of Commons style of oratory, but an excess of gesticulation and synthetic emotion are frowned on. Great speeches are still made, and are appreciated on both sides of the House, but the ordinary Member should eschew anything in the nature of a grand peroration. Above all, the type of speech varies with the form of the business. On the committee stage of a Bill the contributions are briefer and narrower in scope; on a second reading or in a general debate Members will attempt a wider canvas. When speaking a Member may be asked to 'give way' to an opponent who seeks to ask a question or challenge a statement of fact; to refuse to do so savours of cowardice unless time is short or the speech has been previously interrupted. After he has spoken it is also the custom for a Member to remain in the Chamber during the subsequent speech, partly as a matter of courtesy and partly to hear any comment that may be made about his own remarks. The Department concerned with the subject under review is always represented on the Treasury Bench, and the Minister due to reply to a debate normally sits through the greater part of the preceding discussion.

A Member's first speech, his 'maiden' speech, is heard without interruption, and earns a few words of congratulation from whoever follows him in a debate. It is generally agreed that a maiden speech is an ordeal, especially as the novice knows fairly exactly at what time he will catch the Speaker's eye. The novice receives a measure of priority for, within limits, he can choose the time at which he addresses the House; naturally the Speaker cannot allow too many first attempts on any one day, and they cannot follow in immediate succession because of the need for commendation. The convention that a maiden speech should not be controversial has now faded and this leads to some resentment against the prohibition on interruption. Frequently a maiden speech contains references to a Member's constituency. The victor at an important by-election may gain unusual publicity: Miss Bernadette Devlin (Ind. Mid-Ulster), according to a front page headline in *The Times*,[1] 'enthrals packed House'. A. P. Herbert commenced his parliamentary career by protesting against the decision of the Government, which was supported by the Opposition, to restrict the amount of private members' time, and followed his protest by forcing a vote on the issue which the Government won by 232 votes to 5. This performance was described by Winston Churchill as 'a maiden hussy of a speech'.[2]

Much of the routine work of the Commons is unexciting and attracts little publicity. It is inevitable that the news media should concentrate on the more exceptional Members. Thus the independents, the extremists and those with colourful personalities will command attention; leading examples are Bernadette Devlin, Sir Gerald Nabarro (Con. Worcestershire, South), Enoch Powell (Con. Wolverhampton, S.W.) and the Rev. Ian Paisley (Ind. Antrim, North). Of course, there is no connection between the nature and extent of the publicity a Member receives and his (or her) reputation within Parliament itself. Other Members become prominent because they associate themselves with issues that arouse public interest: both Leo Abse (Lab. Pontypool) and Norman St. John Stevas (Con. Chelmsford) have been active in relation to private members' Bills which raise moral issues. It would be pleasant to record that Members became noted for the quality of their contributions to debates but apart from Michael Foot (Lab. Ebbw Vale) it is difficult to find convincing examples.

Physical conditions in the Chamber and parliamentary tradition, enshrined in the rules of debate, are all aids to harmony. Order papers are always available to be waved in congratulation, but there are no

---

[1] April 23rd 1969.

[2] A. P. Herbert, *Independent Member* (Methuen, 1950), pp. 21–30. Herbert represented Oxford University as an Independent 1935–50. Nearly all the autobiographies of Members or ex-Members contain an account of their maiden speeches.

desk-lids to bang. When addressing the House a Member may use notes, but speeches should not be read. Speeches must also be in English. One Member referring to another in debate must refer to the latter not by name but by a descriptive periphrasis in the third person, so minimising the possibility of personal abuse. Thus a Member is described by reference to the name of his constituency, e.g. 'the Honourable Member for Orkney' or by some phrase as 'the Honourable Member who spoke last', 'the Honourable Member below the gangway', etc. Privy Councillors are 'Right Honourable', Queen's Counsel are 'Honourable and learned' and Service officers are 'Honourable and gallant'. This terminology serves to soften allusions to other Members, but how far a Member may go in personal criticism of his fellows depends to a considerable degree on the severity of the Chair: it is out of order to impute discreditable motives to other Members and to accuse them of deceit. Comments on the physical appearance of Members, or about their private lives, are not permitted. A wide variety of abusive descriptions have been disallowed through the years, including 'villains', 'hypocrites', 'murderer', 'insulting dog', 'swine', 'pecksniffian cant', 'cheat', 'stool-pigeons' and 'bastard'. However, Prime Minister Harold Wilson's description of Peter Griffiths (Con. Smethwick 1964–66) as a 'parliamentary leper' was allowed to stand in spite of protests.[1] While a Member is speaking other Members should remain silent or converse in under-tones in order not to interfere with the debate. Should the volume of conversation make it difficult to hear a speech, the Speaker or Chairman will call the House to order. Cries to 'hear, hear', 'question', 'divide, divide', are sanctioned by long usage and are not out of order unless they obstruct the course of business. A Member should not move from his place when addressing the House and offensive weapons should not be brought into the Chamber. Leslie Lever (Lab. Manchester, Ardwick 1950–70) and Simon Mahon (Lab. Bootle) had their swords removed by the Serjeant-at-Arms before they were allowed to enter the Chamber.[2] Apart from the ban on weapons there appears to be no clear-cut regulations governing Members' dress: most Members are not of the age or disposition to follow extremes of fashion. They are allowed to eat in the Chamber but they may not read books or newspapers.

The Commons is usually a well-behaved assembly; if the House does become extremely disorderly, the Speaker will suspend the sitting for a short period. This occurred on November 1st 1956 during the Suez crisis and again on January 25th 1971 when about 35 Members gathered in the centre of the Chamber shouting objections to the Government's intention to impose a time limit on the discussion of the

---

[1] H.C. Deb., Vol. 701, col. 71.   [2] *The Times*, March 12th 1969.

Industrial Relations Bill. If an individual Member is guilty of grossly disorderly conduct, he is normally warned by the Speaker or Chairman and, if the warning does not have the necessary effect, the Member will be ordered to withdraw from the House. In extreme circumstances the Member is 'named' by the Chair—if the House is in Committee, the Speaker is summoned—and a motion is put, without debate, that the offending Member be suspended from the service of the House. Since 1926 the period of suspension has been five sitting days for the first offence, twenty sitting days for the second, and the remainder of the session on any subsequent occasion. It is not always possible to warn Members in advance about their conduct, as at the famous incident when John Beckett[1] seized the Mace. A Member can only be 'named' in this way because of misbehaviour in the House; the use of offensive expressions or the commission of an assault elsewhere in the Palace is treated as a contempt of Parliament, in accordance with the procedure described in the section on privilege.[2] The most recent case of the 'naming' of a Member occurred in 1968 when Dame Irene Ward (Con. Tynemouth) stood before the table of the House and refused to resume her seat as an act of protest against the limitation of the debate on the Finance Bill.[3] Although Dame Irene was disorderly, her conduct was not on a par with Beckett's since her action was premeditated and the Speaker had had advance warning of her intentions.

In the literature of parliamentary reminiscence occasional references are to be found to the question of drink. Because the Houses of Parliament are a Royal Palace, the restrictions imposed by the Licensing Acts do not apply; unusual opportunities exist, therefore, for those so inclined to be unwise. There is no doubt that the Commons are sensitive on this topic. In 1965 Patrick Duffy (Lab. Colne Valley 1963–66 and Sheffield, Attercliffe since 1970) was reported to have said at a public meeting that 'some of the Tories were half-drunk during debates'. Sir Herbert Butcher (Con. Holland with Boston 1937–66) complained that these remarks constituted a breach of privilege, a view upheld by the Committee of Privileges. In a written statement to the Committee, Duffy withdrew his remarks and stressed that he intended no personal imputations.[4] No further action was taken.

The not inconsiderable social aspect of parliamentary life is arranged through non-party groups and committees. In 1970 groups existed to organise and encourage clay pigeon shooting, camping and

---

[1] Labour Member for Gateshead 1924–29, Peckham 1929–31.

[2] pp. 185–97 *infra*.

[3] H.C. Deb., Vol. 766, cols. 893–5.

[4] H.C. Deb., Vol. 706, col. 855 and Privileges, Report; 1964–65 (129) viii.

caravaning, cricket, flying, golf, motoring, tennis, yachting and paint-ing.[1] Many of the trips abroad and the reception of visitors from other countries have a high social content, although there is some educa-tional value as well. The majority of these international contacts are organised through the Commonwealth Parliamentary Association and the Inter-Parliamentary Union. Almost all Members belong to these associations as individuals and the activities are supported by public funds. The C.P.A. was founded in 1911 to facilitate closer understanding and more frequent intercourse between parliamentarians throughout the Empire: this body has done valuable work in recent years by arranging seminars in London on parliamentary procedure for members of the newer Commonwealth legislatures. There are eight sub-groups of the British branch of the C.P.A. who aim to promote closer links with particular Commonwealth countries. The I.P.U. was founded in 1889 to promote peace through international co-operation and embraces countries that do not have democratic legislatures e.g. U.S.S.R. and Spain. There are no fewer than 42 sub-groups of the British section of the I.P.U. but many of these sub-groups are relatively inactive, although Members who belong may be invited to diplomatic receptions.[2]

---

[1] Mitchell and Birt, *Who Does What in Parliament*, p. 46.

[2] There are other non-party groups of Members concerned with international affairs, e.g. the British–American Parliamentary Group, the United Nations Group, the Action for World Development Group and the Group for World Government: these bodies, however, are concerned to press particular policies and are thus similar to other non-party groups described above, pp. 53–4.

CHAPTER 5

THE CHALLENGE TO THE EXECUTIVE—(1) BY THE WHOLE HOUSE

Members and Ministers

The principle of Parliamentary sovereignty means . . . that Parliament has, under the English constitution, the right to make or unmake any law whatever; and further no person or body is recognised by the law of England as having a right to override or set aside the legislation of Parliament.'[1] This classic statement by Dicey sets out the extent of the power of Members, for the authority of Parliament is now effectively concentrated in the House of Commons. The principle of constitutional monarchy precludes royal intervention in matters of political controversy, and the House of Lords, by the Parliament Act, 1949, can delay only non-financial legislation for a period of twelve months. The absolute legal authority of the Commons is exercised through the Cabinet, and the first duty of the Commons is to provide and maintain a Cabinet that will give direction to the business of government.

In a two-party system with strong party discipline the backbencher is not often called upon to play a part in the making or unmaking of governments. At a general election the party that succeeds in winning a majority of seats in the Commons can expect, in normal circumstances, to continue in office until the next election. The leader of the majority party becomes Prime Minister and appoints other Ministers to their offices; backbenchers can take some part in the original nomination of their party leader, but this may be years before the moment of electoral victory.[2] Revolts or murmurs of rebellion against a party leader, in or out of office, are not unknown but they are rarely successful. In the twentieth century no Prime Minister with a firm party majority in the Commons has been forced out of office save by the electorate.[3] The dismissal of a Prime Minister in such circumstances

---

[1] A. V. Dicey, *Introduction to the Law of the Constitution* (9th ed., Macmillan, 1939), pp. 39–40.

[2] Political Promotion is discussed, in Ch. 11 *infra*.

[3] For full discussion on this point see J. P. Mackintosh, *The British Cabinet* (Stevens, 2nd ed. 1968), pp. 428–35. Mackintosh is Labour Member for Berwick and East Lothian.

could occur only if he had suffered great personal failures, probably ill-health and if there were virtually unanimous agreement over a successor.

War-time Prime Ministers have been more vulnerable. So have those who led coalition or minority governments. With these conditions, changes may be forced either by party leaders acting alone and in secret or by strong tides of opinion among backbenchers. A political crisis arising from disagreement within a Cabinet can be settled by negotiations in which the rank-and-file of the Commons are not concerned. The replacement of the Asquith coalition by the Lloyd George coalition in 1916 is one such example: in 1931 Labour Members were astonished when the MacDonald Labour ministry was succeeded by a coalition headed by MacDonald in which the majority of the previous Labour Ministers refused to serve. The resignation of the Baldwin ministry in 1924 and the decision of MacDonald in the same year to seek the dissolution that led to his defeat, were both caused by the actions of the Liberal Party in the Commons, and illustrate the instability which may result when there exist three effective political parties. Yet on three occasions in this century Conservative back-bench Members can claim to have influenced the fate of Governments. A meeting of Conservative Members at the Carlton Club on October 19th 1922, passed by 187 votes to 87 a resolution urging that the Conservative Party should fight the next election independently of the Coalition Liberals. The effect of this meeting was to bring the Lloyd George coalition to a speedy end. On May 8th 1940 the House of Commons approved the conduct of the war by Neville Chamberlain's administration with a majority of 81—281 votes to 200. As the normal Conservative majority was roughly 200 it was clear that a grave erosion of confidence in the Government had taken place. Chamberlain therefore resigned and was replaced by Winston Churchill. L. S. Amery has described[1] how in April 1940 a Watching Committee had been formed of Conservative Members and Peers who were disquieted by the half-hearted conduct of the war: this committee played an important part in the events before the historic vote on May 8th. The third occasion was in 1951 when Conservative Members, by keeping the House sitting for long hours and forcing divisions late at night, caused much trouble to the Labour Government which had but a slim majority. Conservative Members were younger, healthier and more had accommodation in central London that could be reached easily after a late sitting. Earl Attlee in his autobiography commented that the strain placed on Labour Members at this period was very great, and that it was 'not pleasant to have Members coming from hospital at the risk of their

---

[1] *My Political Life* (Hutchinson, 1955), Vol. III, p. 355 *et seq.*

lives to prevent a defeat in the House'.[1] There can be little doubt that the Conservative tactics were a factor in his decision to ask for the dissolution of Parliament that led to the defeat of the Labour Government. These examples show how backbench pressure can be decisive only when the Government is already weak. In 1922 the war-time Coalition had long outlived its *raison d'être*: in 1940 the personal foreign policy of the Prime Minister had proved a failure and the outbreak of war had created feeling in favour of an all-party coalition: in 1951 the Government was carrying on with an exiguous majority. It is, then, in rare circumstances that Members can destroy Governments, but they may endeavour to exert influence at all times.

When the policy of an individual Department is subjected to heavy public criticism the personal future of the Minister at its head is necessarily involved. Ministers are responsible to Parliament for actions carried out in their name, and must reply to questions and debates about the work of their Departments. But does this mean that the Commons can force the resignation of a Minister whose policy has been a failure? Should a vote of censure on a Minister ever be carried in the Commons, the Minister would immediately resign, and probably the whole Cabinet as well: in practice, party discipline among Government supporters prevents dismissals of Ministers through action in the lobbies. The tradition of collective responsibility in the Cabinet enjoins Ministers to come to the aid of a colleague under attack for applying a Cabinet decision. Normally the spirit of comradeship or political tactics induce such support when the cause of trouble is departmental maladministration, for which the Cabinet cannot fairly be blamed. Has party discipline, therefore, removed all sting from the principle of ministerial responsibility? Opposition criticism, however violent and well-founded, is by itself quite unable to depose a Minister. If dissatisfaction spreads to the Government benches the position is uncertain; the Minister may stay, he may be moved to another office, or he may resign. Three factors influence the outcome: the temper of the backbenchers, the views of the Prime Minister and possibly his most senior colleagues, and the attitude of the Minister under fire. The latter may defend himself and cling tenaciously to his post, or be willing to surrender his responsibilities. It is probably impossible for private Members to oust a resolute Minister who is firmly backed by his colleagues but, if there is wavering in Whitehall, opinion in Westminster can be decisive. Even so, the most recent case in which a resignation has been influenced by a backbench revolt is that of Sir Thomas Dugdale[2] in 1954 over Crichel Down.

---

[1] *As It Happened* (Heinemann, 1954), pp. 206–7.

[2] Con. Richmond, Yorks. 1929–59. Now Lord Crathorne.

The political activities of Members are multiplex. They may be public or discreet; they may be individual or collective; they may stem from personal enthusiasms or be prompted by persuasions from extra-parliamentary sources. The more important an issue, the greater the probability that the reactions of Members will be public, collective and dictated by party opinion. The channels for their activities are also diverse. Members may write letters to *The Times* or to their own political leaders: when the prospect of a British withdrawal from Port Said was first mooted nearly 80 Conservative Members were reported to have written letters urging the Cabinet to 'stand firm'.[1] Groups of Members pressing a particular policy may assume a semi-permanent form, e.g. the left-wing 'Tribune' group of Labour Members and the right-wing 'Suez Group' of Conservatives in the nineteen-fifties. Should a group stray too far from official party policy it will attract the displeasure of the Whips and, especially in the Labour Party, issues of party discipline will emerge. Members may also take a leading role in public associations with avowedly political objects—witness the support given by Members to the various associations formed to support or oppose Britain's entry into the European Common Market. Members also ventilate their views by tabling motions on the Commons' Order Paper, not in the expectation of securing a debate, but for propaganda purposes and in order to test the feeling of the House. Other Members who agree with the resolution may add their names; in December 1968 a motion sponsored by Kevin McNamara (Lab. Kingston-upon-Hull, N.) opposing the sale of arms to South Africa rapidly acquired over 130 supporters and was widely believed at the time to have had much influence on the Cabinet decision to retain the ban on such sales.[2] Signatures to motions do provide a useful guide to the opinions of individual Members on issues that cause dissension within parties.[3] An allied technique is to table an amendment to an official motion that is due for debate; in November 1970 100 Labour Members supported an amendment to their own Party's motion on defence policy.

---

[1] *The Economist*, December 1st 1956.

[2] This motion was the cause of much controversy. Labour Whips encouraged their Members to sign but since the motion supported existing policy this is scarcely improper: see *Tribune*, October 16th 1970.

[3] *Backbench Opinion in the House of Commons 1955–59*, by S. E. Finer, H. B. Berrington and D. J. Bartholomew (Pergamon, 1961), is an analysis of these motions. But, as the authors recognise, their evidential value is limited. Some Members are generous with signatures and will readily sign motions with which they have some sympathy. Others are cautious and scarcely ever sign. Where a motion is worded ambiguously—and this may be done deliberately—it is unsafe to make a precise attribution of view to its supporters. It is not unknown for Members to have second thoughts, and subsequently to withdraw their names from a motion.

Meetings between Members and Ministers are frequent and may be held in an atmosphere of intimacy and cordiality, for the Ministers of today are the backbenchers of yesterday and are on good personal terms with most Members, other than newcomers. Under the present Conservative Government a weekly gathering of junior Ministers is addressed by a member of the Cabinet. This arrangement has a double purpose. Not only does it ensure that junior Ministers themselves are more fully appraised of the development of official policy, but it helps them to discuss current issues with backbenchers far more effectively. Many chances for casual conversation occur within the precincts of the House, although with the growing pressure of Departmental business, Ministers—especially senior Ministers—tend to spend more time in their offices. A backbencher may see a Minister by private appointment, probably arranged through the latter's parliamentary private secretary, or he may press a viewpoint on a Minister as part of a formal deputation. In the debating chamber itself many hours are devoted to the examination of Government policy and the ventilation of grievances; in the committee rooms further attention is given to matters of detail. Later sections of this chapter will describe how the work of the Commons is designed to facilitate the examination of executive action, and the advocacy of causes great and small. Private meetings of Members are also of much importance, especially among Members who support the Government of the day. Both the main parties have a series of subject committees, described above,[1] which have watching briefs over the doings of corresponding Ministries. Discussion in these gatherings can be highly influential. There are quite special difficulties in the way of democratic control of foreign affairs and defence policy because of the element of secrecy in diplomacy and strategic considerations. Yet Members are not always powerless: it is more than probable that the withdrawal from Port Said in December 1956 and the subsequent decision in 1957 that British ships should again use the Suez Canal would both have taken place at an earlier date had there not been such great resistance amongst Government supporters to these actions.

There are, of course, many questions on which the division of views cuts across party lines. Matters of conscience are not subjected to the normal rules of party discipline, and may be decided by a free vote in the House.[2] But the normal pattern of parliamentary business is for the 'whips to be on' and Members are expected to support their leaders and to make personal convictions submit to the demands of party orthodoxy. But rebellions do take place, and the seriousness of a

---

[1] pp. 45–53.
[2] Issues of conscience are discussed in Ch. 7 *infra*.

rebellion depends upon the circumstances. If the Opposition is hopelessly uncertain in its attitude to Government policy, as the Conservatives have been over race relations, it will lose face but the position of the Government is unshaken. If Government and Opposition leaders agree, again a backbench revolt will not have major political consequences—although the fate of the Parliament Bill in 1969 provides an exception to this rule. Should any considerable number of Government supporters agree with the Opposition, then the implications of a revolt are grave for it could lead to the humiliation of Ministers and a reduction in the authority of the Cabinet; this situation constantly threatened to arise over the prices and incomes policy of the Wilson administration. In the extreme case, a combination of Government backbenchers with the Opposition could lead to the downfall of the Cabinet followed by a general election. A more probable outcome is that the Cabinet would change its policy. And in the common run of political affairs the stability of the British Cabinet is secured by the ties of party loyalty and the bonds of party discipline.

One further general observation must be made. From time to time Ministers give way and bow to a storm or accept suggestions made by Members: the sum total of such occasions does not represent the extent of the influence of Members. In framing policy Ministers consult interested parties, inside and outside the precincts of Westminster. Unless political principles or expenditure are involved Ministers will usually try to accommodate the representations they receive, and it may be possible to conciliate potential opponents before a word is said in the House. And Members, if they are wise, will try the tactic of private negotiation; it is much easier for a Minister to change his mind before he has publicly committed himself to a particular course of action.

Parliamentary Debates

The function of Parliament as the Grand Inquest of the Nation is carried through partly by discussion of proposed legislation and partly through a variety of debates on Government policy and administration. The table opposite shows the distribution of time in the Commons between various categories of parliamentary business in session 1968–69.

The following sections of this chapter discuss the passage of government legislation, private legislation, question-time, ministerial statements and adjournment debates. Private members' time is considered separately in Chapter 7. The remaining items in the table provide, in general, for a scrutiny of executive actions and allow the Opposition and Government backbenchers some initiative in pressing criticisms. Each session opens with a debate in reply to the Queen's Speech—the Gracious Speech from the Throne—which announces in outline Cabinet policy for the coming year. Normally this introductory debate lasts five days. The Opposition can decide how it wishes to concentrate its attack on the Government but traditionally one day is reserved for foreign affairs. Through a Vote of Censure the Opposition can force a debate on any subject at any time: by convention this right is used but once or twice a session. The fiction that the Commons can control Ministers through the ability to refuse to grant supply— i.e. to vote the supply of money needed to carry on the business of government—is being dropped. The Committee of Supply disappeared in 1967. But Supply Days remain. On these 29 days the Opposition decide how the time available shall be used. Normally topics will be chosen on which the Opposition have strong views or on which the Government is thought to be vulnerable. Supply Days may be spent, with Opposition concurrence, on Government legislation, motions or prayers against Statutory Instruments.[1] Government backbenchers have no rights in the choice of subjects on these occasions.

DISTRIBUTION OF PARLIAMENTARY BUSINESS BY TIME: 1968–69

	%
Government legislation	41·0
Government Orders and resolutions	5·5
Government motions	5·7
Supply debates	11·6[2]
Private members' legislation	6·7
Private members' motions	2·4
Private Bills	1·3
Adjournment motions S.O.9 (emergency procedure)	0·8
Adjournment motions (daily and holiday)	7·0
Business of the House	2·1
Ministerial statements	2·0
Prayers or motions against Statutory Instruments	1·9
Questions	9·5
Debate on Address	2·1
Church of England measures	0·1
Votes of censure, not included under Supply time etc.	0·3
	100·0

[1] This created difficulties in forming the table above: to avoid double counting 6 hours of Supply time spent on a Prayer and a further 31.5 hours spent on Government legislation and motions have been included only as Supply time.

[2] The form of business on a Supply day varies. The total of 170 hours of Supply time included, as a result of Opposition choice, 6 hours devoted to a prayer against a Statutory Instrument, 31 hours on Government business and 61 hours when for technical reasons it was felt to be more convenient to hold the debate on the adjournment motion.

Other debates on policy are initiated by the Government, often after parliamentary pressure for time to debate a particular topic. Reports from Royal Commissions or Departmental Committees may be debated—usually a considerable time after publication. The more important Select Committee Reports may attract the attention of the House. Government White Papers announcing fresh developments in ministerial policy can be discussed and approved—this is often a prelude to legislation. But in particular the House will expect the Government to find time for matters that fall outside the normal range of legislation, notably foreign affairs and defence. A defence White Paper is normally debated. Any fresh problem on the international scene will stimulate demands for a debate. Yet the Commons tend to concentrate on the Government's handling of economic and social affairs, including the way in which Ministers spend the taxpayers' money. Reference has already been made to the peculiar obstacles to parliamentary consideration of foreign affairs and defence which arise through secrecy combined with an absence of legislation. Perhaps Members avoid these subjects because they find them frustrating. Members also know that their constituents, save at moments of acute international crises, are more concerned with domestic bread-and-butter issues.

In 1968–69 the Commons spent rather more time on Government legislation (including delegated legislation) than on general scrutiny of Government policy and administration. But the proportion is not rigid and will vary with the pressures of the period. Those who argue that it is the duty of Ministers to produce legislation that will improve the human condition may be tempted to feel that non-lawmaking discussion is a waste of time. Certainly, consideration of a Bill demands that clear-cut decisions are made; these decisions determine the content of statutes. Productivity is visible. And because controversial measures stimulate pressure-group activity and lead to voting in the division lobbies, they arouse greater interest among Members than a Supply Day devoted to some particular aspect of public administration. It is not possible to show that a Supply debate has precise effects—but how would the executive behave if the prospect of detailed backbench criticism were diminished? The value of a watch-dog is not limited to what he does: one must add on what might happen were he not there.

Debates on White Papers and the reports of commissions and committees serve a very different function. Often they enable Members, including Ministers, to think ahead in public and in advance of action. They test opinion inside and outside Parliament. The Wilson administration started the issue of occasional Green Papers which set out ideas to which the Government was not firmly committed: these documents provided a new opportunity for Members to participate in the formative stage of policy-making. Thus some of the proposals in the first Green Paper on the National Health Service[1] were revised by Labour Ministers after widespread criticism. Even where Government ideas are firmer and reach the White Paper stage, parliamentary debate is still of great use for probing Government intentions. Since 1969 White Papers setting out five-year programmes of public expenditure have given Members fuller material with which to debate long-term economic priorities. This type of preliminary discussion can give Ministers early warning of storms ahead. At the end of the debate on the Labour White Paper on industrial relations, *In Place of Strife*, 55 Labour Members voted against their leaders and about another 30 abstained. Had Ministers taken the hint they could have saved themselves much subsequent embarrassment. It is much easier for the Cabinet to adjust policy before it is committed to anything as precise as a draft Bill. Thus the more time the Commons spend on pre-legislation debate—as opposed to discussing actual Bills—the more influential will Members become.

The Passage of Legislation

Each Bill before it becomes an Act must pass through five stages in the Commons: first reading, second reading, committee, report of committee to the House and third reading. In addition, if the Lords alter the text of a Bill, consideration will have to be given to the Lords' amendments. The first reading is formal and no debate takes place except when the Ten-Minute Rule is used;[2] the Bill is introduced by its sponsors and is ordered to be printed. A general discussion of the principles of the Bill follows on the second reading. The only amendment, if any, moved to the proposal that 'the Bill be now read a second time' is the official Opposition amendment; it is open to Members to put down other amendments on the Order Paper, but these are merely for propaganda. The Opposition amendment may be reasoned, setting out their objections to the measure, or it may advocate delay—'that the Bill be read six[3] months' hence'—which is treated as a demand for a complete rejection of the Bill. The financial resolution in committee of the whole House follows immediately; it is moved by a Minister and authorises expenditure on the purposes of the Bill. Frequently the financial

---

[1] The first (1968) Green Paper should be compared with the Second (1970) Green Paper.

[2] For details see pp. 143–4.

[3] After Whitsun the period of delay proposed is three months.

resolution is agreed to with little or no debate.[1] The committee stage of
most Bills is taken in one of the Standing Committees.[2] These meet on
Tuesday, Wednesday and Thursday mornings and sometimes in the
afternoons when pressure of work is heavy. The Committees consist of
the Minister in charge of the Bill and between 16 and 50 Members
chosen in proportion to party balance in the Commons. Important
Bills go before a committee of about 50 Members; lesser Bills need a
smaller committee. When the Government has a slim majority, their
supporters on the Standing Committees must be assiduous in attendance
if the Opposition is to be prevented from winning minor victories.
Submission of Bills to Standing Committees does restrict opportunity
to join in their detailed examination, but decisions made in committee
may be reviewed by the whole House on the Report stage when further
amendments can be moved by Ministers and other Members. The third
reading follows immediately upon the Report stage and will be formal
unless a Bill has aroused such controversy that its opponents wish to
restate their objections. After that, unless there is disagreement in the
Lords, the Royal Assent will be signified.

The great obstacle to the passage of legislation is the shortage of
parliamentary time. In recent years fresh devices have been arranged
to assist the enactment of measures which command general agreement. It is now possible to refer the second reading of a Bill to a committee: to prevent measures slipping through by this procedure virtually
unnoticed, ten days' notice has to be given of any motion to use this
technique and twenty Members by merely rising in their places can
defeat the motion. The record of the debate in a Second Reading committee is bound with *Hansard*. Bills allowed to proceed in this way
can also have their Report stage before a small committee; but the use
of such Report committees is unusual. Another important saving in
time has been achieved through a revised procedure for the annual
Finance Bill. Before 1968 the committee stage of the Finance Bill was
considered by a committee of the whole House. The Opposition always
put down a high number of detailed amendments to the Government
proposals: it was traditional that several days and one or two nights

---

[1] But in the nineteen-thirties there was much controversy over the drafting of
financial resolutions which was said to restrict unreasonably subsequent debate. Cf.
Procedure relating to Money Resolutions, Select Committee Report; 1936–37 (149)
viii, and Sir W. I. Jennings, *Parliament*, pp. 249–64. This problem was again discussed by the Select Committee on Procedure in 1957: First Report: 1956–57(110) vii.

[2] Very rarely a Bill is committed to a Select Committee, with powers to send for
persons, papers and records, which examines witnesses and memoranda before
determining its conclusions. Select Committees consist of backbenchers only: no
Minister in charge of the Bill is present. This procedure was used in 1966–67 for the
Armed Forces Bill.

should be devoted to this business. One view held that it was crucial to the rights of backbenchers for all of them to be able to object to Government proposals for tax changes that could adversely affect their constituents. In fact, the protracted discussions on the details of a Finance Bill were dominated by the relatively few Members who specialise in financial matters.[1] In 1968 the Wilson Government insisted that the committee stage of the Finance Bill be assigned to a committee of 50 Members: this arrangement proved to be contentious and unsatisfactory. Since 1969 the Finance Bill has been divided into two; those parts which are relatively technical go to a Standing Committee while the more important and controversial aspects remain for consideration by the whole House.

The time taken to turn a Bill into an Act is very variable. At moments of extreme crisis, such as the outbreak of war, wide emergency powers can be conferred on the executive in a single day. Agreement between the major parties always enables rapid progress. Immediately before the 1970 Election a number of measures, including important items, passed hastily on to the Statute Book before the dissolution of Parliament. Among them were the Administration of Justice Bill and the Local Authorities Social Services Bill which authorised the establishment of unified social service departments by local authorities on lines proposed by the Seebohm Committee. Over the former measure the Government had suffered a defeat at the Report stage by 105 votes to 104 when the Commons refused to agree that the new Commercial Court should be allowed to sit in private: the Government accepted this decision in order to allow the Bill to become law before the election.

In normal times the discussion of an important and controversial Bill will be spread over many months. It is the duty of the Opposition to attempt to delay measures which conflict with their principles; not to do so would be regarded as a mark of weakness. Equally it is the business of the Government to ensure the completion of its legislative programme, and this may entail using its majority to restrict the time available for debate. The opportunities for obstruction arise at the committee stage and the Report stage when detailed amendments are proposed and considered: the normal closure motion 'that the question be now put' may be inadequate to prevent interminable discussion. To prevent unreasonable prolongation of arguments the Chair is given the right to select amendments for debate. It is also normal for Government and Opposition to reach informal agreements on the amount of time to

---

[1] The Select Committee on Procedure of 1966–67 wished to keep the committee stage of the Finance Bill on the floor of the House but urged that it should be subject to a voluntary timetable: Fourth Report paras. 14–17; 1966–67 (382) xvi. For further discussion see H. V. Wiseman's chapter in *The Commons in Transition*, ed. A. H. Hanson and B. Crick (Collins, 1970), pp. 182–97.

be spent on controversial items. Sometimes an agreement proves impossible or perhaps an agreement breaks down. The ultimate solution is to pass a 'guillotine' or timetable motion after a two-hour debate in the Chamber. The guillotine motion authorises the establishment of a Business Committee which fixes time limits by which various stages of the controversial Bill must be completed.[1] Voluntary timetabling is far preferable but is not practicable on occasions of great bitterness. On average, motions which enforce formal limitations on debate are required about once each session.[2] A guillotine both anticipates and invites trouble so a Government will not resort to it lightly.

Any restriction on debate can be portrayed as an infringement on the proper rights of Members. It has been a common tactic to waste time in committee on unimportant amendments so that the most vital clauses are not discussed because of the operation of the guillotine. This gives colour to the claim that the Government have allowed inadequate time. The Opposition, be it Labour or Conservative, then protest that a guillotine is dictatorial, and that the Government is determined to ignore parliamentary opinion and to use the House as a mere rubber-stamp for its proposals.

Quite a lot of time spent in Standing Committees is wasted. Normally the meetings start at 10.30 a.m. and last for two and a half hours: in the absence of a timetable there is no sense of urgency. Much of the objections take the form of general policy arguments already heard and rejected at second reading. A protracted committee stage is of

FATE OF GOVERNMENT BILLS: 1962–70[3]

Session	Government Bills	
	Total	Passed
1962–63	43	42
1963–64	64	63
1964–65	66	65
1965–66	36	21
1966–67	103	103
1967–68	65	63
1968–69	54	51
1969–70	63	38

[1] For an example see the timetable motion on the Ports Bill, 1970. H.C. Deb., Vol. 799, cols. 161–206 and 686.

[2] John Palmer, 'Allocation of time: the guillotine and voluntary timetabling' in *Parliamentary Affairs*, Summer 1970, Vol. XXIII, pp. 232–47.

[3] Excluding Provisional Order Confirmation Bills, and Bills under the Private Legislation (Scotland) Act, 1936.

positive effect only where Ministers are unclear or hesitant about the consequences of their proposals and need time for second thoughts.

With few exceptions, Government measures reach the Statute Book; most of those introduced by backbenchers do not. (For a discussion of the special procedural difficulties facing private members' Bills see Chapter 7.) The slaughter of Bills in 1966 and 1970 was due to the dissolution of Parliament in order to hold a General Election. Session 1966–67 lasted for eighteen months and thus produced an exceptionally high tally of legislation. In a normal session all or almost all the Government Bills will pass. However, it will be seen that three failed in 1968–69. The Merchant Shipping Bill was introduced too late in the session to proceed: the Parliament Bill was dropped at the committee stage in the Commons: the House of Commons Redistribution of Seats Bill was lost as the House of Lords failed to agree with the version of the Bill accepted by the Commons. The much-heralded Industrial Relations Bill was also dropped before it was even introduced. Thus 1968–69 witnessed three major set-backs for the Government programme of legislation—an unusual experience for a Cabinet with a firm majority in the Commons.

While few Government Bills are lost completely, it is not uncommon for them to be altered either by suggestions from Members, from peers in the Upper House or through second thoughts by Ministers. On the committee stage, amendments hostile to the principle of a Bill are invariably rejected. But if an amendment appears to be helpful to the purposes of a Bill, the Minister in charge may ask that it be withdrawn so that he may look at the matter again. Then he will consult with his Departmental advisers and, if no objection of sufficient weight is forthcoming, the Minister will himself introduce an amendment to cover the point at the Report stage. Even if the Minister is ready at the committee stage to accept the substance of an amendment immediately, he may doubt whether the precise form of words suggested is satisfactory. Drafting of legislation is a highly specialised task and private Members suffer from the disadvantage that they do not enjoy the legal assistance that is available to Ministers. If by mischance an amendment hostile to Government policy should be carried at the committee stage, the decision can always be reversed at the Report stage on the floor of the House when the Whips can be relied upon to secure a majority for Ministers. Thus the Standing Committee on the Decimal Currency Bill 1969 decided by six votes to five, against Government advice, that the sixpence should be retained: on the Report stage the demise of the sixpence was re-enacted.[1]

---

[1] Subsequently the Lords voted to save the sixpence, but the Commons rejected this amendment. After the Bill became law, and after further pressure from the Commons, the Government relented and the sixpence had a temporary reprieve.

As noticed above, almost all Bills are sent to Standing Committees for detailed examination. Their composition is changed very considerably for each Bill; calls on the time of Members are so heavy that it is not easy to man committees. A Member rarely experiences difficulty in securing nomination to the one considering a Bill that excites his interest. In theory, Standing Committees are non-specialised as implied by their designation through letters—A, B, C, D. In practice, a Bill comes before a selection of Members, including the chief critics of the measure, who are unusually knowledgeable about its contents. The result may be that a Standing Committee, although politically proportionate, does not truly reflect opinion in the House as a whole. Scottish Bills go to a Scottish Standing Committee and any Bill referring exclusively to Wales and Monmouthshire may be referred to a Welsh Standing Committee. In addition the Scottish Grand Committee, consisting of all representatives from Scottish constituencies and up to fifteen other Members, is empowered to discuss the general principles of Scottish Bills that are referred to it. This is tantamount to a second reading discussion.[1] The Grand Committee can also take the Report stage of Bills it has considered in principle.[2]

The burden of Standing Committee work on Members is substantial, partly because it is unevenly shared. In an average session about 130 Members will never be called to one of these committees while others will be heavily involved. In the abnormally long session 1966–67

STANDING COMMITTEES, GRAND COMMITTEES, SECOND READING AND REPORT COMMITTEES 1962–70

Session	No. of committees	No. of Bills examined	Members summoned[3]	No. of chairmen	No. of sittings
1962–63	10	38	489	16	223
1963–64	10	51	514	16	209
1964–65	10	49	529	15	212
1965–66	11	11	326	11	69
1966–67	13	69	550	19	401
1967–68	14	53	514	18	352
1968–69	12	48	478	17	270
1969–70	14	42	437	18	281

[1] When the Grand Committee reports to the House that it has considered the general principles of a Bill, it is open to any six Members to demand a second reading debate in the Chamber. This rarely happens. But see the debate on the Crofters Bill, 1961, H.C. Deb., Vol. 636, cols. 1564–1690.

[2] For further discussion of the Scottish Grand Committee see pp. 134–5 *infra*.

[3] Including chairmen.

James Bennett (Lab. Glasgow, Bridgeton) attended on 70 out of a possible 71 occasions and Harry Gourlay (Lab. Kirkaldy) attended 73 out of a possible 79 meetings. Scottish Members are always potentially the most heavily engaged because of the existence of the separate committees for Scotland. (Welsh Members are less affected because there is little separate legislation for Wales.) It is not surprising that Ministers representing Scottish constituencies answered none of fourteen summonses. The table above shows how the amount of committee work has increased; before 1962–63 the number of this type of meeting never exceeded 200. In terms of pressure on Members' time the growth must be considered in relation also to the substantial burgeoning of select committee activity.[1] To reduce the load the tendency has been to reduce still further the size of Standing Committees and a mere twenty Members are left to examine the details of important and controversial legislation.

Attendance at the official Committee meetings, however, does not exhaust the task of a Member especially concerned with a Bill. An Opposition group of specialists will hold meetings to plan strategy in relation to the committee stage, to draft amendments and nominate spokesmen and consider Government and any other amendments that may be down for discussion. As a counterpart to the Minister in charge of the Bill, the Opposition nominates a Leader who may propose the major Opposition amendments and will make any quick tactical decisions that may be required as the committee stage proceeds. Backbench victories in committee are achieved by pressure rather than by voting: the pressure is supported by the threat of an adverse vote, but Government defeats are rare yet not unknown. The 1971 Immigration Bill was changed against the wishes of the Government so that the grandchildren of British citizens were deprived of 'patrial' status: Labour and Liberal Members supported the amendment together with two Conservatives, Enoch Powell (Wolverhampton S.W.) and Sir George Sinclair (Dorking). Thus although party discipline is strict, it sometimes breaks down. However, Government supporters are normally reluctant to put down important amendments likely to be unacceptable to their leaders. If such an amendment is moved from the Government side and the Opposition refuse to permit its withdrawal, the unhappy proposer is forced either to deny support to his motion in the division or to act contrary to the 'party line'. Thus pressure groups find it difficult to get their ideas ventilated effectively: Opposition Members are more willing to co-operate with them—but their help is the kiss of death. Public proceedings in Westminster often have something of a rubber-stamp quality; in private, the Government are willing to compromise, especially with their own supporters.

---

[1] pp. 115–36 *infra.*

Apart from parliamentary consideration, the content of proposed legislation is the cause of much consultation for Ministers and their advisers with interested bodies of many kinds: discussions on a Bill may continue in the committee rooms of Whitehall after the measure has been introduced into Parliament. The relative importance of these negotiations and the activities of backbenchers depends upon subject-matter. On a topic such as rent restriction, which is of great political moment but on which the aggrieved are not highly organised, the influence exerted by Members is considerable.[1] Where voluntary bodies and professional associations are strongly entrenched, the role of Members in the evolution of policy tends to decline, except in the individual case of a Member who becomes the spokesman of a particular organisation. The danger of Ministers making prior agreements with interested parties is that the outcome of parliamentary debate is prejudged if Ministers cannot modify their position without defaulting on these commitments.

Many Acts of Parliament now delegate power to Ministers to issue rules and regulations which help to fulfil the purposes of the parent Act. This subordinate legislation—officially designated as Statutory Instruments—is very substantial in bulk, and the number of Instruments often exceeds 2,000 a year. Delegated legislation is essential to save parliamentary time and to give an element of flexibility to legislation. It also permits Ministers to consult with interested organisations on points of detail after an Act is passed, but before regulations are issued. In spite of its dangers and some degree of public criticism, delegated legislation is firmly established in the machinery of public administration.[2] The rights of Members to review the regulations vary between different categories of Instruments. Some are 'laid' before the House without any provision for parliamentary control: some are subject to negative procedure—they are 'laid' and become law immediately, or after forty days, unless annulled by a Member successfully moving a 'prayer': some need an affirmative resolution before they come into effect. Discussions on delegated legislation are often brief, especially when an affirmative resolution is required on some uncontroversial matter. Statutory Instruments cannot be amended; they must

---

[1] M. J. Barnett, *The Politics of Legislation* (Weidenfeld and Nicolson, 1969), provides a detailed analysis of the activities of backbenchers in connection with the Rent Act, 1957.

[2] The classic statement of the need for delegated legislation is to be found in the Report of the Committee on Ministers' Powers; 1931–32 Cmd. 4060, xii. The critics include Lord Hewart, *The New Despotism* (Benn, 1929), and Sir C. K. Allen *Law and Orders* 3rd ed. (Stevens, 1965). John Eaves, Jun., *Emergency Powers and the Parliamentary Watchdog* (Hansard Society, 1957), contains an excellent survey of the attempt by backbenchers to keep some check on the extra-ordinary powers granted to the Government in war-time.

be either accepted or rejected by the House. If a vote takes place the Government will win because the Whips are on. Yet there are occasions when the Minister will retreat if he is under pressure from all parts of the Chamber. This is most likely to occur if a prestigious organisation mounts a campaign against a Government Order by lobbying Members; e.g. the Police Federation secured the reconsideration of the Police Pensions Regulations in July 1964.[1] Important Instruments that require positive confirmation may occupy a full parliamentary day; in this category come Orders to redefine parliamentary constituencies and local government general grant Orders. A Member who wishes to invoke the negative resolution procedure will move a 'prayer' against an Instrument. These motions are exempt from the ten o'clock closure; usually the debates thereon start at this hour and they must finish at 11.30 p.m.[2] Until fairly recently time was always found for these 'prayers', but now they may go undebated if the House is heavily engaged with other business after ten o'clock. This change constitutes a little noticed but not unimportant erosion in the rights of backbenchers.

Questions and Statements

Question-time is a major opportunity for backbench Members to claim the attention of the House. Parliamentary reputations, including those of Ministers, are much affected by events at question-time, and Departments of state carry on their work in the knowledge that any action may be the subject of public challenge.[3]

From Monday to Thursday the first hour of the Parliamentary day is devoted to questions, less a few minutes for prayers and any unopposed items of private business. The three types of questions are those demanding an oral answer, which are starred on the Order Paper, those which ask merely for a written reply that appears in the Official Report, and private notice questions. All questions must be put down at least 48 hours before the time of reply, except those by private notice which are dealt with at the end of question-time and are of relative urgency, thus enabling a Minister to make a statement on

[1] H.C. Deb., Vol. 698, cols. 543–77. See also R. G. S. Brown, *The Administrative Process in Britain* (Methuen 1970), pp. 172–7.

[2] Before 1953 there was no time limit. In 1951 the Conservatives used nightly 'prayer' debates as a tactic to harass the Labour Government with its tiny majority. The imposition of the time limit followed the recommendation of the Select Committee on Delegated Legislation, Report, para. 107; 1952–53 (301–1) ix.

[3] The standard work on this subject is D. N. Chester and Nona Bowring, *Questions in Parliament* (O.U.P., 1962). See also Nevil Johnson, 'Parliamentary Questions and the Conduct of Administration', in *Public Administration*, Vol. 39 pp. 131–48.

some matter of immediate public concern. The advantage of an oral answer is that the Ministerial reply can be followed by further supplementary questions; the Member who initiates a question has the prior right to put a supplementary, but other Members may join in subsequently if the Minister's reply is felt to be unsatisfactory, and if the topic is sufficiently exciting. Ministers read prepared answers to the items on the Order Paper, but only intelligent anticipation can protect them against the supplementaries. It is impossible to forecast when a 'row' will develop at question-time; one may develop on any topic should a Minister use an incautious or infelicitous phrase. If a Member is not satisfied with a reply he can give notice to raise the subject again on the motion for the adjournment, and it is in the interests of Ministers to be conciliatory wherever possible. There is a true element of drama in the question-hour: a full House and packed galleries provide a large audience for the occasion. Business is carried on at some speed in order to cover as much ground as possible: the Speaker has constantly to use his discretion in restricting supplementaries. Even so, less than half of the questions down for oral reply are reached before 3.30 p.m.; the remainder obtain answers in the Official Report in the same way as unstarred questions, unless a Member asks for a postponement to a later date. The Prime Minister answers questions at 3.15 p.m. on Tuesdays and Thursdays and so is subjected to fifteen minutes of interrogation. Other Ministries are placed in varying order at question-time and a notice of priority on future days is posted in the division lobby. Each Ministry comes first on the list about every fourth week and it is increasingly common for the whole of question-time to be devoted to the top priority Department on a particular day. To share out the burden of preparatory work, the task of answering questions can be divided between the Minister and one or more junior Ministers. A maximum of three weeks' notice is allowed for questions. So a Member who is keen to question a particular Minister is able to do so provided he watches this timetable carefully. He must put down his question exactly three weeks before his quarry is number one on the list: then will come the opportunity to produce a carefully prepared supplementary.

To save time, a Member who has a starred question on the Order Paper merely rises in his place when his turn comes; if he is not present no oral reply is given and the answer appears along with those to unstarred questions. If an answer is necessarily long and involves many figures it is usual for a Minister to say that 'I will, with permission, circulate it in the Official Report', and the suggestion is normally well received for Members are anxious to save precious minutes. Alternatively, if the reply is long and highly important, the Minister may, with the permission of the Speaker, give it at 3.30 p.m.; like private notice questions this, in effect, lengthens question-time and is a privilege sought infrequently to prevent its abuse. Since 1960, Members have been limited to two starred questions a day. Yet, as noted above, these devices fail to provide for the consideration of all items down for oral reply. There is general agreement in the House that the Speaker should be strict in limiting the number of supplementary questions, but the main trouble is that the supplementaries themselves have become more lengthy and so have ministerial replies thereto. Thirty years ago oral questions were dealt with at the rate of one a minute; now the rate is little more than one in two minutes.[1]

The total of questions seeking written answers is much lower than those for oral response; they are less popular as being unlikely to capture public attention or stimulate executive action. However, items of local interest, personal cases and requests for statistical information are often unstarred. If a Member has exhausted his daily ration of two oral questions, he may use this second-best method of raising further matters. Of course, if a Member merely wishes to obtain information from a Minister and has no wish for interrogation, then a letter might serve his purpose as well as an unstarred question. The difference is that the reply to a letter may not arrive for three weeks while written questions must be answered within 48 hours. Some Members are very active in putting down questions; others do so rarely, if at all. In the session 1969–70 the highest score belonged to Arthur Lewis (Lab. West Ham, North) while other energetic questioners were Mrs. Winifred Ewing (Scot. Nat. Hamilton 1967–70), Edward Taylor (Con. Glasgow, Cacthart) and John Pardoe (Lib. North Cornwall).[2]

Rules governing the admissibility and framing of questions are somewhat complex and no attempt will be made to describe them fully: Campion has produced 38 such rules[3] which cover the main principles. Briefly it may be said that the aim of the question must be to press for information or for action; it must not be hypothetical and it must be addressed to someone who has a clear responsibility for the subject. Normally questions are addressed to Ministers, but they may also be directed to a Member holding an honorary position with special duties— the only remaining example of this kind is the Second Church Estates Commissioner. This responsibility limitation often prevents Members from raising matters of contemporary interest. No action of a local

---

[1] H.C. Deb., Written Answer, Vol. 674, cols. *49–50*.

[2] In the months of November and December 1969 only 239 Members put down questions, i.e. a minority not only of the House but of backbenchers. In the same period one Member asked 37 questions. Procedure. Select Committee Report 1969–70 (198).

[3] Cf. *Introduction to the Procedure of the House of Commons* (Macmillan, 1947), pp. 149–52.

authority may be challenged unless it can be associated with a government department; police forces outside the Metropolitan Police area are supervised by joint committees of local authorities and magistrates, so there are obstacles to raising items about the conduct of provincial police. However, the Home Secretary is responsible for certifying the efficiency of local forces for the purpose of the police grant. He can also under the Police Act, 1964, Section 30, require a report to be made to him about any police activity. Both these powers give Members an opening. They can ask if the Home Secretary is satisfied with the efficiency of force X or whether he will ask for a report on some particular matter. There have also been difficulties over questions on nationalised industries. The theory is that these agencies should carry on their business in an atmosphere of commercial freedom; at the same time Ministers have power to give directions to the industries and have a general, if undefined, responsibility for ensuring that the industries are conducted in the national interest. In practice, the rule here seems to be that any question is admissible which a Minister is willing to answer. And Ministers try generally to be helpful. Questions on some topics are barred in the interests of constitutional propriety. The exclusion covers any reference to the Royal Family, the use of the prerogative of mercy and the ecclesiastical patronage of the Crown. A question that refers to the principles on which honours are awarded will be allowed, but not one which refers to an individual honour.[1] Reference may not be made to any decision of a Court of Law, nor to anything which is *sub judice*. Suggestions may not be made for amending Bills before the House or relating to any topic that has been referred to a Parliamentary Committee or a Royal Commission. There is also a rule against repetition; allusion may not be made to previous debates or questions in the current session. The actual wording is also carefully vetted by the Clerks at the Table who will excise any superfluous matter, epithets, innuendoes and ironical statements. Members are responsible for the accuracy of facts on which a question is based and a short outline of such facts may be included in the form of a question, but extracts from speeches and newspapers are not permitted.

In contrast to the extent of regulations covering the asking of questions, there are none to govern the nature of replies. Courtesy demands that some reply be made, but if it be brief, evasive or otherwise unsatisfactory to the questioner, he can do nothing except to try and elicit further information by skilful supplementaries. On rare occasions answers may be refused on a plea of national interest.

Questions differ greatly in subject-matter and scale of importance.

---

[1] A Member may put down a motion which is critical of an individual award. Whether time would be made available to debate the motion is uncertain.

They are also prompted by a variety of motives. A Minister may be asked to comment on some recent development affecting his department in order to allow the questioner to put a supplementary which expresses a particular point of view. On issues of party controversy a question may be used to express a direct challenge to the policy of the Government. Other questions are of a local or 'constituency' character; others are technical, or of limited public appeal, but reflect the special interests of the questioners; others are about personal cases including the affairs of servicemen, pensioners and hospital patients. The above categories are not mutually exclusive and two or three may apply to many questions. In addition, should a Minister wish to obtain publicity for some new aspect of the policy of his department, he may arrange for a government backbencher to ask an appropriate question. Members who use question-time attract press coverage at least in local papers. They also bring themselves to the attention of party leaders.

Parliamentary questions are an accurate indicator of the changing political and economic situations. Many are highly topical and the volume of questions directed to any one Minister will reflect the varying degree to which his responsibilities excite public interest. Unemployment or industrial unrest will increase the prominence of the Secretary of State for Employment. The total of questions is also associated with the general level of political excitement: in periods of calm it is lower than at moments of acute controversy. It is dangerous to quote a figure for the daily average as conditions change. Naturally, Opposition Members tend to be the more active interrogators and, unless the Government has a large majority, most questions come from the Opposition side of the House. A Government supporter who intervenes consistently in the question-hour to embarrass his leaders will become unpopular with his party, but displays of independence occur daily on the Government benches; Labour Members give much attention to employment and the social services while Conservatives more frequently engage the Minister of Agriculture.

The drafting of replies is undertaken by senior civil servants and this task is given regular precedence over other administrative duties. Much care is given to their form which, although strictly truthful, will present departmental actions in the most favourable light possible and attempt to minimise the scope for successful supplementaries. Ministerial time is also consumed; a Minister, if he is wise, will study the implications of each question—with the aid of his advisers—to prepare himself for supplementaries. It follows that here is one sure method of bringing obscure, local or personal matters to ministerial attention. As a Minister is normally better informed than his critics, he usually defeats them in verbal battle; still, if a Minister has a weak case, pressure at question-time may lead to a subsequent modification of policy. By common consent, parliamentary questions are a most valuable safeguard against bureaucratic excesses, for they ensure that, at quite short notice, any official action may have to be publicly defended by the responsible Minister. Whether the opportunity is used to the fullest advantage is doubtful. A fair amount of time is spent on party debating points; unless party leaders become involved, these pocket battles go unnoticed by the mass media. Routine party sparring has no effect whatsoever on the conduct of public affairs. Would it not be preferable for question-time to be shared more equally among backbenchers? If all Members, other than Ministers, chose to use it occasionally for constituency or fairly specialised matters, the result would be not only greater variety but also more positive. One minor step in this direction would be to insist that a Member's daily ration of two oral questions could not be both directed at the same Minister.

As noted above, a private notice question on an important and urgent topic may be dealt with at the end of question-time. This arrangement has a number of advantages. It provides for emergencies; it extends the time available for questions; it permits a bigger number of supplementaries. But an alternative procedure is a ministerial statement made with the permission of the Speaker. A statement is followed by questions and brief comments. Any debate is irregular since there is no formal motion before the House—but the Speaker allows Members a little latitude. Statements have now become an accepted means of announcing fresh Government policies and at busy periods there may be more than one each day. Comments on statements are less spontaneous than reactions at question-time. The press may have anticipated what is to be said and the Shadow Minister who has to respond is given a copy of the statement at least half an hour before it is heard in the Commons.

Adjournment and Private Members' Motions

There are three types of adjournment debates: major debates which form the main business of the day; three-hour emergency discussions; and brief opportunities for backbench initiative. As a procedural device it is highly convenient because it allows speeches to range widely, unrestricted by the terms of a reasoned motion. The famous two-day debate in May 1940 on the conduct of the war which led to the resignation of the Chamberlain Government was held on the question 'that this House do now adjourn'. There may be an agreement between the parties that an adjournment debate should be restricted to a particular topic, but this arrangement can always be broken. On December 9th 1970 part of the adjournment debate on foreign affairs was devoted to the breakdown of power supplies caused by the industrial action of the electricity workers.

Under Standing Order No. 9, the motion for the adjournment may also be used in an emergency to raise a matter of public importance, although there are many procedural difficulties in the way of obtaining such a debate. At the end of questions a Member can move the adjournment of the House to discuss some recent development; the Speaker will not accept the motion unless the subject is specific, urgent and of sufficient gravity. If the Speaker accepts the motion, and forty Members support it, a three-hour debate is held next day after question-time.[1] This delay gives all concerned time to prepare for the discussion which normally arouses considerable interest. Requests for an emergency debate come usually from Opposition Members and they do place a heavy responsibility upon the Speaker who has to decide whether a topic is admissible within the terms of the Standing Order. Before 1967 rulings from the Chair had become increasingly restrictive and seriously limited the ability of the House to force immediate discussions on serious incidents at home and abroad. In particular the stipulation that no matter could be considered unless it fell within the responsibility of Ministers drastically reduced the application of this procedure to foreign affairs. In July 1957 there was a short debate on a motion which regretted the Speaker's refusal to accept an emergency adjournment on British military action in Muscat and Oman.[2] If rules about urgency were lax, the system might well be abused; since it was allowed to operate less than once a year, disuse seemed a stronger possibility than abuse. However, in 1967 the Select Committee on Procedure recommended modifications to the Standing Order which would permit wider discretion to the Speaker.[3] Subsequently the rules were changed. In particular, the ban on topics falling outside the responsibility of Ministers was softened: the position now is that the Speaker 'shall have regard to the extent to which (the subject) concerns the administrative responsibility of Ministers or could come within the sphere of Ministerial action'. The emergency debates now average four per session and the vast majority have some international implications. Backbenchers enjoy a refreshed element of flexibility in the parliamentary timetable and one which adds to the attention paid to Parliament by the news media.

The daily adjournment debates are of more common concern to Members as they provide regular opportunities for initiative. Half an hour at the end of business is given to a discussion introduced by a

---

[1] The prearranged business continues for three hours after the normal closing time. So the House has a late sitting.

[2] The motion moved by Wedgwood Benn (Lab. Bristol, S.E.) was withdrawn at the end of the debate. The Speaker may not be criticised inferentially but only on a specific motion regretting some aspect of his conduct. H.C. Deb., Vol. 574, cols. 880–911.

[3] Procedure, Second Report paras. 10 and 11: 1966–67 (282) xvi.

backbencher, and should all other items be disposed of before 10 p.m. on Mondays to Thursdays or before 4 p.m. on Fridays, the adjournment debate may still continue until 10.30 p.m. or 4.30 p.m. respectively. This procedure may not be used to raise issues for which the Government has no responsibility. The increased popularity of the adjournment led to the institution in 1945 of a fortnightly ballot to determine its allocation, but subsequently this method was felt not to make the best use of the time available. The arrangement now is that a Member wishing to use the adjournment notifies the Speaker in writing of the matter he wishes to raise. From this information the Speaker selects the topic for the adjournment debate each Thursday evening, and in so doing endeavours to give priority to important constituency grievances and matters of topical interest. Members who are not chosen in this way are entered in a weekly ballot to determine the allocation of the adjournment on other nights of the week. A Member unsuccessful in a ballot does not have his name carried forward to the next without making a fresh application: a Member successful in a ballet is automatically excluded from the next one. The last day of the session and the days immediately before the adjournment at Christmas, Easter, Whitsun and for the summer recess are also devoted to discussions initiated by backbenchers. Members wishing to speak on these days notify the Speaker, who again has the task of allocating the time available and does not necessarily limit each item to half an hour.

Many adjournment debates arise out of matters originally raised at question-time, when an interrogator is not satisfied with the reply received, but sometimes broad issues of policy are raised. The normal form of these short discussions is for the time to be shared fairly equally between the Member introducing his case and the ministerial reply, usually given by the Junior Minister of the appropriate department. Brief interventions may also be made by other Members. A minimum of 48 hours' notice of the subject must be given to enable the preparation of the ministerial reply. Occasionally there is no discussion on the adjournment motion and for this there are three main reasons. The Member may decide not to pursue the particular issue; the problem to be raised may have been settled; the Member due to speak may not be in the House when the adjournment is moved. The last possibility is strengthened by the erratic times of adjournment debates for, while normally they commence at 10 p.m., the parliamentary timetable is very variable. Other business frequently continues until later, and occasionally ends earlier, than the usual hour. The table opposite shows the use made of this facility on every sitting day in April 1971, including the holiday adjournment on the 8th for the Easter recess.

It will be noted that almost all the subjects are constituency matters, sometimes personal cases. The adjournment permits much fuller ventilation of a grievance than can be secured at question-time, although it is rare for a Minister to concede anything that has already been refused publicly. Matters of wider import tend to be raised only during the longer adjournment discussions immediately prior to a recess. Very occasionally a Member will abandon his right to the adjournment in order to allow a Minister to make an emergency statement: on November 22nd 1968, J. Boyd-Carpenter (Con. Kingston-on-Thames) did so to allow the Chancellor of the Exchequer to make an announcement about increases in purchase tax and excise duty.[1]

ADJOURNMENT MOTIONS: APRIL 1971

Day of month	Subject	Number of speakers including Ministers
1	Strath of Kildonar	2
2	(Friday, House counted out)	—
5	Mr. M. F. McEvoy (Conviction)	2
6	Lincoln (Unemployment)	2
7	Compulsory Purchase Order (Cardiff)	2
8	Lanarkshire (Unemployment)	4
	Tourist Industry	4
	Civil Service (Women)	3
	Amphetamines	3
	World Population	2
	Bradford (Economic Prospects)	3
Easter Recess		
19	Overseas Aid (Research Centre)	2
20	European Economic Community (Inshore Fishing Industry)	3
21	British Railways (Closed Shop)	2
22	Bolton (Industrial Obsolescence)	4
23	Planning Applications (Perivale)	2
26	Terminal Patients (Treatment)	2
27	Brost Forge Company	2
28	Archway Road, Islington	2
29	Local Government Reform (Scotland)	4
30	A1 Road (Middlesex)	2

[1] H.C. Deb., Vol. 773, cols. 1790–1805.

Motions in private members' time provide a further opportunity for backbenchers similar to the recess adjournment debates. Twenty Fridays are allocated to private members' Bills and motions and a further four half-days are provided for motions. The distribution of Fridays between Bills and motions has been changed from time to time but is now twelve for Bills and eight for motions. So the parliamentary timetable has twelve slots for private members' motions in a normal session,[1] five hours on each of eight Fridays and approximately three hours on four other days. Twelve separate ballots are held to decide which Members shall have the good fortune to use this facility and in each ballot three names are drawn. Accordingly three motions are put down for each occasion, but usually the whole time is occupied by the debate on the first motion; in the session 1970–71 only twice was a significant amount of time available for the second motion of the day. Most of the subjects involve social and economic issues, and often produce constituency-orientated speeches, e.g. on the problems of a particular industry. A foreign affairs topic may be raised but this is fairly unusual. Many of these discussions follow orthodox lines of party controversy but others produce general agreement in the House and are regarded as an opportunity to ventilate a problem rather than as a challenge to Government policy. The essential difference between a private member's motion and a recess adjournment debate is that the former can end in a decision. A motion by an Opposition Member that is critical of the Government is normally talked out. Less contentious ones may be accepted. Occasionally an Opposition Member will challenge a division, but this will not happen on a Friday because attendance on a motion Friday is often very poor as Members feel that other engagements should have priority. On Fridays the House is even less compelling as a debating society than as a legislature.

This does not imply that time devoted to motions is ill-spent. Many have a topical character or provide a chance to ventilate a problem that would not otherwise be discussed. They also may allow a Member, unplaced in the ballot for Bills, to bring his pet subject to the attention of the House. On a matter like rural transport Members are enabled to make 'constituency' speeches. And if motions give a little relaxation to Members, they may do good in countless ways.

---

[1] An opportunity to debate private members' motions may be lost if it happens to clash with an emergency debate under Standing Order 9. In February 1971 Gregor Mackenzie (Lab. Rutherglen) missed the chance of introducing his motion on unemployment in Scotland because of the emergency debate on Rolls Royce. See H.C. Deb., Vol. 811, cols. 107–8 and Standing Order 3.

CHAPTER 6

THE CHALLENGE TO THE EXECUTIVE—(2) BY COMMITTEES

An assembly of over 600 Members is limited in the tasks it can perform. The House of Commons is well suited to the discussion of broad principles of policy which can be transformed into legislation; it can ventilate particular grievances; it can both echo and stimulate the voice of public opinion. But it cannot exercise intense scrutiny of matters of detail and items of administration. A body of this size cannot usefully study complex memoranda dealing with a particular problem, nor can it engage in the cross-examination of witnesses. So the House has developed a tradition of nominating committees to deal with specific issues. These Select Committees have commonly been given power 'to send for persons, papers and records'. Reports are submitted to the House and may or may not get much further attention. As ministerial control over the Commons developed in the nineteenth century and as the quality of the civil service improved, the number of such *ad hoc* investigations declined. However, another type of Select Committee emerged, sometimes known as sessional committees because they are appointed regularly each session. These bodies engage in detailed review of some aspect of national administration. In recent years there has been much argument inside and outside Parliament about the appropriate extent and value of these regular investigations. They give Members an opportunity to study government at close quarters and to air views arising out of this experience. The discussion on the role of Select Committees is very largely a discussion on the proper role of a backbencher in Parliament.

There are two groups of these committees. One is essentially concerned with considering reports from permanent expert staff; this category covers the Public Accounts Committee and the Select Committees on Statutory Instruments and on the Parliamentary Commissioner for Administration. None of these have been controversial. The other group conducts enquiries themselves and includes the Expenditure Committee which replaced the Estimates Committee in 1970, the Nationalised Industries Committee and the various 'specialised' Select Committees. They have the assistance of a clerk from the permanent staff of the Commons together with some help from the Commons' Library. This group has caused varied disputes. Should these bodies be allowed specialist assistance? Should they be allowed to travel abroad? How large should they be? Should they be allowed to form sub-committees? And what should they enquire into? Obviously not all these issues have become contentious in relation to each committee. Between 1965 and 1968 it gradually became accepted by Ministers that committees could travel abroad and engage limited and temporary expert staff.[1] In 1968 £7,000 was provided for overseas visits. A liaison committee of Select Committee chairmen was formed to administer this grant and co-ordinate committee activities. All this represented a modest victory for those who favoured an extension of Members' functions.

One other difference between the two groups of committees is significant. When Members meet to consider reports from permanent staff, the meeting is in private; this is because the proceedings carry a suggestion of error or culpability by civil servants. When Members conduct an *ad hoc* investigation themselves no such suggestion need arise; instead the intention is to focus public attention on a sector of a public service and so the meetings are often open to the public.

Legal and Financial Committees

The most highly specialised Select Committee is that on Statutory Instruments, or the Scrutiny Committee as it is commonly called, which undertakes a regular review of delegated legislation. It was first established in 1944 in accordance with a motion moved by Hugh Molson.[2] Eleven Members serve on the Committee, most of whom have legal experience, and they have the assistance of the Counsel to the Speaker; Government supporters are in a majority but the Chairman is drawn from the Opposition. It is not concerned with the policy of Statutory Instruments but with their constitutional propriety and can, therefore, proceed in a non-political atmosphere. The terms of reference instruct the Committee to inspect every Statutory Instrument, or draft of a Statutory Instrument, laid before the House and to consider whether the special attention of the House should be drawn to it on any of the following grounds:

(i) that it imposes a charge on the public revenues or contains provisions requiring payments to be made to the Exchequer or any Government Department or to any local or public authority in

---

[1] Martin Partington, 'Parliamentary Committees: Recent Developments', *Parliamentary Affairs*, Autumn 1970, Vol. XXIII, pp. 366–79, gives full details.

[2] H.C. Deb., Vol. 400, cols. 202 *et seq*. A Committee on these lines had been proposed in 1932 by the Committee on Minsters' Powers, Report, pp. 67–70, Recommendation XIV B; 1931–32 Cmd. 4060, xii. Molson was Conservative Member for Doncaster 1931–35 and High Peak 1939–61.

consideration of any licence or consent, or of any services to be rendered, or prescribes the amount of any such charge or payments;

(ii) that it is made in pursuance of an enactment containing specific provisions excluding it from challenge in the courts, either at all times or after the expiration of a specified period;

(iii) that it appears to make some unusual or unexpected use of the powers conferred by the Statute under which it is made;

(iv) that it purports to have retrospective effect where the parent Statute confers no express authority so to provide;

(v) that there appears to have been unjustified delay in the publication or in the laying of it before Parliament;

(vi) that there appears to have been unjustifiable delay in sending a a notification to Mr. Speaker under the proviso to subsection (1) of section four of the Statutory Instruments Act, 1946, where an Instrument has come into operation before it has been laid before Parliament;

(vii) that for any special reason its form or purport calls for elucidation;

(viii) that the drafting of it appears to be defective.[1]

Only a small number of Orders earn adverse comment from the Committee; in session 1968–69 the total was eleven. Criticisms most often arise under paragraphs (iii), (vii) and (viii). The latter items are concerned with precision and clarity. Only paragraph (iii) might permit straying into the forbidden realm of policy and the Committee is cautious when reporting Orders under this heading. Its Reports are not debated by the House although material from them is sometimes used in 'prayer' debates. The Committee serves a limited 'watchdog' function which tries to ensure that the civil service observes correct procedures and constitutional propriety in relation to delegated legislation.

Should the duties of the 'Scrutiny' Committee be widened? Sir Gilbert Campion, then Clerk to the House, suggested to the Select Committee on Procedure in 1946 that the Scrutiny Committee might inquire into grievances arising from Instruments already in operation.[2] To some extent this function is now covered by the Parliamentary Commissioner for Administration. Sir Gilbert also proposed that the Committee might enquire into 'the effectiveness of Instruments as an exercise of the powers delegated'.[3] But such a phrase can imply very

---

[1] The eighth paragraph was added to the original terms of reference in 1967 at the suggestion of Graham Page (Con. Crosby).

[2] Third Report, p. xlv; 1945–46 (189-1) ix.

[3] *Ibid.*, p. xi. Similar proposals have been made more recently by the Study of Parliament Group: *Procedure.* Sixth Report Appendix 4 1966–67 (539) xvi.

broad investigations into administrative method. It would take the Committee far beyond its established role as a watchdog of constitutional propriety. Certainly such a task could not be attempted without the provision of great additional resources.

A curious feature of the Scrutiny Committee is that it is not expected to offer reasons for its decisions. The Committee itself finds this unsatisfactory. A special report issued in 1971 proposed that brief explanations should be given to the House for its findings and that its terms of reference should be made more flexible by allowing it to report an Instrument on any ground which does not impinge on the policy merits of an Instrument.[1] The report also suggested that any Instrument reported to the House that was subject to negative procedure should automatically be transferred to the affirmative resolution category.

Scrutiny of financial administration has been divided between two sessional committees. One is concerned with the accounts of money already spent; the other considers proposed future expenditure. The Public Accounts Committee, the oldest sessional committee, was first established in 1861. It receives reports from the Comptroller and Auditor-General on the appropriation accounts which show how money has been spent. The Comptroller's salary, like that of the Speaker and the Judges, is a direct charge on the Consolidated Fund and so does not have to be approved each year by Parliament. This ensures his independence from Ministerial influence. The Comptroller is assisted by a specially trained staff of some five hundred auditors who have continuous access to departmental accounts. Any expenditure which is not clearly covered by the authority of estimates approved by Parliament, which is wasteful and uneconomic, or which has unusual features will be reported to the Public Accounts Committee. The Committee has fifteen members, a quorum of five, and a Chairman drawn from the Opposition who has had appropriate Ministerial experience. The Chairman plays an important role in guiding the work of the Committee; he does much of the questioning of witnesses that appear before it and, before each meeting, he will discuss with the Comptroller the subjects to be examined. The witnesses are the accounting officers[2] of the Departments whose spending has elicited criticism from the Comptroller, and representatives of the Treasury are also present. Questions to witnesses may be prolonged and highly technical; they are clearly the result of much careful preparation on all sides. In contrast to the Estimates Committee, the work of the P.A.C. is essentially expert in character, and has also something of a judicial quality since it is concerned with the

---

[1] 1970–71 (260).

[2] i.e., Permanent Secretaries, the chief officials of Departments.

legality of expenditure. Witnesses are not summoned for pure explanation, but may be called on to defend departmental actions; their presence implies a hint of culpability. Adverse reports from the P.A.C. are treated with the greatest seriousness in Whitehall and are followed by corrective action. Reports are made to the Commons, but they are also directed at the Treasury which writes Minutes on the recommendations to the Departments concerned. These Minutes have much persuasive weight. Herbert Morrison, drawing on his ministerial experience, testified to this effect before the Select Committee on Procedure.[1] The P.A.C. and the Comptroller are normally treated by the Treasury as valuable allies in restraining unorthodox expenditure. The P.A.C. is, indeed a major cautionary force because it is able to base its work on the findings of the Comptroller and his staff.

The annual expenditure of the British Government is now of the order of £12,000 million.[2] The pattern of this expenditure is set out in the annual Civil, Army, Navy and Air Force estimates, which run to hundreds of pages and are published each February about two months before the start of the financial year to which they refer. How can this burden of paper help Members to shape their views on the desirability of spending money in the way suggested? The problem has baffled and largely defeated Members throughout the twentieth century. A Select Committee on Estimates was appointed between 1912 and 1970 with gaps in both world wars when detailed estimates were not published. The terms of reference instructed the Committee to suggest economies consistent with the policy implied in the estimates. Members on the Committee were faced with four immediate difficulties: the sheer bulk of their raw material; the impossibility of making significant investigations between February and the start of the period to which the estimates referred; lack of staff; the extent to which questions of policy were barred. The last two items of this catalogue require further comment. The staff of the Estimates Committee consisted of one or more of the clerks on the staff of the House of Commons supplemented after 1966 by very limited outside expert assistance. Its resources were in no way comparable to those of the Public Accounts Committee. The limitation on policy enquiries was thought to be a major constitutional issue because of the theory that Ministers are responsible for policy to the House as a whole and not to any committee. So the Estimates Committee was supposed to be limited to a consideration of the more economical administration of existing policies, not with the policies themselves. But the precise boundary here must be ill-defined and is

---

[1] Third Report, Minutes of Evidence. Q. 3227; 1945–46 (189–1) ix.

[2] Current figures will be found in the Annual Abstract of Statistics: Consolidated Fund Revenue and Expenditure Account.

sometimes unrealistic. If a group of Members set out to consider the financial administration of Concorde, then the basic issue of whether the project should continue cannot be totally erased from their minds. In fact the Committee did not appear to be over concerned about their exclusion from the forbidden territory of policy. William Hamilton (Lab. Fife, West) when chairman of the Estimates Committee told the Select Committee on Procedure: 'We can at the moment, I think, get pretty near to policy'.[1]

Before 1939 the Estimates Committee was notably unsuccessful and generally ignored. After 1945 its pattern of work changed and it generated more interest and enthusiasm. Less attention was paid to the actual estimates. Instead a number of investigating sub-committees were established and each was given one or two topics to investigate. They proceeded by gathering written evidence and by calling witnesses from government departments, local authorities and elsewhere. In 1965–66 and 1966–67 the whole range of Government spending was divided out between the sub-committees which could thus enjoy some functional specialisation. This arrangement ceased in 1967 when the size of the Committee had to be reduced to permit the appointment of other new Select Committees. In recent years the sub-committees sometimes moved away from Westminster and travelled abroad. The size of the Estimates Committee fluctuated and was once as high as 43. Work was carried on in a non-party spirit: any disagreement about the content of a report probably did not follow party lines.

The level of industry of the Committee was considerable; Members seemed to enjoy the work for it added to their knowledge of the business of government and led to visits of observation at interesting places. Certainly, their endeavours were of value to students of public administration as much information was produced that would not otherwise have been published. How far the Reports had influence is arguable. It was the practice for Departments to respond to criticisms from the Committee in published statements and so its opinions did earn serious official consideration. From 1960 onwards the Commons allocated three days per session, including two Supply Days, to discussion of the work of the Estimates Committee and the Public Accounts Committee.[2] This may have done something to strengthen the impact of the Reports, for civil servants are sensitive to parliamentary criticism; if a Department rejected suggestions from the Estimates Committee there was always the possibility that the argument would be carried further in the Chamber. Just occasionally a report made an immediate and obvious

---

[1] Fourth Report: 1964–65 (303) viii; q. 387, p. 91.

[2] A. H. Hanson and H. V. Wiseman, *Parliament at Work* (Stevens, 1962), pp. 271–8, describe events leading to this innovation.

impact. The Sixth Report of 1964–65 on Recruitment to the Civil Service[1] caused both the appointment of the Fulton Committee on the Civil Service and stimulated the Treasury to try to get more recruits for the administrative grade from the provincial universities. In general, however, the House as a whole showed little interest in the Committee's activities. Members are too concerned with the continuous political battle to become eager about recommendations for administrative change that have little or no political content. Few parliamentary questions were generated by Estimates' reports. The Committee was well respected, sometimes useful but contributed little to an effective control of public expenditure.[2]

The limitations of the Estimates Committee must not be considered in isolation for they were linked to the nature of the financial information provided by the executive and to the traditional methods of accountancy practised by the Treasury. Taken together these have made many Members feel either that the volume of public spending is slipping out of control or that the control system does not ensure that liabilities and priorities are assessed efficiently. The national accounts are kept on a cash-book basis that records monies spent: they also start afresh each year, in that authority to spend money does not continue automatically from one year to the next. The estimates show neither future commitments, nor the consequences which immediate spending may have for later years. Further, the moral restraint implied by an estimate, that it sets a firm ceiling on the amount that could be spent under a given heading within a financial year, has been eroded because steadily rising costs due to inflation have rendered inevitable an ever-increasing number of supplementary estimates needed to authorise inevitable additional expenditure.[3] During the nineteen-sixties the Government came to recognise the need for longer-term surveys of expenditure and annual White Papers now review spending programmes over a five-year span. To match this development the Select Committee on Procedure recommended[4] in 1969 that the Estimates Committee be replaced by a Select Committee on Public Expenditure which would have a number of functional sub-committees each of which would have a threefold task. It should study the long-term expenditure projections

---

[1] 1964–65 (308) vi.

[2] Nevil Johnson, *Parliament and Administration* (Allen and Unwin, 1966), gives a full review of the work of the Estimates Committee between 1945 and 1965.

[3] To pursue this rather technical subject adequately would be beyond the purpose of the present volume: see *inter alia* Gordon Reid, *The Politics of Financial Control* (Hutchinson, 1966), A. H. Hanson and B. Crick (eds.), *The Commons in Transition* (Collins, 1970), Ch. 4, and E. L. Normanton, *The Accountability and Audit of Governments* (Manchester U.P., 1966).

[4] 1968–69 (51) xv.

in its field and compare them with earlier figures: it should assess the
expenditure implications of ministerial policy and assess success in
obtaining these objectives: it should continue the work of the Estimates
Committee by inquiring into the effectiveness of departmental administration.

The new Conservative Government accepted this proposal[1] and
the Expenditure Committee was appointed for the first time in session
1970–71. It has 49 Members and has created a steering sub-committee
and six functional sub-committees dealing with economic and financial
matters; defence and foreign affairs; the environment and home affairs;
the social services; education and the arts; industry and agriculture.
The pattern of organisation is very similar to the defunct Estimates
Committee. The non-party approach is stressed in the nomination of
chairmen: Edward Du Cann (Con. Taunton) presides over the full body
but three of the sub-committee chairmen are Conservative and three
Labour.

The sub-committee concerned with finance and economics, chairman Dick Taverne (Lab. Lincoln), immediately directed its attention to
the general system of supervision of public expenditure with particular
reference to the contents of the annual Command Papers issued to
explain details of the longer-range planning of expenditure. The
framing of these future programmes now has a more important influence
on the pattern of spending than do the annual estimates which tend
merely to set out the financial implications of policies already accepted.
A report[2] from the Expenditure Committee noted that it was difficult
to construct a new form of parliamentary control which would develop
alongside the new techniques of long-term planning. It recommended
that the House should debate the realities on which the forecast figures
are based, what programmes 'are estimated to cost, what their objectives are and whether alternative programmes would or would not
represent a better allocation of available resources and money'.[3] The
Committee's task is to ensure the availability of information so that
Commons debates on public spending can be effective. Unhappily,
the House as a whole seems no more interested in the Expenditure
Committee than it was in the defunct Estimates Committee.

Nationalised Industries

The institution of many socialised industries in the period after 1945
created a new problem of parliamentary control. Earlier public

---

[1] Green Paper, *Select Committees of the House of Commons*, October 1970,
Cmnd. 4507 and H.C. Deb., Vol. 806, cols. 618–735.

[2] 1970–71 (549).   [3] *Ibid.*, para. 14.

corporations—the British Broadcasting Corporation, the Central Electricity Board and the London Passenger Transport Board—had functioned with a minimum of public supervision; their activities were largely uncontroversial and, except for the B.B.C., they made no claim on state revenues. But the second generation of public corporations governed large-scale industries and services whose efficient operation is vital to the national economic well-being. The theory of nationalisation followed by the Attlee Labour Government contained two central principles: that these undertakings should be monopolies removed from the privately-owned sector of the economy, and that they should retain the freedom for enterprise enjoyed by other commercial bodies. This desire to combine the advantages of public ownership, private ownership and private enterprise led to difficulties in deciding the relationship that should exist between the new corporations and Parliament. If Parliament could not supervise these bodies, what guarantee was there that they would be conducted in the national interest? Alternatively, if the corporations were subjected to daily parliamentary criticism, much of it activated by political motives, it was feared that their boards and officials would be dominated by a spirit of caution. Initiative and imagination might be frowned upon lest their results incurred displeasure.

In the nineteen-fifties there was much hostility among Conservative Members to nationalisation. Labour Members wished to protect the new public corporations from searching public investigation that could provide ammunition for their critics—at least until the corporations were more firmly established. Conservative Ministers were dubious about granting wide powers of investigation to a committee of backbenchers. Against this unpromising background the Select Committee on Nationalised Industries had a slow and painful birth. Initially the Committee was precluded from inquiring into:

(a) Matters which have been decided by, or involve the responsibility of, Ministers.
(b) Wages, conditions of employment, and other questions normally decided by collective bargaining.
(c) Matters which fall to be considered through formal machinery established by statute.
(d) Matters of day-to-day administration.

In November 1955 the Committee issued a short Report[1] which stated that their present terms of reference left 'insufficient scope to make inquiries or to obtain further information regarding the Nationalised Industries which would be of any real use to the House'. After

---

[1] 1955–56 (120) ix.

twelve months' delay the Select Committee was re-appointed in spite
of objections from the Labour Opposition. The revised terms of reference instructed the Committee 'to examine the Reports and Accounts
of the Nationalised Industries' and within this more flexible rubric the
Committee settled down to work on similar lines to those adopted by
the Estimates Committee. Each session a particular nationalised industry
was investigated. Officials from the industry and the parent Ministry
were summoned to give evidence and a mass of data has been collected.
More recently the Committee widened its outlook by taking evidence
from Ministers, private industry, trade unions and other experts.
The terms of reference were extended in 1965 to cover the Post Office
and in 1969 the Independent Television Authority, Cable and Wireless
and the Bank of England were added. The proposal to investigate
the Bank of England caused some friction with the Treasury; ultimately
it was agreed that confidential functions of the Bank be excluded,
particularly the operation of monetary and financial policy. The Wilson
Government refused to agree that the ambit of the Committee should
be extended to other commercial undertakings in which the state has a
controlling interest: this restriction was severely criticised in the Commons and accepted by a vote of 101 to 61 after both Labour and
Conservative Members on the Committee had objected to the
limitation.[1]

The Select Committee has a chairman from the Government
backbenches. In 1966 its size was increased from thirteen to eighteen
Members and it received the right to appoint sub-committees. This
enabled more than one enquiry to be carried out at the same time. It
also allowed small sub-committees to be nominated to take evidence
abroad. Since 1967 some of the Committee's hearings have been held in
public. A major restraint on the Committee has been lack of staff.
Initially, it was proposed that there should be a staff headed by an
officer of great administrative experience with a status equal to that
of Comptroller and Auditor-General.[2] The Conservative Government
resisted the idea. The Committee has had to content itself with one,
later two, clerks from the House of Commons. The clerks may play a
rather larger role in the work of the Committee than some Members
might care to admit, particularly in framing the first drafts of reports.
More recently the part-time services of individual experts have been
obtained to help with particular enquiries. Were the Committee given
more facilities there is no doubt that its work could be better prepared
and more effective. It is not simply that more resources are needed:
equally important is the need to establish the Committee on a more
permanent basis, to avoid re-appointment each session, so that future

---

[1] H.C. Deb., Vol. 777, cols. 1181–1272.   [2] 1952–53 (235) vi.

enquiries can be planned in advance and adequate time made available to organise research.

A survey of its reports will show that two issues have dominated the mind of the Committee. One is the nature of the relationship between the responsible Minister and the board controlling an industry. The other is the financial situation of an industry, particularly in relation to pricing and investment policies. Financial tests are the obvious means of checking the efficiency of a commercial undertaking. They also raise the question of how far an industry is being run on business lines or how far decisions are being taken for political or social reasons. The Committee have sought to establish to what extent Ministers have encouraged public undertakings to charge uneconomic prices, to maintain uneconomic services or make investment decisions that could not be financially justified. Ministers have power to issue directives to public corporations and these directives must be published: few of these formal instructions have been given. The Committee has suspected that much ministerial influence has been exercised informally, perhaps across the lunch table. Political pressure, not least by Conservative Ministers, may force nationalised industries into doing things that otherwise would not have been done and, since the pressure is informal, Ministers may seek to escape responsibility. In a special Report, *Ministerial Control of Nationalised Industries*,[1] the Committee has suggested that a single Ministry be responsible for supervision of the nationalised industries. It was thought that this would unify and clarify relations between the Government and public boards. The Committee urged that Ministers should be clearly responsible for deciding how far nationalised industry should respond to social needs and that the cost of meeting social needs should be met, not by the industries, but by the taxpayer. Where appropriate, these additional costs could be met by social grants included in Departmental estimates for which Ministers would be responsible and would have to justify to Parliament. These ideas were too uncomfortable to be acceptable to Ministers. Nevertheless, the Report does demonstrate that the Committee is able to raise fundamental questions without dividing on party lines.

Debates in the House on nationalised industries have perhaps been better informed as a result of the Committee's labours. The significant question, however, is what impact they have had on Ministers and Boards. Some changes have certainly followed the lines of the Committee's suggestions: whether similar changes would have been made without the Committee's intervention cannot be known. David Coombes has summarised the position: 'The Committee has not so far succeeded

---

[1] 1967–68 (371) xiii. For criticism of this Report see W. A. Robson in *Political Quarterly*, January 1969, Vol. 40, p. 103.

in deflecting the government from any policy on which it was firmly set. But it had often influenced the government to undertake reviews of current policy and to formulate policy where none existed.'[1] Ministries and Boards have been stimulated by the parliamentary probing. It seems that the Report on British Railways affected methods of judging schemes for capital investment; that the structure of the gas industry was influenced by the Report on that industry; that the Report on the Post Office had some impact on its subsequent reorganisation; that the Report on ministerial control stimulated fresh thought about the pattern of relationships between Departments and Boards.[2] In retrospect, some of the fears expressed when the Committee was first established now seem exaggerated if not absurd. Lord Morrison suggested that the managers of nationalised industries 'might well find it trying and nerve-racking to be put through the mill at the House of Commons'.[3] The idea that a septennial interrogation would weaken the vitality and potential risk-taking of public corporations out of awe for a Commons' committee attributes to Members a degree of majesty they do not possess. One of the early critics, Ian Mikardo, has publicly recanted: as Chairman of the Committee during the period of the Wilson Government he became convinced of its value.[4] The fact that the Committee has worked with remarkable harmony in what could be a highly controversial field is a tribute to the farsightedness of Members who have served on it. Trivial matters have been avoided. Issues arousing contemporary excitement have been avoided. So also has anything relating to collective bargaining. There have been no party rows and the work has moved forward with a collective wish to find means of improving the efficiency of the publicly controlled sector of the economy.

Viewed in this light, the success of the Select Committee on Nationalised Industries helped to pave the way for further parallel committees appointed to scrutinise other areas of public administration. These developments are considered in the following section.

Specialised Committees

Almost since the start of this century schemes have been put forward for the establishment of parliamentary committees that would specialise

---

[1] *The Member of Parliament and the Administration* (Allen and Unwin, 1966), p. 191.

[2] Ian Mikardo in a contribution to *Parliamentary Scrutiny by Committee* (Pergamon, 1970), p. 69. Mikardo has been Labour Member for Reading 1945–59 and for Poplar since 1964.

[3] *Government and Parliament* (O.U.P., 1954), p. 281.

[4] *Parliamentary Scrutiny by Committee*, pp. 55–7.

n particular sectors of public affairs. Details have varied with an assort-
ment of ideas about the constitution, function and *modus operandi* of
the committees. But there has been a common belief that Parliament, as
at present organised, lacks both the information and the opportunities
to enable it to play an effective role in the government of the country.
The real decisions, it is said, are made in Whitehall. Westminster is
divorced from Whitehall. Parliament in Westminster becomes a unit
for the formal registration and legitimation of decisions made elsewhere. To end this isolation, Members are urged to break down the
barriers by forming committees to discuss problems of policy and
administration with Ministers and civil servants. In this way Members
could come to participate in the real business of government.

In 1907, Fred Jowett, then a Labour Member for Bradford, proposed
that a separate Commons committee be appointed to supervise each
Government Department. The senior Minister in a department would
be chairman of the committee which would examine all legislative and
administrative matters within its scope before they were discussed in
Parliament. Departmental documents would be available to these
bodies. Obviously the scheme was conceived on the local government
model which did not fit the established relationship between Cabinet
and Commons depending as it does on party loyalty and party discipline. The Jowett plan tended to discredit later and more sophisticated
plans for Commons committee work. Another obstacle to change
has been that the advocates of reform of Commons procedure have
tended to hold left-wing political views.[1] Possibly the most eloquent
explanation of how specialised committees might work was set out by
Harold Laski in his *Grammar of Politics* which is still worthy of quoting:

'They would work, not as makers of policy which is primarily,
as I have argued, a ministerial function, but in part as a consultative organ and in part as a means of bringing to the legislature a
definitely competent opinion upon the working of the administrative process. They ought to have access to all papers except
those of an especially confidential kind. They should be able
to summon public servants before them for the taking of evidence
upon particular questions. They should have regular meetings with
the minister at which his policy, and particularly his legislation, is
discussed and explained . . . They would have no power to
prevent the introduction of legislation, and no authority to
dictate ministerial methods. Their business, like that of the King of

---

[1] For fuller discussion of schemes of reform before 1960 see Peter G. Richards,
Parliament and Foreign Affairs (Allen and Unwin, 1967), Ch. VIII.

England, would be to advise, to encourage, and to warn, with the addition that, in the process, they would also learn.'[1]

Backbench dissatisfaction on both sides of the House led to the appointment in the session 1958–59 of a Select Committee on Procedure. A. H. Hanson and H. V. Wiseman presented a memorandum to the Committee urging the establishment of committees broadly on the lines of the Laski plan.[2] Simultaneously Bernard Crick produced a Fabian pamphlet on the same theme.[3] But the Procedure Committee was unimpressed and brushed aside the idea of specialised committees.[4] Six years later the Procedure Committee again returned to the question: at this time there were more younger Labour Members in the Commons seeking an outlet for their energies. In 1964 the Procedure Committee received evidence from a small newly-created body of political scientists and members of the staff of Parliament known as the Study of Parliament Group. While the Group proposed specialised committees on the Laski model, it urged that they should be concerned with less controversial topics—scientific development, crime, machinery of administration, housing and land use, the social services.[5] This modification was introduced in order to meet the objection that the new brand of committee would be unable to do constructive work if it became another forum for the party political type of argument.[6] The Group broadly accepted that if specialised committees were to succeed, they would have to observe the non-party traditions of the Public Accounts Committee and the Estimates Committee.

Change in Parliament comes slowly. The Procedure Committee moved forward towards the proposition advocated by the Study of Parliament Group but in a way which emphasised evolution and continuity. Its proposal was that the Estimates Committee should ask its sub-committees to specialise in separate fields of government activity and, equally important, that the terms of reference of the Estimates Committee should be widened so that matters of policy were no longer excluded specifically from its purview. The Government was even more cautious, perhaps because of its tiny majority: the Estimates Committee was allowed to form sub-committees on a functional basis

---

[1] *Grammar of Politics* (Allen and Unwin, 1925), p. 350.

[2] Their memorandum was subsequently published in *Public Law* (1959), pp. 272–92.

[3] Later developed into a fuller study *The Reform of Parliament* (Weidenfeld and Nicolson, 1964).

[4] 1958–59 (92) vi.

[5] 1964–65 (303) viii; pp. 131–142.

[6] This objection was set out in my *Honourable Members* (Faber, 1959), p. 252.

but its terms of reference were unaltered. However, after the 1966 Election the position changed. The Wilson administration had secured a firm majority and felt perhaps a need to provide occupation of mind for their young and keen backbenchers. A new Leader of the House, Richard Crossman (Lab. Coventry, East), was willing to experiment. After consultation with the Opposition, two specialist committees were formed, one on science and technology and the other on agriculture. There was an immediate distinction between these two bodies; one was to investigate a subject, the other was given a particular Government Department to examine. In session 1967–68 the Agriculture Committee was replaced by a fresh Select Committee linked to the Department of Education and Science.[1] Three further Select Committees were established in session 1968–69 to consider Race Relations, Scottish Affairs and the Ministry of Overseas Development. The Race Relations Committee was the result of initiative not from backbenchers but from the Home Secretary, James Callaghan (Lab. Cardiff S.E.).

The creation of these specialist committees has been the most important parliamentary innovation of recent years and is worthy of detailed examination.[2] Both their constitution and composition caused friction. The selection of Members has been done through the Whips and this caused muttering about the power of the 'usual channels'. All the chairmen have been drawn from the Government backbenches. Often the chairmen are ex-Ministers. The size of the committees has varied but was commonly about sixteen. Since there is a shortage of Members able and willing to serve on some committees, rather smaller numbers might be more suitable. However, the higher figure does enable the formation of sub-committees that can take evidence simultaneously. The Select Committee on Education created as many as five sub-committees. The record of attendance has been remarkably consistent: between 1966 and 1970 it averaged around 66% for all the Select Committees except Agriculture.[3] For this Committee the attendance

---

[1] Work on the final report of the Agriculture Committee was not completed until February 1969.

[2] A considerable literature on this field has already developed. Eight Members have given their views in a symposium, *The Growth of Parliamentary Scrutiny by Committee* (Pergamon, 1970). There are two chapters on the subject by H. V. Wiseman and Nevil Johnson in *The Commons in Transition* (Collins, 1970). Other articles include Roger Williams 'The Select Committee on Science and Technology' in *Public Administration* (1968), Vol. 46, pp. 299–313; G. T. Popham and D. Greengrass, 'The Role and Functions of the Select Committee on Agriculture', in *Public Administration* (1970), Vol. 48, pp. 137–52; M. Partington, 'Parliamentary Committees—Recent Developments', and D.R. Shell, 'Specialist Select Committees', both in *Parliamentary Affairs* (1970), pp. 366–404.

[3] A Member has only to make a brief appearance in the committee room to be recorded as present.

record was 66% in 1966–67, 52% in 1967–68, 58% in 1968–69. When the size of the Committee was increased the new Members tended to stay away, especially on the Labour side: Andrew Faulds (Smethwick) and Clifford Kenyon (Chorley 1945–70) were never present.

The Agriculture Committee had a stormy history. Initially it contained no Members representing Scottish constituencies since its task was to review aspects of the work of the Ministry of Agriculture— a Ministry whose functions do not penetrate north of the Border. After protests, two Members from Scotland were added. Subsequently, in December 1967, the size of the Committee was further increased from sixteen to twenty-five. Surely this is an unwieldy number to undertake a parliamentary inquiry? Since there was also much talk about the shortage of Members available for committee work, this move was very strange. As the Agriculture Committee had shown a degree of initiative and independence that was displeasing to the Government, the addition of extra Members can be interpreted as a move to dilute enthusiasm. Later in the session Ministers decided, in the face of strong objections, that the Committee was not to be re-appointed. An argument developed over how far specialist committees should be permanent. Should the benefits—and difficulties—of committee investigation be centred continuously on one Ministry, or should the searchlight of enquiry be allowed to move round? Ministers were determined that benefits and difficulties should be shared.

Another source of friction has been the choice of subjects for investigation by Select Committees. The Agriculture Committee decided to start operations by an enquiry into the consequences for British agriculture of entry into the European Economic Community. Politically this topic was highly sensitive, although not in the orthodox party dimension. The Education Committee started more circumspectly with a survey of the schools' inspectorate but then went on to enquire into student relations. This investigation achieved wide publicity, aroused some student disorder and covered the work of universities and local education authorities. Here the ground for criticism was that the Committee had strayed away from its original purpose—to scrutinise the work of the Department of Education and Science. The Race Relations Committee chose to study job opportunities for coloured school leavers; again local authorities were involved through the youth employment service. Local government, through the associations of local authorities, expressed disquiet at the unexpected intervention of Select Committees in their field of public responsibility. For many years local authorities have resented the extent to which their affairs have been supervised or directed by government departments: the Select Com- mittees were regarded as another unwelcome central intrusion into local autonomy. Only once has the Government asked for a particular topic to be investigated: after the *Torrey Canyon* disaster in 1967 the

Select Committee on Science and Technology were requested to study coastal pollution. The matter was referred to a sub-committee and a report subsequently appeared. However, the request was ill-received by the Committee and some Members felt that it was a move to deflect attention from the on-going enquiry into the nuclear reactor programme.

For staff the specialist committees have had to rely essentially on the clerks of the House of Commons. But after some pressure and delay, authority has been given for the appointment of one or more expert advisers working on a part-time basis. There is widespread objection to any idea that the Commons should build up a large separate staff that would challenge the competance of the civil service, as this would lead to duplication, waste and institutional rivalry. The function of the expert adviser is merely to suggest to the committee profitable lines of enquiry and to help the committee clerk and the Research Division of the Library to assemble information for the assistance of Members.

The tendency has grown for committees to take evidence in public. However the press have shown little interest in the proceedings even when Ministers have appeared to give evidence. Earlier fears that grave constitutional difficulties would follow were Ministers and civil servants to be cross-examined by Select Committees have proved unfounded. Civil service witnesses have showed caution when the questioning has turned to issues of policy. So far no Minister has been unwilling to discuss policy. Witnesses from outside central government have been uninhibited. Yet there have been problems over obtaining other information from Whitehall. The specialist committees are given 'power to send for persons, papers and records' but there is no power to ensure that such requests for information are answered. The Agriculture Committee asked the Foreign Office for certain reports which the Foreign Office refused to provide and asserted in a formal Command Paper 'Government departments cannot accept a general obligation to produce all papers for which a parliamentary committee asks, particularly those relating to internal administration'.[1] This statement was a basic challenge to the original concept of specialised committees— that they should scrutinise the administration rather than the policy of government departments.

Select Committees have in the past almost always conducted their business at Westminster. Members serving on the specialised committees have displayed an urge to travel, not merely within the United Kingdom but also abroad. At first this desire was resisted by Ministers, perhaps because of the expense, but even more because the Foreign

---

[1] Cmnd. 3479, para. 3.

Office saw diplomatic difficulties about the desire of the Agriculture Committee to visit Brussels.[1] The Select Committee on Science and Technology wished for some of its Members to visit Europe and America to assist its study of the nuclear reactor programme.[2] After some argument both Committees were allowed to travel. As from the financial year 1968–69 a sum of £7,000 was set aside in annual estimates for travel by Select Committees, the fund to be administered by the liaison committee of Select Committee chairmen.

The reports of specialised committees appear to have had little influence on government departments. Sometimes a formal official response has been made to their recommendations and sometimes not. The reports should have had some effect in educating public and parliamentary opinion—notably on carbon fibres.[3] Information has been brought together and published which was otherwise not easily available, e.g. on defence research.[4] Only a minority of reports have been debated in the Chamber. Divisions in committee on party lines have been avoided with the perhaps surprising exception of the Committee on Science and Technology where the recommendations on the nuclear reactor programme caused a Labour/Conservative split.[5] The Government also rejected the recommendations of the same committee on coastal pollution. This led to an Opposition challenge in the Commons and a vote with the Whips on: the chairman of the sub-committee that had studied the subject, Sir Harry Legge-Bourke (Con. Isle of Ely), spoke in the debate from the Opposition front bench[6] and thus made a serious dent in the attempt to create a tradition that specialised committees act on a non-party basis.

A major criticism of the specialised committees is that they tended to move away from the role originally envisaged for them, the scrutiny of government administration. Instead they have occasionally studied topics where the responsibility of government departments is but marginal, e.g. student unrest, or they have tended to become a pressure group favouring a particular policy—perhaps in support of a Ministry. The Select Committees on Overseas Aid and Scottish Affairs consisted not of an average cross-section of Members but rather of groups of Members who were especially keen on helping under-developed areas or of helping the Scottish economy. Two other factors dull the impact of these specialised committees. Their enquiries tend to be a little academic; they are, indeed, attempts to discover truth. In consequence, they are removed from the immediate anxieties of making decisions; they are also set apart from the clash of party conflict. Results of

---

[1] 1966–67 (378) xvii, paras. 17–29.   [2] 1966–67 (381) xix, paras. 3–8.

[3] 1968–69 (157).   [4] 1968–69 (213).   [5] 1966–67 (381) xix.

[6] 1967–68 (421–1) xv and H.C. Deb., Vol. 785, cols. 105–17.

these labours may be worthy but they are politically unexciting. The other feature is the present multiplicity of public enquiries by royal commissions, departmental committees and a host of other bodies. Another committee of investigation has no novelty value for the news media. So their activities are overlooked. Their reports may go unread even by other Members faced with a mass of material awaiting their attention.

Disappointment with the impact made by specialised committees has helped to revive criticism of the whole concept. The original objection was twofold. It was argued that the committees would attempt to intervene in the normal processes of departmental administration and policy. If they were ineffective they would be a waste of time: if they became a real nuisance to Ministers, then Ministers would use their political authority to frustrate committee activities. The experience of the Agriculture Committee provides support for this view. The second criticism, strongly advanced by two prominent Labour Members, Michael Foot (Plymouth, Devonport 1945–55 and Ebbw Vale since 1960) and John Mendelson (Penistone), is that the only place to challenge the Government is in the Chamber of the House. Committee activity diverts Members from the basic political conflict between parties. Ministers will retreat, not from adverse committee reports, but from sustained argument and challenge in debate. This view also became more persuasive after 1969 when the Wilson Government failed to carry through important aspects of its declared policy through opposition in the Chamber.

It is true that advocates of specialised committees are trying to minimise the party element in political conflict by urging that Members should spend more time on an aspect of parliamentary work where the party dimension is weak. If a committee worked too closely with a government department, it would cease to scrutinise and stimulate; instead it would become a clique of departmental supporters. In the words of Sir Kenneth Wheare, committees can become buffers or duffers. There would be special difficulties in the way of forming specialised committees on foreign affairs and defence because s ome information in these areas must be confidential. Were Members on such committees not given access to confidential material, it is arguable that their reports would be of little value: were access to classified information granted, then they would not be able to explain fully the basis of their opinions to parliamentary colleagues. Backbenchers would come to have first and second class status in relation to foreign affairs and defence, depending upon whether or not they sat upon the relevant committee. To a lesser extent the same situation could develop in relation to Members sitting on other specialised committees.

In spite of doubts and criticisms, most Members who have served on these bodies seem enthusiastic. Certainly, the Agriculture Committee protested bitterly when it was disbanded.[1] Backbenchers who belong to specialised committees are not a typical cross-section of the House because they tend to be 'full-time' Members who devote almost all their energy to parliamentary affairs. They feel that this unusual committee assignment brings them closer to the heart of government, to Ministers, to civil servants and the evolution and operation of policy decisions. Here is a fresh interest, a new role, perhaps a little more status and travel. The unimportant backbencher may make his presence felt just a little. He may help to frame sections of a committee report.

The incoming Conservative Government decided not to turn its back on the new specialised committees.[2] Instead, the experiment has been adapted and continued in those areas where it is most likely to make a positive contribution or satisfy the aspirations of Members. As described above[3] the Estimates Committee has been transformed into the Expenditure Committee with wider terms of reference; nevertheless, the approach will be more confined than that of the specialised committees because of the concentration on public spending. Some of the committees established under the Labour Government still remain— those on Science and Technology, Race Relations, Overseas Aid and Scottish Affairs. The size of some committees has been reduced. No successor has appeared to the Agriculture and Education committees. It is notable that the departmental type of committee has disappeared apart from the special case of Scottish Affairs: the retention of a body to survey conditions north of the Border is perhaps a modest concession to nationalist sentiment.

Regional Committees

The regional committees for Scotland and Wales require separate treatment because they cut across the normal distribution of functions. They also create special problems.

The Scottish Grand Committee comprises all 71 Members representing Scottish constituencies and up to 15 Members added to make its party composition more similar to that of the House as a whole. This is a debating committee which deals with three classes of business— Scottish legislation, Scottish Estimates and discussion of Scottish matters. Unless 10 Members of the Commons object, the general principles of any Bill relating only to Scotland can be considered by this body at not more than two meetings each lasting $2\frac{1}{2}$ hours. Such a debate is tantamount to a second reading in the Chamber. The Grand can also take the Report stage of any Bill which it has already considered

---

[1] 1968–69 (138) vi.   [2] 1970–71 Cmnd. 4507.   [3] pp. 121–2 *supra*.

in principle. The committee stage will go to one of the two Scottish Standing Committees. Thus it is possible for every effective stage of a Scottish Bill to be dealt with outside the Chamber save for the third reading which is usually a formality. Scottish legislation can thus go ahead without impinging on the timetable of the Commons.

Not more than six times a session the Opposition can choose one or more Scottish Estimates to be debated in the Grand Committee. The procedure is similar to that of a Supply Day in the Chamber. On not more than two other days the Government can propose 'matters' to be considered; the arrangement here is not unlike the consideration of a Government motion in the Chamber.

The Scottish Grand does provide a separate forum for the affairs of north of the Border. It keeps Ministers of the Scottish Office closely in touch with Scottish Members. Its functions could be expanded. Scottish questions might be transferred from the Chamber to the Grand Committee; this would permit both more time for Scottish questions and more time for other types of question in the Chamber. The idea, however, has been resisted by Scottish Members since they do not want to lose the greater publicity always obtained for questions in the House: while enjoying separate facilities, they do not wish to give up other rights. Another difficulty associated with the Grand Committee is the question of voting. Divisions are rare. Some Members feel they are improper. The position of Members added to provide a party balance is obviously artificial and unsatisfactory. It is not surprising that their attendance is sometimes poor. As from 1970 the situation became more delicate since even with the addition of 15 backbench supporters, the Government cannot hope for a majority.[1]

A Welsh Grand Committee was established in 1960.[2] It is a pale reflection of the Scottish predecessor since it has no legislative role and a separate Ministry for Wales did not emerge until 1964. Up to four discussions are held each year on topics concerning the Principality: the topics are chosen through the usual channels but the Opposition has the initiative. All 36 Members for Wales sit on the Committee with 5 other Members added. When Conservatives are in office a large number of added backbench supporters would be necessary to ensure a Government majority. An imbalance does not matter since a vote in the Welsh Grand is of no practical importance. There is very little law that relates only to Wales. Should such a Bill come forward there is a provision that the committee stage can go before a standing

---

[1] Twenty-three Conservatives were elected from the 71 Scottish constituencies in 1970. One is a Deputy Speaker who cannot vote. Eight are Ministers whose regular attendance at the Grand Committee cannot be expected.

[2] For an account of its activities see R. L. Borthwick's article in *Parliamentary Affairs*, Summer 1968, Vol. XXI, pp. 264–76.

committee composed of all Members from Welsh constituencies plus added Members. This arrangement was instituted in 1907 but it remained unused until 1962.[1]

The device of the specialist select committee was extended to Scotland in 1969. It has already been stressed that select committees work on a non-party basis and every effort is made to secure a unanimous report. This consensus is based on agreement between Conservative, Labour and Liberal Members and does not extend to Nationalists. Accordingly when the Scottish Affairs Committee was preparing its report on Economic Planning in Scotland,[2] Mrs. Winifred Ewing (Scot. Nat. Hamilton 1967–70) produced a separate report. The Committee rejected the Ewing version by 9 votes to 1, but it was still printed as part of the proceedings of the Committee and attracted some publicity in Scotland. If minority or extreme opinions gain representation on select committees, it is clear that the committee can be used as a platform for the dissemination of unorthodoxy. No select committee on Ulster affairs is likely to be created because no British Government could hope to excercise effective control over its activities. Were such a body to be instituted, it would surely become a forum for partisan argument.

Are regional committees anything more than a sop to nationalist sentiment? Perhaps it is surprising that in 1970 the Conservatives agreed to continue the Scottish Select Committee when other select committees disappeared. Regional debates do give Scottish and Welsh Members extra opportunity to press constituency problems, especially economic difficulties. There is an element of equity here since these areas are less prosperous than England. Regional committees could also help to relieve the overcrowded Commons' timetable. Switching Scottish legislation away from the Chamber does make a small contribution, but it depends upon the co-operation of the Opposition which will not be obtained for controversial Bills. Nor may the Opposition co-operate if they are trying to make difficulties for the Government in the management of the Commons' business. The other limitation is that Scottish and Welsh Members are not willing to barter their traditional rights for fresh regional facilities. So questions to Scottish and Welsh Ministers still consume time in the Chamber and in 1960 the Welsh Members successfully resisted the idea that the Welsh Grand Committee could be allowed to replace the normal 'Welsh Day' debate in the Commons.

---

[1] So far this type of Welsh committee has been used only for fairly uncontroversial private members' Bills. The committee stage of the Welsh Language Bill, 1967, was taken on the floor of the House.

[2] 1969–70 (272).

Members and Civil Servants

A common criticism of the Civil Service is that it stifles initiative and insists on excessive adherence to prescribed administrative routines. This, it is said, leads to a lack of inventiveness, the desire for a quiet life and failure to see the problems of tomorrow. In order that no indiscretions shall be committed each grade of civil servant has a limited power of decision; matters exceeding the competence of an official must be passed up to the next step in the hierarchy. A civil servant is responsible to his superiors and ultimately his Minister; the supreme crime for him is to cause his Minister embarrassment. The result of the activities of Members may well be to strengthen the inherent tendencies to official caution beyond desirable limits—the problem of how far parliamentary commentary would damage the efficiency of nationalised industries is one that applies to all Departments of State. It also increases the cost of administration, for much care is given to the preparation of evidence for Select Committees and to the content of Ministerial replies and speeches. Senior officials give top priority to parliamentary business; other matters are perforce delayed. The price of parliamentary inquiry is high, but it must be paid to secure some protection from bureaucratic actions. The financial aspect is of less significance than the cost of fear and frustration. Left-wing critics who favour large-scale and imaginative state action are distressed by the effect of the restraining voice of Parliament, even although its value is admitted. Civil servants may well think of legislators as interfering busybodies, or as lobbyists seeking special favours. The Member, for his part, is convinced of his duty to make representations in response to complaints that come his way: much experience of such complaints may make him feel that the Civil Service is unsympathetic, parsimonious, inflexible and adept at procrastination, however much he may respect the officials he happens to encounter. The anonymity of the Civil Service is also irritating. Most of the decisions that Members challenge are made by officials and are, of necessity, unknown to Ministers. The cloak of Ministerial responsibility shields the individual administrator from criticism and also safeguards his independence, for no civil servant feels that his personal future depends on willingness to act in a way that is pleasing to influential Members. After the Crichel Down inquiry, in which details of public administration received unparalleled publicity, there was some demand among Members for wider retributive action against officials who were criticised in Sir Andrew Clark's Report.[1] Crichel Down also led to an official restatement of the limits of the doctrine of Ministerial responsibility,[2] which may be summarised

---

[1] 1953–54 Cmd. 9176, xi.   [2] H.C. Deb., Vol. 530, cols. 1290–1.

as follows. If a civil servant carries out a direct order from a Minister or acts properly in accordance with the policy laid down by the Minister, the responsibility of the Minister is absolute. If a civil servant makes a mistake, but not on an important question of policy, the Minister should acknowledge the mistake and accept responsibility, although not personally involved, and subsequently take corrective action within the Department. If a civil servant acts reprehensibly there is no obligation on the Minister to defend actions of which he has no knowledge and which he believes to be wrong, although he must still account for his stewardship to Parliament. But these principles may not provide a clear prescription covering any particular case, for the extent to which a policy has been laid down by a Minister (or by his predecessors, and not countermanded) can be a matter of argument. The restatement of these rules is unlikely to have satisfied Members who felt that civil servants enjoy too great a degree of security of tenure; that while exhaustively conditioned to avoid mistakes, the public official is over-protected if he errs. Meanwhile the anonymity surrounding the Civil Service is being slowly eroded as its senior officers come to make more frequent public appearances in Parliament and elsewhere—a development welcomed by the Fulton Committee on the Civil Service.[1] To insist that civil servants must always hide away behind the skirts of the theory of ministerial responsibility is wholly unsatisfactory. Equally, Ministers are legally and politically responsible for their policies; they must not be allowed to dodge blame by imputing inadequacy to their permanent advisers.

At present Members come into contact with the more routine work of civil servants mainly through complaints from constituents. Traditionally there have been two avenues for Members to take up complaints: a letter could be sent to the responsible Minister or a question could be asked in the House. Neither process was likely to provide much satisfaction for the person with a grievance. The letter to the Minister does bring the case to his personal attention but normally his reply is prepared by civil servants and supports, perhaps with fuller explanation, the action already taken. A question in the House is even less likely to provide satisfaction for here the Minister is protecting his officials from a public challenge. If at all possible a Minister will avoid admitting any error. Unless a major political storm developed, as over Crichel Down, there has been no possibility that a Member could obtain an independent enquiry into a constituent's grievance. To remedy this situation a report by JUSTICE in 1961, *The Citizen and the Administration*, urged the appointment of a parliamentary official to investigate complaints on the lines of the Scandinavian Ombudsman.

---

[1] p. 92; 1967–68 Cmnd. 3638 xviii.

The contemporary Conservative Government rejected the idea. However, the proposal was later adopted by the Labour Government and in 1966 the office of Parliamentary Commissioner for Administration (P.C.A.) was instituted.

The British form of this office is based on the precedent of the Comptroller and Auditor General. Like the Comptroller, the P.C.A. is the servant of Parliament, not the executive. His salary is a permanent charge on the Consolidated Fund. He has a staff to assist him. He reports to a Select Committee of the Commons whose chairman is a senior Opposition Member. When considering his reports the Select Committee can call for evidence from government departments. Here the similarity ends. The P.C.A. does not carry out an audit function: his task is to seek out maladministration by the Civil Service. But what is the meaning of 'maladministration'? It is perhaps rather easier to recognise than define. The most formal explanation was set out in the Crossman catalogue 'bias, neglect, inattention, delay, incompetence, ineptitude, perversity, turpitude, arbitrariness'.[1] Put more simply, maladministration would seem to cover any case where a civil servant's action had been improper or inadequate. The concept does not extend to every situation in which a government department is required to make a discretionary decision. Thus if a department is authorised to give or withhold grants to particular types of applicant, an unsuccessful claimant is not entitled to use the P.C.A. to have his claim reviewed unless he can provide *prima facie* evidence of maladministration as defined above.

Complaints cannot go to the P.C.A. direct from the public. They must be forwarded through Members or Peers. Any Member can send any complaint, so an individual with a grievance is not confined to action through the Member representing his own constituency. There are two reasons why complaints cannot go directly to the P.C.A. First, Members act as a sieve and help to reduce the volume of work falling on the P.C.A. and his staff. Second, this arrangement reduces the possibility that the P.C.A. will seem to usurp the historic task of Members to care for the interests of constituents: in no way does the P.C.A. replace Members. He is their assistant. If the P.C.A. feels that there is a basis for a complaint, he will ask the Department concerned for comments. He has the right to inspect relevant departmental documents. His findings are reported both to the Department and to the Member. However, there is no requirement on the Member to transmit the report to the complainant. If the P.C.A. advises remedial action— either in terms of departmental procedures or in making recompense to the individual concerned—his views are only advisory. He cannot

---

[1] Speech of the Leader of the House on the second reading of the Parliamentary Commissioner Bill 1966: H.C. Deb., Vol. 734, col. 51.

overrule a ministerial decision. Nevertheless, the opinions of the P.C.A. carry great weight: if he recommends compensation, then compensation is paid. The main limitation on the P.C.A. is that so much of public administration lies outside his jurisdiction. He is barred from local government including police, from public corporations, administrative tribunals, the armed forces, consular services, hospitals, contractual arrangements with government departments and personnel issues in the Civil Service. About 50% of the cases sent to the P.C.A. by Members are *ultra vires*. Why do Members submit so many cases that cannot be examined? Do they send along complaints about local government as a form of campaign to get the system extended? Are they ignorant of the extent of the powers of the Commissioner? Or do Members want letters from him, regretting his inability to investigate, as a means of satisfying constituents? This last explanation seems the most probable. A high proportion of complaints about the public services do concern hospitals, police and certain branches of local government, so it is inevitable that Members find that the P.C.A. can be of limited help in dealing with individual grievances.

The Select Committee for the Parliamentary Commissioner for Administration issues both general and special reports on the operation of this complaints machinery. The special reports deal with particular issues or cases which are of public importance, e.g. the claims for compensation from the former inmates of the prisoner-of-war camp at Sachsenhausen or the delay in prosecuting those alleged to have been concerned with an auction ring at the sale of the Duccio painting. The Select Committee does not act as a court of appeal against the findings of the P.C.A. It does provide him with general support and has urged him to interpret his powers more broadly. Thus the Committee defended their Commissioner against criticism from Foreign Secretary George Brown (Lab. Belper 1945–70) over the Sachsenhausen affair[1] and asked him to consider both the quality of the process for making particular types of decision and the quality of individual decisions.[2] So the P.C.A. can now consider whether a rule system is so harsh as to cause unreasonable hardship: if it does the Department concerned can be asked to re-examine its rules and also consider whether those adversely affected should be compensated. The reference to the quality of a specific decision has encouraged the Commissioner to look for maladministration through bias and perversity where individual applications have been rejected. But it must be emphasised again that the role of the P.C.A. is wholly advisory.

---

[1] For a full discussion of this case see the article by C. K. Fry in *Public Administration* (1970), pp. 336–57.

[2] 1967–68 (258) xiv.

One of the arguments used by the Macmillan Government to reject the Ombudsman idea was that such an official would interfere with the responsibility of Ministers to Parliament. Instead, the P.C.A. has increased the reality of ministerial responsibility by forcing civil servants to explain and justify their actions more fully than before. The valid objection to complaints machinery is that it may make public servants more cautious and less helpful on the basis that the less that one says the less opening there is for complaining about what is said. How far the P.C.A. does inhibit civil servants cannot be known. On balance, the office appears to be a modest success. Around fifty cases of maladministration are uncovered each year; the largest category of these arise from unreasonable delay by the Inland Revenue due to under-staffing.

The importance of the system lies in the probability of its extension. Already parallel arrangements have been made in Ulster. There is pressure to extend the jurisdiction of the P.C.A. to include hospitals and the armed forces. The Wilson administration accepted the need for the Ombudsman concept in local government. One other possibility is that the P.C.A. could report to the Select Committee on administrative rules that cause harsh treatment of individuals so that the rules could be amended by fresh legislation. Such a development would extend his duties beyond the original concept of maladministration. Were he to work on these lines, the P.C.A. would tend to become a general adviser to Parliament on the fairness of public administration rather in the same way as the Comptroller and Auditor General gives advice to the Commons on public expenditure.

How to secure democratic control of the mass of government action is an intractable problem in the modern state. The effective political difficulties in the way of making the doctrine of ministerial responsibility imply penalties for Ministers who incur widespread parliamentary displeasure were discussed above. The main devices fashioned by Parliament to bring the work of the executive under review have also been outlined; their operation was shown to be partial, uneven and somewhat spasmodic. They are not without effect, but any closer connection between Members and Government Departments would impose demands on the time of the former which could not fail to have other repercussions on the character of the House of Commons.

CHAPTER 7

NON-GOVERNMENT LEGISLATION

Private Members' Bills

The growth of the influence of Ministers over backbenchers is well illustrated by the increased Government dominance of the parliamentary timetable. Backbenchers now determine the character of business on 24 occasions during the session: these are known as 'private members' time'. At the commencement of the nineteenth century one day a week was reserved for the Government, in 1837 the Government took a second day, and in 1852 a third day. More restrictions on the initiative of backbenchers came in 1902 when it was agreed that Government business should have precedence at all sittings, except on some Fridays and on half of certain Tuesdays and Wednesdays. A further rearrangement in 1927 gave private Members precedence on about eight Wednesdays and thirteen Fridays. Even this slim ration could be abolished in any session if the Cabinet, backed by the Whips, demanded the whole time of the House, as in 1928–29, 1931–32, 1934–35 and between 1939 and 1948. In 1948–49 the Attlee Labour Government was persuaded to grant ten Fridays for private members' Bills and since 1950 the Standing Orders have allowed backbenchers 20 Fridays, ten for Bills and ten for motions. Four extra half days, Mondays or Wednesdays, were added in 1959 for the discussion of motions. In the 1966 Parliament sixteen out of the twenty Fridays were allotted to Bills but in 1970 Conservative Ministers changed the proportion to twelve Fridays for Bills and eight for motions.

Members wishing to use these opportunities enter a ballot: a single draw is held on the second Thursday of the session for the right to introduce Bills. Half the Fridays for Bills are occupied by second reading debates, and the remaining half is given to those Bills that have already advanced furthest along the road to the statute book; the highest priority goes to any Bill for which Lords' amendments are awaiting consideration, and the lowest priority to any Bill the second reading of which is not completed. This is to ensure that Bills which have most nearly finished the parliamentary journey shall not be lost through shortage of time.

There exist two methods of introducing Bills other than by obtaining a place in the ballot, but they offer little prospect of time for discussion and, therefore, of ultimate enactment, unless the proposals are exceptionally uncontroversial. Under Standing Order No. 37 a Member may present a Bill without obtaining leave from the House and the Bill shall be read a first time without any questions being put and shall be printed. Bills introduced in this way are termed Unballoted Bills. They receive no further consideration unless one of three things take place: an unopposed second reading is allowed—the Government provides time for debate—or all balloted Bills down for discussion on any Friday are disposed of before the end of the sitting. The second and third possibilities are highly unlikely. A Member who hopes to get an unopposed second reading will bring forward his Bill at the close of the main debate on a Friday, but the attempt will fail if any other Member shouts the single word 'Object'. It is, therefore, essential to conciliate all interested Members, including the Department(s) concerned, before such a Bill can succeed.[1]

Another means whereby private Members may initiate legislation, the Ten-Minute Rule, was revived in November 1950 through a Government defeat on the issue by 235 votes to 229.[2] Under the Ten-Minute Rule (Standing Order No. 13) one Bill may be introduced at the end of question-time each Tuesday and Wednesday with a short speech not exceeding ten minutes. A single speech of similar length may also be made in opposition, and then the motion for leave to introduce the Bill is put. The Bill may be unopposed or there may be a division: if the Bill is unopposed, or is successful in a division, it is available for further consideration in the same ways that apply to the unballotted Bills described in the previous paragraph. The right to use this facility is distributed on a first-come first-served basis. In November 1969, Robin Maxwell-Hyslop (Con. Tiverton) stayed at the Commons overnight to be first in the queue when the Public Bill office opened to receive Ten-Minute Rule Bills for the 1969–70 session. He handed in 70 notices on behalf of himself and other Conservative Members to pre-empt all the time available under Standing Order 13 for the whole session. After protests in the Chamber,[3] Opposition leaders intervened and it was agreed that 14 days should be left vacant for the use of Labour Members. This is a good example of how a smart trick can fail because it gives general offence to the House.

The Ten-Minute Rule procedure introduces an attractive element of flexibility into the parliamentary timetable. When it results in a division, no Whips are on. If a Bill cuts across the lines of party controversy, both sides may be hopelessly divided. A good attendance is assured because the discussion takes place normally within half an

---

[1] The 1967 Act sponsored by Leo Abse (Lab. Pontypool) to amend the law on homosexuality was introduced under this Standing Order and given Government time. Such cases are rare. They will occur only when Ministers wish an issue to be brought before Parliament but do not care to take the initiative themselves.

[2] H.C. Deb., Vol. 480, col. 976.   [3] H.C. Deb., Vol. 792, cols. 639–50.

hour of the end of question-time. Here is an admirable opportunity to command the attention of the House with no need to win a place in a ballot, and a better audience is available than for an adjournment motion.

Two quite separate purposes may be served by the Ten-Minute Rule. The short speech that it permits a Member to make may succeed in satisfying any opponents to his measure and may smooth the path towards an unopposed second reading.[1] Alternatively, it permits a Member to make a demonstration on some more controversial topic in the hope that the interest and support aroused by the brief introduction may improve the chances of legislative action in a subsequent session. Among recent social reforms, the abolition of capital punishment and theatre censorship and the change in the law on homosexuality, were all assisted by preliminary ventilation under this procedure.

The one serious hope for the backbencher who wishes to promote important legislation is the ballot. Yet the obstacles in his path are formidable. The number of Bills brought in under the ballot depends on the time available for them. In the 1966 Parliament with 16 Fridays available, 27 Bills were introduced: in 1970 with only 12 Fridays available, 20 Bills were introduced. An increasing number of Members enter the draw. In the nineteen-fifties the total was between 250 and 300 while recently it has been between 350 and 400. This rise is due partly to the participation of some Members in the 'Shadow Government'; previously the ballot was regarded as a wholly backbench affair. Even more important is the growing appreciation of Members that private members' Bills provide them with a major opportunity. Because the ballot is so popular, it follows that a Member with a keen desire to legislate on a particular subject will find that his chances of a good place, i.e. the first six, are worse than one in fifty. Not all Members who join the competition have a Bill they wish to introduce: if favoured by fortune they can get a Departmental Bill from the Whips' Office or they can go to the aid of a colleague who has a Bill ready but who was unlucky in the draw. A Member who wins a high place can be besieged with offers of Bills.

Members successful in the ballot present their Bills in dummy form on the fifth Wednesday of session. The three-week gap between ballot and presentation allows time to decide how to use the opportunity. At this stage nothing more than a short title for the Bill is required but a sponsor must ensure that his Bill is printed seven to ten days before

---

[1] Three minor measures became law under this procedure in 1969–70. They were the Education (School Milk) Bill introduced by Kevin McNamara (Lab. Kingston-upon-Hull N.), the Food and Drugs (Milk) Bill introduced by Alfred Morris (Lab. Manchester, Wythenshawe) and the Road Traffic (Disqualification) Bill introduced by Niall MacDermot (Lab. Lewisham N. 1957–59 and Derby N. 1962–70).

the day fixed for second reading. Not to allow reasonable time to study the text of a Bill provides a legitimate source of complaint. The time needed for drafting and preliminary consultations may affect the choice of date for second reading.

Drafting of legislation is a highly specialised art only understood fully by the limited group of official parliamentary draftsmen. With occasional exceptions when Ministers are sympathetic, the services of these official practitioners are not available to a backbencher. So sponsors need help. They may obtain it from the House of Commons' clerks in the Public Bill Office who, through experience, acquire something of the art. Help may come from other Members with legal training or from an interest group who are pressing for a particular change in the law.

Members are allowed to choose a second reading Friday in the order of their precedence in the ballot. Three or four Bills fall due to be considered on each of these days: if the debate on the first Bill occupies the whole of the time available, the other Bills due to be discussed on that day go to the end of the queue and will almost certainly die for lack of time. Alternatively, the time left for the second (or third) Bill may be too brief for any reasonable discussion of it to take place, and the Bill will be 'talked out' without any decision having been reached. Only Members who secure one of the first six places in the ballot are guaranteed a full hearing, and probably about six out of the twenty Bills fail to obtain any attention at all. It is possible that the debate on the first Bill will be unnecessarily prolonged in order to obstruct the passage of another and highly controversial Bill due for examination on the same day. Members who draw a higher number than six choose a Friday when the preceding Bill(s) seem so uncontroversial as to require but a short debate. Thus George Strauss (Lab. Vauxhall), tenth in the ballot in 1967, decided correctly that the Adoption Bill would not consume much time and so would leave room for adequate discussion of his Bill to abolish stage censorship by the Lord Chamberlain. It is also good tactics, *ceteris paribus*, to choose an earlier Friday rather than a later one so that a Bill will have a higher place in the queue of measures waiting for consideration by Standing Committee.

A further problem is to keep the House in session. On Fridays the call of constituencies and the week-end encourage Members to be absent from Westminster. A Member introducing a Bill must do his own 'whipping' to keep his supporters present; if opponents stay away from a division, 40 Members are still needed to obtain a second reading even if the Bill on the Order Paper commands virtually unanimous support. When a Bill is supported by a majority of Members present it is still sometimes difficult to obtain a decision on the second reading, for opponents will try and avoid a vote. If no decision is reached by 4 o'clock, the Bill is 'talked out' and it is improbable that time will be available for further consideration. The sponsor of the Bill can claim to move that 'the question now be put', but the Speaker may refuse the motion if he is of the opinion that the Bill has not been adequately discussed: in practice, the Speaker will always permit a division on the first Bill of the day when it has been debated for five hours. So the first six Members drawn in the ballot are guaranteed a vote on the second reading of their Bills. Even when the closure motion is accepted by the Chair and is carried by a majority, it still needs 100 Members in support to be successful: in January 1971 the Divorce (Scotland) Bill was delayed when the closure failed with a vote of 71 to 15 in favour.[1]

The Standing Committee which examines the detail of a private member's Bill is composed as far as possible of Members who have showed an interest in the measure. If the Bill is carried by a majority vote at second reading, then the Committee should reflect the balance of opinion in the House. Thus the sponsor is sure that a majority will favour the principles of his Bill. But it does not follow that the majority of the committee will favour each separate clause. Even more serious is the possibility that the Bill's opponents will put up a determined fight by tabling a large number of amendments. No guillotine or timetable motion is available to aid a private member's Bill. Thus a determined filibuster can kill a controversial measure, e.g. the successful campaign by Sir Cyril Black (Con. Wimbledon 1950–70) against the 1968 Sunday Entertainments Bill. Even when a Bill has emerged from committee it must pass the report stage in the Chamber. Here time is even more limited as all other balloted Bills compete for attention. It is clear that no private member's Bill that meets severe opposition can survive the report stage unless the Government agrees to make extra time available. The Wilson administration accepted this should be done when a substantial body of parliamentary opinion is shown to be in favour of a change in the law. Time can be obtained by allowing the House to have additional or extended sittings so the progress of Government business is not affected. Two devices are available. The House can continue to sit after the normal 10 p.m. closure—if necessary all night. Alternatively a four-hour session may be held starting at 10 a.m., enough to complete a second reading but probably insufficient time for a contentious report stage. Both these techniques were needed to pass the Divorce Act, 1969, sponsored by Alec Jones (Lab. Rhondda West). If a Bill passes safely through report, then success at the third reading should be assured.

The final hurdle is the House of Lords. More than once the Upper House wrecked attempts to abolish capital punishment. Yet since the

---

[1] H.C. Deb., Vol. 810, col. 1547.

advent of life peers the atmosphere has changed considerably. None of the controversial private members' Bills passed during the Wilson administration were impeded by their Lordships. Bills to reform the law on homosexuality and abortion passed the Lords before the Commons. A Bill to liberalise the position regarding Sunday entertainments has been passed by the Lords but has failed several times in the Commons.

Pressure groups can play an influential role in backbench legislation, whipping up support or objections both inside and outside Parliament. Sometimes a Bill forms a battleground between opposing organisations e.g. the tussle between the Abortion Law Reform Association and the Society for the Protection of the Unborn Child over the Abortion Act, 1967. The activities of pressure groups are limited, however, by the Standing Order which forbids the introduction of any proposal to spend public money other than on the recommendation of the Crown. Only the Government, therefore, can bring in a Bill which seeks to impose a charge on the national revenues. If a private member's Bill implies incidentally an amount of State expenditure, it can proceed only if an appropriate resolution is moved in Committee of the whole House by a Minister. This is a most valuable safeguard against any abuse by Members of their right to introduce Bills, for it eliminates the possibility of their trying to obtain financial benefits for their constituents or other sectional interests.

The fate of a Bill depends on two factors—its general character and the quality of the preliminary negotiations undertaken with interested parties. The more important the subject of a Bill and the wider its scope, the more likely it is to arouse objections from sectional interests, other Members and Ministers. If a sponsor is able to announce that he has the support of the appropriate outside bodies and the Government indicates something approaching benevolent neutrality, his Bill may obtain a second reading without a division. The more unexciting a Bill, the better are its chances of survival. If only part of a measure is contentious, it may succeed if the disputed sections are dropped. Thus, in 1963, the Matrimonial Causes and Reconciliation Bill sponsored by Leo Abse (Lab. Pontypool) was severely truncated on the report stage. The Bill had originally two purposes—to facilitate reconciliation between estranged couples and to permit divorce after seven years' separation. After the Bill had a successful second reading, some sections of religious opinion campaigned strongly against any extension of grounds for divorce. It became clear that the whole Bill, including the reconciliation section that was everywhere applauded, would be lost through shortage of time unless the controversial proposals were withdrawn. Abse was forced to delete the divorce through separation clause, much against his will.

The value of private members' time must depend upon how the facility is used. If Opposition Members use their luck in the draw to produce measures that constitute a basic challenge to Government policy, then their proposals will be defeated after a party-style row. There is a tradition that party whipping is not applied to private members' Fridays, but Ministers will always be able to secure the defeat of a Bill to which they object deeply. If Government backbenchers use their luck in the draw to put forward minor Departmental Bills that could not find a place in the timetable of Government legislation, then the Fridays linked to the ballot will not be very exciting. It used to be the fashion to decry the importance of private members' Bills. Harold Laski argued that if a matter were important enough to require legislation, then responsibility for the legislation should rest upon the Government. Further, he asserted that the sponsor of a private member's Bill was in a hopelessly weak position since no new law would pass unless Ministers approved of it.[1] This view is over-simple. There are many matters on which Ministers may not agree among themselves, especially on topics that fall outside the normal range of party controversy. On questions that have religious or moral implications, Ministers may avoid action in order not to give offence to some of their own supporters: under these circumstances a private member's Bill may be the sole way to ventilate the problem. Even if a backbench sponsor does not get his measure on to the statute book, he may still prod a Government into action. Edward Bishop (Lab. Newark) extracted in 1969 a promise of Government legislation in the following session as the price for dropping his Matrimonial Property Bill. The Younger Committee on privacy of the individual established in 1970 was stimulated by the Bill on this subject brought forward by Brian Walden (Lab. Birmingham, All Saints) in November 1969.

Despite the procedural obstacles, much important legislation has been steered through the Commons by backbenchers. Pre-war examples are A. P. Herbert's Marriage Act, 1937, and Ellen Wilkinson's Hire Purchase Act, 1938. After the war came the Defamation Act, 1952, sponsored by Harold Lever (Lab. Manchester, Cheetham), the Obscene Publications Act, 1959, sponsored by Roy Jenkins (Lab. Birmingham, Stechford) and the Legitimacy Act sponsored by John Parker (Lab. Romford 1935–50 and Dagenham since 1950). The most famous campaigner was Sydney Silverman (Lab. Nelson and Colne 1935–68) who, after many attempts succeeded in securing the abolition of capital punishment.[2] In the 1966 Parliament private members' legislation

---

[1] *Parliamentary Government in England* (Allen and Unwin, 1938), p. 166.

[2] At the 1964 Election the Labour Opposition pledged itself to find time for a private member's Bill on this subject which would be allowed a free vote. This promise was duly repeated in the Queen's Speech in 1964. Thus Silverman's Bill to abolish capital punishment had the unique distinction of being mentioned in the Gracious Speech from the Throne.

reached a new peak of importance.[1] The measures passed included the reform of the law on homosexuality,[2] abortion,[3] contraception[4] and divorce[5] and the abolition of theatre censorship.[6] It is difficult not to feel that many items in this catalogue made a greater impact on the daily lives of men and women than many Government measures.

Private Bills

Private Bills form a quite separate category of legislation. They are introduced by petition from persons, companies, local authorities or other public bodies to acquire powers not available under public law. The second and third readings of these Bills frequently go through 'on the nod', without opposition and without discussion. If when the second reading is moved any Member says 'object', the consideration of the Bill is postponed for several days. This interval may allow the promoters to conciliate the Member who obstructed its passage. Should further attempts to obtain an unopposed second reading fail, the Chairman of Ways and Means will put the Bill down for discussion one day at 7 p.m. when the main business is interrupted. Private Bills run into trouble for political reasons, or because they offend local interests able to persuade Members to represent their views in the House.[7] Once a second reading is secured, with or without debate, a Private Bill goes forward to the committee stage. If a petition of objection has been lodged against a Bill, it is sent to a small committee of four Members who must have no interest in the Bill, either personally or as representing their constituencies. What constitutes an 'interest' in these circumstances may sometimes raise delicate questions of conscience. The committees are so small that the attendance of all their Members is essential, and if a Member fails to be present at a sitting he is reported

---

[1] For full discussion see Peter G. Richards, *Parliament and Conscience* (Allen and Unwin, 1970).

[2] Sponsor, Leo Abse (Lab. Pontypool).

[3] Sponsor, David Steel (Lib. Roxburgh and Selkirk).

[4] Sponsor, Edwin Brookes (Lab. Bebington 1966–70).

[5] Sponsor 1967–68 William Wilson (Lab. Coventry South): 1968–69 Alec Jones (Lab. Rhondda West). The driving force was Leo Abse.

[6] Sponsor, George Strauss (Lab. Vauxhall).

[7] In 1971 two Labour Members, Michael English (Nottingham, West) and James Wellbeloved (Erith and Crayford), proposed to object to 22 Private Bills in order to impede the progress of Government business. This action was to be a protest against the guillotine on the Industrial Relations Bill. They were, however, persuaded to abandon this tactic since it would have delayed important improvement schemes by many local authorities.

to the House. Proceedings in an Opposed Bill Committee are quasi-judicial in character; the objectors put forward their case through parliamentary counsel—lawyers with experience of this work—and the arguments for the promoters are similarly presented. After the evidence has been heard, the witnesses withdraw and the Committee decides its view on the disputed clauses; the report of the Committee is normally accepted by the House without discussion. A Private Bill that stimulates no objection goes to the Unopposed Bills Committee, consisting of five Members, including the Chairman of Ways and Means and the Deputy Chairman, whose task is to see that the Bill conforms to the relevant precedents, or to be satisfied with the justification for failure to do so.

The total of Private Bills appears to be increasing: in session 1968–69 there were 54 while the average figure in the early nineteen-sixties was near 35. Nearly all these Bills gain the Royal Assent. In 1968–69 only 4 out of 54 were unsuccessful. However, 9 out of the 54 were opposed. The Welland and Nene (Eppingham Reservoir) Bill was challenged at both second and third readings, being opposed by the National Farmers Union, the Country Landowners Association and the Rutland County Council. Nine meetings were required at the committee stage to consider the conflicting evidence. Ultimately on third reading the Bill passed by 75 votes to 65. Just occasionally a Private Bill raises an important question of principle—for example, the attempt in 1971 by the Isle of Wight County Council to impose a landing charge on visitors to the island was withdrawn in face of Government objections before their Bill was debated in the Commons.[1] Thus Ministers have influence over this category of legislation although the whips are off whenever the House votes on a Private Bill. These local measures provide Members with a little more variety and extra freedom.

Church of England Measures

The Church of England, as an Established Church, is in a quite different position from other religious bodies. The explanation of its special position is to be found in events of the sixteenth century. At the time of the Reformation and the dispute between Henry VIII and the Pope the Monarch became supreme in all matters, spiritual and temporal. This close relationship between the Crown and the Anglican Church ensures that this church officiates at all great religious ceremonies associated with the affairs of state. But while the Established Church

---

[1] Other sections in the same Bill, to control 'pop' festivals on the island, ultimately became law after some opposition.

enjoys privileges, it also suffers limitations. The authority of the Monarch over the Church has passed to Parliament. Bishops are still appointed by the Crown but are nominated by the Prime Minister. Legislation affecting the government of the Church, including matters of worship and doctrine, is subject to parliamentary approval.

The procedure for passing Church Measures through Parliament is now laid down in the Church of England Assembly (Powers) Act, 1919. By this Act Parliament delegated the right to initiate legislation to the Church Assembly (since 1970, the General Synod), but both Houses of Parliament retain a right of veto over such legislation. Thus the Church can revise the rules relating to its own affairs and then seek parliamentary approval of the changes. Except for the Prayer Book Measure of 1927 and 1928, Church business has passed through the Commons with little opposition. In the fifty years after the 1919 Act, a total of 155 Church Measures have received the Royal Assent. According to the Church of England report, *Church and State*, the Commons have 'acted with steady consideration and courtesy towards the Church of England'.[1]

The Synod subjects a Measure to a procedure similar to the three readings of a Bill in Parliament. Once through the Synod, a Measure is sent to its Legislative Committee which is responsible for the submission of the Measure to Parliament. Together with an explanatory memorandum the Measure is received by the Ecclesiastical Committee of Parliament consisting of 15 Members of each House. The Members from the Commons are selected by the Whips 'through the usual channels': those chosen usually assent to Christian views but they are not necessarily supporters of the Anglican Church. Sometimes it seems there is a little difficulty in finding Members who are willing to serve. The Ecclesiastical Committee is essentially a sounding-board for parliamentary opinion. If any serious objection to a Measure is likely to be forthcoming, this should appear from the Committee's report. A report goes first to the Legislative Committee of the Synod, and will not go forward to Parliament unless the Legislative Committee so desires. If a report is not presented to Parliament, the Measure dies. This arrangement ensures that the Synod is given early warning of parliamentary dissent and is thus given the opportunity to withdraw any Measure that may arouse controversy. A Measure that is presented to Parliament needs only a simple affirmative resolution from both Houses for the Royal Assent to be given.[2]

---

[1] Church Information Office, 1970, para. 60.

[2] The Maud Committee on the *Management of Local Government* proposed that this system be applied to legislation promoted by local authorities as it is simpler and cheaper than Private Bill procedure. H.M.S.O., 1967, para. 289.

On average, three Measures come before the Commons each session; most of them are of minor importance and are quickly dispatched. In 1964 the Vestries of Ministers Measure was debated for three hours and a minority of evangelicals challenged a division.[1] Two hours were needed for the Prayer Book (Alternative and Other Services) Measure, 1968. Debates no longer contain the ferocity aroused in the nineteen-twenties over the Prayer Book. Of course, there is no party whipping on Church business; this is essentially a matter of conscience. During the great clash over the Prayer Book in 1927–28, Cabinet Ministers voted in opposite lobbies. Church Measures are introduced by the Second Church Estates Commissioner,[2] who is always a Government back-bencher, and he also has to negotiate with the Government Whips to find time for Church business. In 1970 the post was filled by Marcus Worsley (Con. Chelsea) who was also parliamentary private secretary to the Leader of the House: such a close link between the Government and the Church representative is unusual.

Why should the Commons discuss and determine the affairs of a particular religious organisation? Only a minority of Members are active supporters of the Anglican Church and some Members are devoted to other faiths. Reginald Sorensen, a non-conformist minister, has confessed to a feeling of almost 'indecent embarrassment as if I were being involved in a domestic discussion in the House of my neighbours'.[3] Many Members avoid the embarrassment by taking no part in this type of business. Some Members feel that to dodge the problem by absence is to disenfranchise those of their constituents who are supporters of the Established Church. It is also arguable that so long as a particular Church is allowed to embody the spiritual will of the state, at least at religious ceremonies, then there must be some democratic supervision of the doctrines of the Church. The anomalous situation can be ended only by some form of disestablishment. The *Church and State* report proposed that authority to order the form of worship be granted to the General Synod. In the meantime the problem is not acute because of the general lack of interest and activity in Church affairs. Were the Church to be consumed by dissension over its internal management, Members might well feel they had neither the time nor the competence to settle the issues involved.

---

[1] H.C. Deb., Vol. 699, col. 1933.

[2] The Second Church Estates Commissioner is appointed by the Prime Minister and holds office under the Crown but is not a member of the Government. He answers parliamentary questions relating to the business of the Church Commissioners. He may delegate this duty to another Member so it is possible for a parliamentary question on Church affairs to be answered from the Opposition benches.

[3] H.C. Deb., Vol. 699, col. 1910. Sorensen was Labour Member for Leyton 1929–31, 1935–64. Now Lord Sorensen.

CHAPTER 8

MEMBERS AND THEIR CONSTITUENCIES

The Impact of Local Opinion

Representation does not consist merely of putting forward party views at Westminster. There is, in addition, the constituency aspect of representation. With the current interest in participation in government as part of the democratic urge, there is increasing pressure on Members to concern themselves with the details of local problems and to make appropriate representations to the central government. The 'good constituency Member' will take up personal cases and intervene to assist other essentially local causes. What this implies and how it is done depends partly on the Member, partly on the constituency. A Minister cannot engage in public protest against a government decision which offends some of his electors; any action he takes must be discreet and private. Some constituencies generate more grievances than others. Middle-class areas are more articulate than working-class areas. A parliamentary constituency that coincides with the boundary of a local authority will have a natural focus through which opinion can express itself for transmission to an individual Member. Local industrial depression and threats of redundancy provoke more disquiet than do prosperity and security. From these rules one can see the difficulty of producing the profile of a highly contented constituency: wealthy areas with the least economic distress also have the highest proportion of people who may take political or social initiatives.[1]

On the majority of these local concerns, party differences largely disappear. The Member will find that opinion is unanimous that action should be taken about aircraft noise,[2] coastal pollution, the withdrawal of rural buses or a proposal to close a railway. In 1971 some Members were under strong pressure to resist the Government's plan to reform the structure of local government. Any action a Member can take to promote prosperity in his constituency will be welcome. In matters of this kind there need be no conflict between the Member and

---

[1] A detailed study of the constituency work of Sheffield Members is provided by William Hampton, *Democracy and Community* (O.U.P., 1970), Ch. 4.

[2] Barker and Rush describe the efforts of Marcus Worsley (Con. Chelsea) following on constituency complaints about aircraft noise: *The Member of Parliament and his Information*, pp. 221–30.

his constituency, although if he pleases his constituency a government backbencher may irritate his Whip.

Yet there are many other political questions, even moral questions, on which a Member may clash with some of his constituents, notably his local party executive. How should a Member act in such circumstances? This is the classic controversy in the theory of representative government. Nearly sixty years before the first Reform Bill, Burke made his famous speech to the Electors of Bristol in which he argued that an elected Member must use his own judgement at all times and was not a mere delegate appointed to carry out the instructions of those who sent him to Westminster.

'Certainly, gentlemen, it ought to be the happiness and glory of a representative to live in the strictest union, the closest correspondence, and the most unreserved communication with his constituents. Their wishes ought to have great weight with him; their opinion, high respect; their business, unremitted attention. It is his duty to sacrifice his repose, his pleasures, his satisfactions, to theirs; above all, ever, and in all cases, to prefer their interest to his own. But his unbiassed opinion, his mature judgment, his enlightened conscience, he ought not to sacrifice to you, to any man, or to any set of men living. These he does not derive from your pleasure; no, nor from the law and the constitution. They are a trust from Providence, for the abuse of which he is deeply answerable. Your representative owes you, not his industry only, but his judgment; and he betrays, instead of serving you, if he sacrifices it to your opinion.

'. . . If government were a matter of will upon any side, yours, without question, ought to be superior. But government and legislation are matters of reason and judgment, and not of inclination; and what sort of reason is that, in which the determination precedes the discussion; in which one set of men deliberate, and another decide; and where those who form the conclusion are perhaps three hundred miles distant from those who hear the arguments?

'To deliver an opinion, is the right of all men; that of constituents is a weighty and respectable opinion, which a representative ought always to rejoice to hear; and which he ought always most seriously to consider. But *authoritative* instructions; *mandates* issued, which the member is bound blindly and implicitly to obey, to vote, and to argue for, though contrary to the clearest conviction of his judgment and conscience—these are things utterly unknown to the laws of this land, and which arise from a fundamental mistake of the whole order and tenor of our constitution.'[1]

---

[1] Edmund Burke, *Speeches and Letters on American Affairs*, pp. 72–3 of the Everyman edition.

Similar views to those of Burke have been expressed by other eminent writers. In his *Representative Government* (1861), J. S. Mill argued that pledges should not be required of a parliamentary candidate, although the voters were 'entitled to a full knowledge of the political opinions and sentiments of the candidate'.[1] Walter Bagehot, in *The English Constitution* (1867), objected to any increase in the influence of constituencies over Members because it would lead to the pursuit of less moderate policies urged by those who lack understanding and responsibility.[2] The case against turning Members into delegates of the constituents was again pressed with great cogency by Lord Bryce in *Modern Democracies* (1921). It would lead to four unhappy results: men of independent outlook would not enter Parliament; the value of parliamentary debate would be diminished; the power of local party committees would be increased; the power of the Cabinet would be increased.[3] But Bryce did not advocate complete freedom for Members. They should not act contrary to any promises made at their election, and a Member who leaves one party and joins another should resign his seat; but on issues on which no pledge has been given, or which have emerged since his election, a Member should be free to follow his conscience.

Sir Ivor Jennings' well-known work *Parliament* (1939), contains a subsection on 'Members and their Constituencies',[4] but in i t will be found no echo of Burke. The reason is that Jennings recognised the overriding character of party considerations in both the selection and the parliamentary activities of Members. Voters support a party and not a candidate, and Members are those fortunate enough to have been adopted by the dominant party in a constituency. Once elected the behaviour of a Member is dictated by considerations of party loyalty. He will, of course, advance the interests of his constituency when possible, deal with individual grievances, be concerned with the prospects of local industries and the like, but when the sheep-dogs bark he will be shepherded into the appropriate lobby. On Jennings' analysis, constituency opinion becomes unimportant except perhaps as a reinforcement to party discipline. His concern was different from the other commentators noted above for he aimed to explain behaviour rather than prescribe it. Yet the reactions of constituents are now more complex than Jennings indicated. Recent events have shown that Members may encounter serious trouble from local supporters on matters where the Whips are silent.

---

[1] Ch. XII of *Representative Government* is a discussion of pledges.

[2] Cf. p. 129 of the World's Classics edition.

[3] Vol. II, p. 387 (Macmillan).

[4] pp. 26–30 (Cambridge U.P.).

Members who are subjected to local criticism seek aid by invoking the spirit of Burke. They stress the need for Members to exercise independent judgement; that the British tradition of democracy is for constituencies to send representatives, not delegates, to Westminster. One might expect this line of argument to be more acceptable to local Conservative Associations than to local Labour parties. The Labour Party has a tradition of debating and voting upon resolutions to determine party policy. A representative from a ward can be sent to a constituency executive with instructions to vote in a certain way: likewise constituency representatives to the annual Labour Conference can be mandated to support particular policies. Conservative Associations spend less energy on debating policy and voting on motions; for Tories the idea of a mandated delegate is less common and less acceptable than it is to Labour supporters. Nevertheless, recent experience suggests that Conservative Members suffer at least as much local pressure as Labour Members. Staunch Tories do not expect to hand out instructions to their local Member. They do expect their Member to uphold Conservative values and local interests. They see no reason to continue to support anyone who strays too far in the direction of liberalism. This is not contrary to Burke's teaching. The Burke argument is that representatives must not receive instructions from the populace: he did not say that a representative is entitled to continuous support irrespective of his opinions.

Certainly local Conservative Associations appear to become rather less tolerant. In the post-war period the Conservatives developed a mass-membership which they had not sought previously. All members can participate in the affairs of a local Association. This democratic arrangement ensures that it is not too difficult for rank-and-file grievances to be ventilated at constituency level. Controversy among local Tories is most likely to develop in suburban-type constituencies where the party has a large membership. The Labour Party operates a system of indirect democracy. At constituency level the local organisation is controlled by a committee composed of delegates from ward or parish units and from other affiliated bodies, notably trade union branches. Such formal and complex constitutional arrangements may make it easier to smother dissatisfaction. The path of wisdom for any Member is to live a little apart from his local party organisation in order to give himself more freedom of action: this must not be taken too far, or made too obvious, lest the Member be accused of neglecting constituency interests. The essential need is to avoid entanglement in any disputes among local party supporters. At the same time Members must fulfil a public relations function as standard-bearers for the party in the constituency and help to keep the organisation in fighting trim. Enthusiasm must be sustained between elections. So attendance at political dances, political bazaars and political meetings is a regular part of the 'week-end in the country'. The general run of constituency speeches by Members is dreary. Addressing the faithful, Members feel their task to be the restatement of current party policy; excitement is likely only at moments of crisis or if some local controversy stirs feeling. Clearly, it would be tactless for a Member to use a branch meeting to ventilate the doubts about the wisdom of party leaders or party attitudes which he may express in private.

On most issues the formation of a clear party line at Westminster provides protection against local criticism. The safeguard disappears under three separate conditions: if a Member rebels against party policy; if the party is itself split; if a 'free vote' is allowed, possibly because the question involves moral or religious considerations.

The greatest constituency campaign against rebel Members was that launched against left-wing Conservatives who objected to the 1956 invasion of Suez.[1] Apart from Cyril Banks (Pudsey 1950–59), who resigned the Tory whip, three others were rejected or 'frozen out' by their local party organisations. Anthony Nutting (Melton 1945–56) left Parliament immediately. Sir Frank Medlicott (Lib. Nat. Central Norfolk 1939–59) and Nigel Nicolson (Bournemouth East and Christchurch 1952–59) were not renominated at the next general election. The Bournemouth case became the classic example of a struggle between a Member and the local party caucus. Nicolson was already unpopular with some Bournemouth Tories through his objection to capital punishment and after he opposed the Suez expedition his local Association chose a fresh prospective candidate, Major Friend. Nicolson continued to be a Member at Westminster in receipt of the Conservative whip and dealt with constituency business as usual. This situation lasted nearly two years. Then reports began to circulate that Major Friend had links with the League of Empire Loyalists, a small very right-wing organisation highly unpopular with Conservative leaders as it had repeatedly attempted to disrupt the final rally at the annual Conservative Conference addressed by the Prime Minister. Major Friend thereupon withdrew, leaving the Bournemouth Association in grave disarray. One section of local Conservatives had always supported Nicolson and they were greatly strengthened by the Friend débâcle; another section, strongly critical of Nicolson, wanted to find a third candidate. It was decided to hold a referendum of members of the local Association to decide whether Nicolson should be readopted and many people then joined the Association in order to obtain a vote. The final result was very close: Nicolson was rejected by 3,762 votes to 3,671. This referendum was unprecedented in British politics, and is the

---

[1] For full discussion see Leon D. Epstein, *British Politics in the Suez Crisis* (University of Illinois Press, 1964).

nearest we have come to the American pattern of primary elections to
elect candidates. It is unlikely to be repeated often, for parties find such
well-publicised displays of disunity highly embarrassing.

It is instructive to compare the troubles of left-wing Conservatives
with the position of the right-wingers. When eight of the latter resigned
the Conservative whip in 1957—a step much graver than abstention
in a single division—there was no report of constituency objection to
their conduct. Only Members who are thought to be too near the political centre encounter hostility from local supporters, although in the
Labour Party this truth is limited by the case of those suspected of
Communist sympathies. Labour Members who lost the whip in 1954
and 1963 were in no danger from their local associations. The Labour
equivalent of a left-wing Conservative is a right-wing deviant. Stanley
Evans (Lab. Wednesbury 1945–57) approved of the Suez invasion.
He was called on to resign by the Wednesbury Labour Party and
complied.

At the end of the historic Common Market debate in October 1971
no less than 108 Members, 69 Labour and 39 Conservative, voted
contrary to officially approved party policy. Some encountered considerable hostility from their constituency Associations, e.g. Neil
Marten (Con. Banbury) and Dick Taverne (Lab. Lincoln). There is no
firm evidence to show that constituency pressure had any effect on
the votes of Members. And the subsequent repercussions were mild.
Dissident Conservatives could claim that technically they were not
rebels since the Government had allowed a free vote; they could also
argue that their views coincided with public opinion as reported in
opinion polls. Dissident Labour Members were in a more difficult
position as they were accused of providing Ministers with a majority,
but they could assert that their attitude towards Europe had been wholly
consistent and in tune with the policy of the previous Labour Government. Inevitably, unorthodox action by a Member which is also
contrary to the trend of public opinion must be a target for
criticism.

Even Members with orthodox voting records at Westminster
suffer local hostility. Before the 1970 Election Terence Higgins (Worthing), Nigel Fisher (Hitchin 1950–55 and Surbiton since 1955) and Sir
George Sinclair (Dorking) each had to fight off attempts to replace
them as Conservative candidates. In each case the complaint was that
the local Member was too progressive or liberal in outlook. The heaviest
assault came from Surbiton; Fisher enjoyed much sympathy from
Conservatives at Westminster who demonstrated their support by
electing him to the Executive of the 1922 Committee for the first time.
Also in 1970 one Labour Member withdrew after a dispute with her
local party. This incident is more unusual since it does not fit into the
normal right-wing left-wing dimension of political argument. Margaret

McKay (Clapham 1964–70) became deeply immersed in the Arab-Israel conflict as an advocate of the Arab cause: constituency dissatisfaction arose not simply through the nature of her opinions but through the amount of time and attention their Member was devoting to the politics of the Middle East.

If a Member has no very firm opinions of his own on a particular subject, then constituency pressure may have some influence on his actions, particularly where the 'party line' is blurred or non-existent. On December 22nd 1965, the Commons voted on the imposition of oil sanctions against the regime in Rhodesia. The official frontbench advice was to abstain. However, 50 Conservatives voted against oil sanctions, and 31 others voted in favour. As in the Suez case, some of the left-wing deviants had trouble with their local Associations, notably Terence Higgins (Worthing) and Richard Hornby (Tonbridge), formerly Parliamentary Under-Secretary at the Commonwealth Relations Office. There were no reports of the 50 right-wingers suffering local criticism. This figure of 50 equalled approximately one-sixth of Conservative Members at that time, but the fraction conceals significant geographical variations. Devon and Cornwall contain a strong body of liberal opinion hostile to social policies pursued in Rhodesia: only one of the dozen Conservatives from this area voted against oil sanctions—Greville Howard (St. Ives 1950–66) who had already decided to retire at the next election. Hampshire has a considerable concentration of Service personnel, active and retired, and wealthy persons likely to have financial interests abroad: half the Conservatives from this area voted against oil sanctions.

Private members' Bills provide further examples of a link between constituency opinion and Members' votes at Westminster.[1] Support for the unsuccessful Sunday Entertainments Bill came largely from South-east England. The same area was also the most favourably disposed to the reform measures on abortion and homosexuality. Members from the South and West of England were more hostile to the abolition of capital punishment than those from any other region except Ulster. A comparison of the voting records of Members from North-west and North-east England shows the former to have been more tolerant of homosexuality and the latter more tolerant of Sunday entertainment. Some variations are related to party affiliations: Conservative strength in the South and West of England is related to the attitude of Members from this area towards capital punishment. But explanation in terms of party is usually inadequate. In the 1966 Parliament the proportion of Scottish Members who were Conservative was lower than that in the Commons as a whole, yet the opposition from Scottish Members to the

---

[1] See my *Parliament and Conscience*, Ch. 9.

bills on homosexuality, abortion, divorce and Sunday entertainment was greater than that from any region of England or Wales. Again the differences shown above between Members from North-west and North-east England on homosexuality and Sunday entertainment cannot be explained in party political terms.

Equally it does not follow that Members' voting behaviour is a direct result of constituency pressure in relation to a particular bill. If Scottish Members oppose the legitimation of homosexual conduct it may be that they are expressing personal opinions and are not simply reacting to a local lobby. It is not unreasonable to expect a typical Scotsman to have calvinistic tendencies.

Political influence may flow in the other direction. A Member may have some impact on the attitude of his local constituency party. This is difficult to demonstrate through lack of precise information. One small piece of evidence is available. In 1960 the annual Labour Conference at Scarborough voted in favour of unilateral renunciation of nuclear weapons: the following year the Conference at Blackpool reversed this decision. According to Hindell and Williams[1] fourteen Labour constituency parties represented by a Labour Member in the Commons changed sides in this controversy between 1960 and 1961 and abandoned the unilateralist view: in only one out of fourteen cases was the local Member a left-winger who supported the unilateralist policy. Thus it seems that Labour parties adjusted to the view of the local Member and not *vice versa*.

It is important to distinguish between local party opinion and views in the constituency as a whole. Traditional political wisdom believes that a good candidate is not worth more than 500 votes at a general election. One suspects that this estimate is a little low. Even so, if a backbencher busies himself with constituency welfare work, the dividend, in terms of votes, will not be high. At an election the retiring Member is essentially at the mercy of the national 'swing', subject to the presence or absence of third-party candidates and occasionally to major changes in the social composition of his constituency. What he, as an individual, has said or done counts for little. Electors are excited chiefly by 'bread and butter' issues of material well-being: they make judgements about party policies and national party leaders. Immigration is the only social controversy likely to make an impact on voting behaviour and here the effect will be pronounced only in particular cases.[2] It is sometimes argued that voting is affected by the attitude

---

[1] 'Scarborough and Blackpool', in *Political Quarterly* (1962) Vol. 33, pp. 306–20.

[2] David Butler and Donald Stokes: *Political Change in Britain* (Macmillan, 1969), Ch. 15. In 1970 there was an above-average swing to the Conservatives at Clapham: the Labour candidate, Dr. Pitt, was coloured.

of a Member to a controversial 'issue of conscience' which has been the subject of a free vote on a private member's Bill. But the average elector simply does not know how his Member has voted at Westminster. Voting at a general election can only be affected by a non-party issue in the isolated case where a Member had played a prominent part in a national campaign. Sydney Silverman's crusade to end the death penalty almost certainly damaged the Labour cause in Nelson and Colne. Humphrey Berkeley (Con. Lancaster 1959–66) lost his seat due to a swing twice the national average and this may have been connected with his sponsorship of a bill to reform the law on homosexuality. No parallel cases can be cited for the 1970 Election. The conclusion must be that it is difficult for an individual Member to upset local voting patterns but not nearly so difficult to upset his local party executive.

So far this discussion of tension in a constituency has been based on disagreement with a Member's opinions. Yet the trouble may be personal. Occasionally a Labour Member is rejected because of his age. Conservatives are more willing to retire at an earlier age, no doubt through their greater financial security. In 1970 a remarkable incident demonstrated that a long-serving Member can still command widespread support. Stephen Davies, Labour Member for Merthyr Tydfil since 1934, was refused renomination on grounds of age. Davies was then 83. He contested the seat as an Independent Labour candidate and was re-elected. Another Member not renominated in 1970 was Reader Harris, Conservative Member for Heston and Isleworth since 1950: when the selection was made Harris was awaiting trial on charges arising out of the collapse of the Rolls-Razor washing machine organisation. Alleged lack of attention to constituency business may lead to an attempt to disown a Member—in February 1971, Percy Grieve (Con. Solihull) survived a motion of no confidence brought before his Conservative Association based on suggestions in the *Birmingham Post* that he had neglected constituency duties in favour of his legal career. An earlier case in 1962 contained a religious element. Patrick Wolrige-Gordon (Con. East Aberdeenshire) was a zealous supporter of the Moral Rearmament movement, and his activities on its behalf made the local Conservative executive feel that he neglected the constituency. Ultimately the executive decided to find another candidate for the next election. Wolrige-Gordon then conducted a campaign in his constituency against the executive and won a handsome victory at a general meeting of the Conservative Association.[1] These examples do show that a Member under attack for personal reasons is potentially in a

---

[1] Austin Ranney: *Pathways to Parliament* (Macmillan, 1965) pp. 75–6. Ranney also gives further examples of friction between Members and their local supporters.

strong position should he decide to fight his cause. Constituencies are now tolerant of matrimonial upsets. Divorce has not been an issue since Nigel Fisher moved from Hitchin to Surbiton in 1955.

A Member who resigns from his party must expect to be disowned by his local supporters. Such a Member is in a weak moral position because he is acting contrary to commitments made at the previous election. If a Member does change sides in the Commons his electors have no immediate legal remedy: the recall is unknown to the British Constitution.[1] So a Member who leaves his party normally remains in Parliament: not since 1955 has a Member surrendered his seat in such circumstances.[2] However, it is fairly uncommon for a Member to desert his party. In the nineteen-sixties 2 Labour Members did so as they developed right-wing sympathies.[3]

A Member who stays with his party although opposing it on a major issue must expect to have a difficult interview with his constituency executive committee. The greatest crime a Member can commit in the eyes of his local constituency Association is to appear to have some sympathy for the views of his political opponents. A local party organisation exists primarily not for political debate, but for political struggle; ardent party members, especially among Conservatives, are not to be deflected by the alleged rights or wrongs of a current controversy. If the wisdom of party policy is questioned publicly in a way that suggests some slight merit for the views of opponents, party enthusiasts are scandalised. Nowhere is this more true than in Ulster. But the duty of a Member is to represent his constituency as a whole— not merely his most articulate supporters. A resolution passed by a meeting of a Member's constituency Association is indicative only of the sentiments of those at the meeting; they may not coincide with majority opinion in the constituency as a whole, or among those who voted for the Member at the previous election, or even among all those who belong to the local party organisation. No single gathering can claim to speak for a whole constituency. And government cannot be

---

[1] The 'recall' is a device used in some states in the U.S.A. whereby a petition signed by a given proportion of voters has the effect of making an elective office vacant. The incumbent can then defend his stewardship by contesting the ensuing by-election.

[2] Sir Richard Acland resigned from the Labour Party owing to his opposition to the manufacture of the hydrogen bomb. He also gave up his seat in the Commons intending to defend his cause at the by-election, but he was overtaken by the dissolution of Parliament and was forced to stand at a General Election, under probably less favourable circumstances: Member for Barnstaple as a Liberal and then a Commonwealth supporter 1935–45, Labour Member for Gravesend 1948–55.

[3] Alan Brown (Tottenham 1959–64) and Desmond Donnelly (Pembroke 1950–70).

conducted by continuous plebiscite. A Member who follows his inclinations is merely doing his duty, provided that he does not contravene earlier *professions de foi*.

Through his status, a Member commands an initial amount of respect. If he takes care to husband goodwill by good constituency service, then he will be in a strong position to override criticism on a particular topic. Personal reputation is important, especially among opinion leaders in the local party organisation. It is easy to underestimate the amount of tolerance that exists. In all parties there are constituency committees which dislike strongly some aspect of their Member's opinions but they continue to support him with good grace. A Member is more likely to arouse active and public opposition from the party faithful if his majority is secure: dissension in a marginal seat offers a prospect of victory for opponents. Further, as was argued above, Members with very central or moderate views are more suspect than those with extreme views. An extremist is not the best candidate for a marginal seat but, once elected, he is safer from challenge by local supporters than a moderate representing a safe seat.

Members can have no right to the permanent loyalty of their constituency parties. Equally, however, enthusiastic party adherents should not be over-hasty in denouncing Members who show independence of mind. A parliament of puppets is in the interests of no one. And the Whips are quite strong enough to maintain an adequate standard of party discipline without further support from the constituencies. This self-denying ordinance must be a difficult prescription for active party workers to swallow, for why should they canvass, subscribe and drive at elections to aid the return of a Member who does not please them? The candidate as an individual is thought to be a negligible quantity, for he owes all to his adoption by the party. Yet as the more lively of amateur politicians in the same party rarely agree among themselves, a Member cannot satisfy them all if he departs from dreary repetition of party platitudes. A Member of merit must sometimes cause offence to some supporters. The growth of party membership, notably in the Conservative Party, means that more people now feel that their Member has some obligation to them. In the small political association with a largely inert membership, sources of friction may be removed in the secrecy of a committee room. In a large-scale organisation which includes ward branches, women's branches and Young Conservatives, public controversy is more likely. Members are perhaps not the most sensitive of men and women, but adverse comment from your 'own side' must be unpleasant and disquieting. There is much in favour of the growth of active political life at the constituency level, for it helps to strengthen the reality of democracy: it is an unhappy paradox that increased interest in politics may weaken the independence of a legislature.

The Welfare Officer Role

Constituency business occupies a significant proportion of Members' time. Although many of the tasks must become tedious, they are carried out, in general, with a marked degree of goodwill and enthusiasm. There is political benefit to be gained from building a reputation for being a 'good constituency man', but it is quite wrong to suggest that Members bestir themselves to deal with the problems of electors out of a shrewd calculation of advantage; willingness to give service to others is a traditional feature of the public life of this country. It is now an established social custom that those who have a grievance against a public authority may carry the plea to their Member, and parliamentary candidates know that a penalty of success is that they are expected to become a sort of Citizens Advice Bureau-cum-preliminary court of appeal. How far Members can really assist constituents with complaints is considered below, but a Member is thought to have done his duty if he takes a sympathetic interest in the troubles brought to him and communicates with the appropriate authority.

A majority of Members find it convenient to live in or near their constituencies, for their diaries contain many local engagements, especially at weekends. Before adoption, candidates from distant part-are frequently asked if, once elected, they will come and reside in the area: a negative response diminishes chances of selection. In geos graphically small, densely populated urban neighbourhoods it is less likely that a Member will have an address within the actual constituency, but he will normally be sufficiently near to keep in close touch with the area. Many invitations are received for non-political occasions, including charitable and sporting functions, religious services, or educational gatherings. It is common for Members to hold an (honorary) office in a variety of local bodies. A small number of Members have active links with local government. Back in the House, Members are pursued by those, curious about parliamentary institutions, who make requests for tickets (Admission Orders) to obtain entrance to the Strangers' Gallery and listen to a debate. When the House is not sitting Members are frequently seen ushering groups of visitors around the Palace of Westminster.

The more important type of constituency problem is that which is collective in character. Growing unemployment in an area will always engage the attention of the local Member. Irrespective of party, a recession in the cotton trade will agitate representatives from Lancashire constituencies: recession in the motor industry will lead the Members for Coventry to urge the Government to take action to ease the position: the political strength of farming grows from the large number of Members it can summon to its aid. Controversial changes in local government structure have been difficult to bring about because of the extent to which they stimulate constituency pressure on Members. In any local disaster, for example severe flooding, the local Member will be active in doing whatever is possible to secure relief. Each part of the country is keen to secure a good share of services provided by the Government; parliamentary representatives are urged to complain about alleged shortcomings in hospital accommodation, postal organisation, broadcasting and television reception, the number of local offices of government departments, etc. Major planning issues affecting local amenities and land use, e.g., the siting of airports, also stimulate local opinion. The examples could be multiplied endlessly, and a glance through a volume of *Hansard* will show how Members raise in the House a great variety of items that are of concern to their electors: it is on matters of this nature that backbenchers supporting the Government most easily voice criticism of the policies of Ministers.

Correspondence received by Members tends to fall into four main groups: individual expressions of opinion of topical issues; circulars from national organisations seeking support for a wide range of causes; general constituency problems, as discussed above; requests to give assistance in personal problems. On average a Member receives around one hundred items of mail each week;[1] a little over half will come from outside his own constituency and relate to national rather than local issues. But this average figure can be seriously misleading as fluctuations from the norm can be extreme. A Member who suffers or enjoys much publicity at the centre of a major controversy will have a heavy volume of correspondence. Enoch Powell (Con. Wolverhampton, S.W.) is reputed to have received over 65,000 letters in 1968 after a speech in Birmingham on immigration. Labour and Conservative Members have broadly equal quantities of mail but constituency correspondence seems to be heavier in rural or semi-rural areas. There are several explanations for this variation. Members for urban areas may hold more frequent 'surgeries' to hear about complaints and difficulties. It is easier in the towns to attend a 'surgery' as travelling distance will be less. The slower pace of life in the countryside may allow more time for literary composition. Above all, letter-writing is a middle-class activity and letters tend to come from retired people, the commercial and professional classes rather than from the proletariat. An average figure for the time Members claim to spend on their correspondence is between $1\frac{1}{2}$ and 2 hours daily. Labour Members spend longer than Conservatives largely because they can afford less secretarial help. There is a general tradition that a Member does not deal with a personal case from outside his constituency, but this convention can be

---

[1] The remainder of this paragraph is based on the detailed research of Barker and Rush: *The Member of Parliament and his Information*, Chs. II and IV.

ignored when a correspondent indicates dislike of his own Member for personal or party reasons. There is a tendency for active Liberal supporters to send their problems to one of the few Liberal Members. Nearly all Members hold surgeries. Some do so weekly, others fortnightly, others monthly. Newer and younger Members are the more conscientious. All Members can tell stories comic, tragic and pathetic about those who come to these interviews. Some are social casualties, often with housing difficulties. Others have failed to get satisfaction from some public body and come to their Member as a final resort. Occasionally, a visitor to the surgery is a rogue. And some requests are simply unreasonable, e.g. for help in filling up an income-tax return.

The growth of this type of social casework is a product of the philosophy of the Welfare State: it is assumed that the processes of public administration should provide for those in need. No one disputes that a Member should concern himself with the prosperity of his constituency. A simple extension from the general to the particular requires the Member to take an interest in individual well-being, especially where the public services are involved. But the welfare officer role is a significant additional burden on Members. It is arguable that they spend their time more valuably when they give attention to broad, national issues rather than to personal cases. There are wide differences of view among Members on this question. Some feel that the welfare function does occupy too much time; that demands made upon them are unreasonable; that people who seek their help are not typical electors; that welfare activity does little to aid understanding of the public mind. Other Members assert that personal casework is a natural and proper part of their duties; that they get real satisfaction from it; that it leads to a fuller appreciation of social and economic conditions. Not surprisingly Labour Members are rather more tolerant of their welfare work than Conservatives. But the difference here is not wholly based on party. Irrespective of political affiliation, Members with previous experience in local government accept casework more readily. Again irrespective of party, ex-public schoolboys are the least content to fulfil a welfare role.[1]

A Member can offer a constituent various forms of practical help as well as sympathy. He can explain which public authority is responsible for a service and provide its address. He can help to draft a letter to the body concerned. If already there has been correspondence that failed to produce satisfaction, the Member can write personally to the local authority, the public board or the responsible Minister as the case requires. He may try to relieve distress through a voluntary organisation. Some Members from urban areas have a local councillor

---

[1] *Ibid.*, pp. 194–6.

to assist them with local government problems. If a matter relates to a Government Department there are other possibilities. Instead of writing a letter, a Member can put down a parliamentary question or refer the issue to the Parliamentary Commissioner for Administration. In the first instance most Members normally write a letter; should this fail to produce a convincing response they then try one of the other alternatives.

Why are Members approached by people with a grievance? Presumably because it is hoped that more favourable treatment can be secured through their intervention. Were it true that a Member could exert influence to secure abnormal generosity by public authorities— the practice would be an abuse and a denial of fair and equal application of the law. In fact a Member can guarantee nothing more than that a case will be re-examined in the light of established procedures. Just occasionally when a Member takes up a complaint he may discover that a plain mistake has been made. Where an element of administrative discretion is involved, a Member may argue that his constituent should be given more favourable consideration in the light of special circumstances: this need involve no change in existing practice or regulations. Alternatively, if the decision on a case is inevitable within existing rules, a Member may wish to urge that the rules are unduly harsh and should be changed. By taking a complaint to the responsible Minister, a Member can ensure that he does understand the details of a particular type of situation. The Member can then exert pressure to secure a change in policy. But it is far more difficult to obtain an alteration of policy than it is to have a mistake rectified.

When a Member decides to take up a case with a Government Department, his first move, as noted above, is usually a letter to the Minister. Such a letter does have some preferential treatment as compared with one from the general public. It is important that the nature of this preference should be understood, but as practice varies between Departments only an outline description can be given. Correspondence from the public is sorted in a Department's registry and despatched to the appropriate section of the office. It will proceed up the hierarchy of civil service grades until it reaches an official sufficiently senior to have the authority to send an answer. The ultimate destination depends, therefore, on the complexity of the issues raised; letters do not get past the level of Higher Executive Officer (H.E.O.) unless they are of a non-routine nature, although replies on topics that look awkward or unusual are scrutinised by a Principal or Senior Executive Officer (S.E.O.). Letters will not rise even as far as an H.E.O. if they appear to come within a category that may be dealt with by the lower grades. The danger is that a junior officer will decide that a letter merits a stock answer without appreciating factors in the case which demand more competent consideration. In contrast, the letter from the Member to a Minister has a quite different career. It goes to the Minister's private office and is handled by the private secretary to the Minister, probably a Principal, who sends an immediate acknowledgement to the Member. The registry encase the letter in a special type of file which indicates that it must have prior attention over other business. It tends to miss some lower levels of the hierarchy on the upward journey and the reply is considered carefully by a Principal or S.E.O. who, when satisfied, will pass the file up to an Assistant Secretary: whether the reply is reviewed by even higher officials, an Under Secretary, Deputy Secretary or the Permanent Secretary himself, will depend upon the conventions within the Department and the delicacy of the issues at stake. Probably in a majority of cases the file will be sent back to the private secretaries' office by the Assistant Secretary, and the reply will then be placed in front of the Minister personally for signature. How far Ministers read what they sign is a question that defies analysis: it is reasonable to suppose that junior Ministers have more time in which to be conscientious. There is a possibility that a Minister will be dissatisfied with the answer prepared and give instructions that the case be further examined. Yet if he wishes to amend any decision the senior civil servants concerned will have an opportunity to advise him as to the possible implications of any alteration; to create a precedent may—according to the circumstances—constitute a new departure in policy affecting all subsequent cases of a similar nature. The strict tradition is that the Member's letter does not call forth a different decision from that which would be given to any other analogous case, unless very rarely it induces a Minister to initiate a change in policy.

What emerges, then, is that although Members' letters get preferential treatment, they do not win any special favours for those on whose behalf they are written. Since the Minister's correspondence has priority they are dealt with more speedily. In addition, since they are considered by senior officers, the replies will be more carefully scrutinised. Whether the replies are also fuller is less certain. A lengthy explanation which attempts to justify departmental practice may smooth away doubts in a Member's mind, but it may also provide grounds for further argument and correspondence, or even discussion in the House. Alternatively, a complete statement might be so long and technical as to be virtually incomprehensible; or it could involve an improper, and therefore impossible, disclosure of confidential information. The general character of the replies prepared to send to Members varies, in fact, between Departments and within Departments. Possibly the greatest advantage of a Member's letter is that it suffers no danger of receiving a stock answer that is inappropriate to the case.

A Member who is not satisfied about a constituent's problem may be mollified if the Minister arranges to see him by appointment.

Before the interview the Minister will have been carefully briefed by his officials. This technique is of value, especially when the Department is not prepared to commit to paper some of the grounds that have guided the decision. Perhaps Ministers and their permanent advisers are over-cautious in suppressing information, but it would be unwise of them to rely always and entirely on the discretion of Members, many of whom have a habit of passing ministerial replies back to complainants. In the greater freedom of conversation, however, it may be possible to give satisfaction to the supplicant Member. To relieve a hard-pressed Minister it is sometimes arranged for a Member to discuss a case with a permanent official, but no civil servant will talk business with a Member without the consent of his superiors.

Each personal case raised by a Member consumes much administrative manpower. Because the time occupied is largely that of senior officials, the cost is considerable. The volume of work thus created varies very greatly between Departments and between different sections of the same Department: while some Principals scarcely ever see a Member's letter, others are faced with a succession of them. In a section that suffers a sudden increase of parliamentary attention there is a grave danger that other important work relating to policy formation may be seriously impeded. If the delayed modifications of policy are related to the cause of Members' letters, a vicious circle could be created: even if this be a rare event it is always a logical possibility. When a flood of correspondence is broadly of a single nature it becomes easier to produce a stereotyped reply. To civil servants, Members may seem tiresome or worse. Some Members appear incapable of seeing more than one point of view, that of their constituent. Others can never be placated since they are fundamentally opposed to the policy which it is the task of officials to administer, and may seem to specialise in collecting grievances of a particular kind. Yet while the cost of trying to satisfy Members is heavy, it must be borne, since it forms another means of making the executive reconsider and justify its actions; the 'checks and balances' in our system of government are precious.

A Member who finds that private negotiation with the Minister about a personal case is of no avail can proceed to raise it in the House either by a question or on the motion for the adjournment.[1] Although this is another important constitutional safeguard it is not likely to produce satisfaction: what is not conceded in private is rarely granted in public. Common advice to new Members is 'If you want to get something done, try writing to the Minister: if you want to make a row, raise it in the House'. For the Member who does ventilate constituency

---

[1] See above pp. 105–13.

business in the Chamber, there is the advantage that his local electorate will see that he is active in working for their interests.

There remains the possibility that a Member can submit a constituent's grievance to the Parliamentary Commissioner for Administration. The functions of this official were described above.[1] Inquiries among Members show that they feel the P.C.A. to be of limited value. Partly this is because he is confined to central government and so cannot deal with matters that arise from local government, hospitals, public corporations and other bodies: partly the difficulty is that his role is limited to the investigation of maladministration. For the most part, no doubt, Members understand these restrictions. The man-in-the-street does not. There is a general impression that an organisation has been created to deal with complaints about the actions of public officials. So anyone with a grievance may go to a Member and ask him to send it to the P.C.A. The Member may know quite well that a particular subject is *ultra vires* for the P.C.A., or he may suspect that the case is ill-founded. What is the Member to do? If the constituent presses his request vigorously, the easiest way out is to send the matter to the P.C.A. knowing full well that it will be a fruitless enterprise. The strong-minded Member will be a better sieve: he will explain the limitations of the complaints machinery, refuse to pass the matter on and will so risk a little unpopularity.

One other aspect of the welfare officer role that sometimes worries Members is the possibility that it may lead to litigation. If a Member takes action on behalf of a constituent, how far is he protected against an action for libel? This question became acute in 1957 when the London Electricity Board threatened action against George Strauss (Lab. Vauxhall) because of the contents of a letter he wrote to the Paymaster General.[2] In spite of their growing correspondence with Ministers, the Strauss case was the first time such correspondence had led to a threat of Court action against a Member. This issue had not arisen before for three main reasons. First, correspondence from a Member to a Government Department is not normally communicated to a third party. Second, a lawsuit is a difficult and expensive venture. Third, a prospective plaintiff would find it difficult to succeed as the defendant Member would plead qualified privilege. Qualified privilege is quite distinct from parliamentary privilege and is an established part of the law of defamation. Where a man, in performance of a legal or moral duty, publishes a defamatory statement about another, honestly believing it to be true and material to the performance of his duty,

---

[1] pp. 139–40.

[2] The relation of this case to parliamentary privilege is discussed below, pp. 187–9.

he cannot be ordered to pay damages even should the statement be shown to be untrue. The defence of qualified privilege is vitiated if the plaintiff can show to the satisfaction of the Court that the defendant was activated by malice—but malice is not easy to prove. Thus, so long as a Member chooses language that does not cast doubts on the *bona fide* of his complaint, he appears to be protected by the existing law.[1]

How should Members act when they receive a communication from a constituent containing some allegation that is defamatory? Many grievances heard by Members are real and do deserve investigation: others are merely the products of weak or disordered intellects. Clearly, Members cannot themselves institute inquiries to discover beyond doubt whether a charge is well or ill founded. The easiest way out of the problem is to pass the complaint to the Minister or the Parliamentary Commissioner with the addition of a compliments slip. But not all such cases involve the central government. Indeed, they may not relate to public services at all. Members feel, quite properly, that they have a duty to try to aid constituents who write in distress. Where the distress involves some serious allegation against a third party, Members also have a duty to consider the interests of the third party. A letter like that received by James Callaghan[2] (Lab. Cardiff, S.E.), from a lady alleging that her doctor had twice made an improper suggestion to her, does create a difficulty. But provided a Member's action is not malicious, he is protected by the doctrine of qualified privilege. This was reasserted in 1971 when Reginald Freeson (Lab. Willesden, East) successfully defended a libel action brought by a firm of solicitors which he had reported to the Law Society following upon a number of complaints from his constituents.

---

[1] See the correspondence columns of *The Times*, the issues dated 11th, 16th and 19th July 1958.

[2] His letter to *The Times*, July 19th 1958.

CHAPTER 9

MEMBERS AND THEIR INTERESTS

The interests of Honourable Members must, in great measure, depend on the sorts of people who are elected to the House of Commons. This, in turn, rests on the choices of the constituency selection committees. But the outlook of Members is also affected by factors that need play no part in the process of local nomination—their sources of income, their previous experience and their personal or non-political enthusiasms. Full information about the private lives of Members is not available, and it follows that no complete analysis of Members' interests can be attempted. Yet a study of the standard works of reference does reveal both a similarity of background among certain groups of Members and the great diversity of their connections. There must be few types of activity in Great Britain that cannot find, when necessary, a friend in the Commons.

The description in Chapter 1 of the social experience of Members is highly relevant to the pattern of their interests which will reflect their age, sex, education, social status, religion, etc. In some cases membership of a particular association will have an important influence on a Member's opinions and, indeed, on his selection as a parliamentary candidate. A large number of Members are sponsored by trade unions under an arrangement which gives the local constituency party substantial help with election expenditure. The interests of trade unions will never be overlooked in a House that normally has over a hundred union nominees. In 1970 a total of 23 unions sponsored 112 successful Labour candidates; the largest group were the Mineworkers with 20, followed by the Transport and General Workers Union with 19, the Amalgamated Union of Engineers and Foundrymen with 16 and the National Union of General and Municipal Workers with 12. The total of sponsored Members given above does not include those assisted by the National Union of Teachers for this Union does not limit its assistance to Labour candidates: the N.U.T. has a scheme under which it may contribute not more than 50% of the election expenses, subject to a maximum of £400, of up to 4 candidates from each of the Conservative, Labour and Liberal Parties. In 1970, 5 candidates aided by the N.U.T. were elected—William Hamling (Lab. Woolwich West), John Jennings (Con. Burton-on-Trent), Michael Roberts (Con. Cardiff, North), Edward Short (Lab. Newcastle-upon-Tyne, Central) and George Thomas (Lab. Cardiff, West).

The Co-operative Movement also sponsors parliamentary candidates but here the position is different because the Co-operative Party is a separate political organisation. Under an agreement between the Labour Party and the Co-operative Party it is possible for the constituency Labour parties to nominate up to 30 joint Labour and Co-operative candidates: in these constituencies the Co-operative Party makes a major contribution to election expenditure. Seventeen Lab–Co-op Members were elected in 1970: this figure has remained remarkably steady over the years. The Co-op Members hold separate meetings at Westminster and elect a Chairman but *not* a Leader. Naturally, they all take the Labour whip and their separate identity tends to be lost within the Parliamentary Labour Party. However, Co-op Members do pay special attention to the interests of the consumer and were critical of the Labour Government's decision to impose Selective Employment Tax.[1]

In addition to assistance with election costs it is common for trade unions to give their Members other forms of help which may include direct monetary payments, reimbursement of expenses incurred through parliamentary duties and the provision of clerical or research facilities. The monetary payments are modest in amount and tend not to keep pace with the fall in the value of money.[2] Among the most generous unions is the N.U.T. whose sponsored Members are entitled to a personal allowance of £350 per annum. In addition, a member of the N.U.T. elected to the Commons other than as an N.U.T.-sponsored candidate may also apply for this allowance, but the number of Members obtaining remuneration must not exceed four from any one political party.[3] Members who obtain money from the Union agree to make themselves acquainted with Union policy and 'within the bounds of parliamentary practice and constitutional usage to have regard to such policy'. The formula indicates that the Union expects assistance from its Members but recognises also that it would be improper for the Union to attempt to give them instructions. But from time to time there have been allegations that other Unions have attempted to exert influence over sponsored Members and echoes are revived of the W. J. Brown case.[4] In July 1968 Will Howie (Lab. Luton 1963–70), not himself a sponsored Member, resigned from D.A.T.A. and warned the

---

[1] T. F. Carberry, *Consumers in Politics* (Manchester Univ. Press, 1969), Chs. 11 and 13.

[2] For an official statement of the nature and implications of the sponsoring system see the memorandum submitted by Douglas Houghton (Lab. Sowerby), Chairman of the Parliamentary Labour Party, to the Select Committee on *Members' Interests (Declaration)*, 1969–70 (57) Appendix III.

[3] In 1964 the four sponsored Labour Members all obtained official positions, three in the Government and one as Deputy Speaker. The Union was thus deprived of any voice on the Government backbenches.

[4] See pp. 193–4 *infra*.

Union's officials that they were risking a breach of parliamentary privilege by coercing or bullying sponsored Members to oppose the Government's prices and incomes policy. Exactly three years later a complaint that an official of the T.G.W.U. had attempted to exert pressure on his Union's sponsored Members in relation to the Common Market issue was referred to the Committee of Privileges.[1]

While sponsored Members would reject any idea that their unions were entitled to give them instructions, there can be no doubt that these sponsoring arrangements do substantially increase union influence within the Parliamentary Labour Party: the fate of the Wilson Government's projected Bill on industrial relations provides an irrefutable example. Nevertheless, the relationship between the unions and the political side of the Labour movement is ambivalent. Although the unions are keen to have strong parliamentary representation, they are equally determined not to be dominated by parliamentarians. When serious strikes are discussed in the Commons few precise suggestions generally come from the Labour side of the House. The reason is simple. It is understood in Labour circles that the conduct of strikes and wage negotiations is the business of union leaders, not of politicians. Another illustration of this combination of love and fear is that most unions do not permit Members to serve on their executive committees and many unions also restrict the right of their full-time officials to become parliamentary candidates.[2] Walter Aldritt (Lab. Liverpool, Scotland) resigned from the Commons in 1970 in order to resume his career as a full-time union official. It is notable that senior union officers tend to prefer union office to the prospect of life in Parliament. This choice may be due to a sense of loyalty to the union or it may arise from a feeling that an industrial role is more likely to provide opportunities for the exercise of leadership and authority.

The 'other side' of industry is even more fully represented in the Commons. According to Andrew Roth's detailed study of this topic, *The Business Background of M.P.s*, over half of the Members have, or have had, substantial connections with some branch of industry or commerce, including a substantial majority of Conservatives and a

---

[1] H.C. Deb., Vol. 821, cols. 1058–76. The official attitude of the T.G.W.U. towards its sponsored Members was explained by the assistant general secretary at the Union's 1971 Conference. The union would not put pressure on a Member beyond argument in support of its collective decisions. If a Member differed from the Union he had a right to express his own views, but if he was often out of sympathy with the Union then the Union might prefer to nominate someone else at the next election. (*The Times*, July 17th 1971). Even if Union support were withdrawn a Member could still be re-elected provided he retained the loyalty of his constituency Labour Party and, of course, of the electors.

[2] V. L. Allen, *Power in Trade Unions* (Longmans, 1954), pp. 152, 244–5.

significant minority of Labour Members. Of course, a Member who joins the Government must abandon other lucrative employments; this prohibition covers company directorships save those connected with private family estates and philanthropic undertakings. A Minister must also dispose of any shares he may hold in companies concerned with the business of his own department: Basil de Ferranti (Con. Morecombe and Lonsdale) resigned the post of Parliamentary Secretary to the Ministry of Aviation in July 1962, after a few weeks in office, as he had been unable to make satisfactory arrangements to sell his holdings in Ferranti Ltd. But once out of office a Member can resume his business connections and it is common for Conservative ex-Ministers on the backbenches to join the boards of large companies. Members may hold 'top brass' positions in industry—the definition of 'top brass' covering Chairman, Deputy Chairman, Partner in a large concern, Managing Director or General Manager—or they can have other associations with business, as executives, consultants or major share holders. Many younger Members who come to the Commons from positions in industrial management will certainly be introduced into board rooms as time passes.

Personal links between business and the Commons are growing for a variety of reasons. Since 1950 the country squire type of Conservative has been in decline and more Labour Members have professional and academic qualifications. The low parliamentary salary leads Members from all parties to seek additional income. In particular there has been a sharp rise in the number of Members concerned with public relations and advertising, but the range of business concerns with which Members are associated is extremely wide. It covers all the major sections of industry and commerce including, for example, banking, insurance, aircraft, motors, brewing, publishing and various forms of engineering. A spokesman in the House is usually available for most large-scale forms of trading activity. The world of business—in the same way as the trade unions—keeps a watchful eye on all projected developments in public policy and, when appropriate, sympathetic Members are carefully briefed. The Confederation of British Industry regularly approaches Members in this way.

Local government also maintains strong links with Parliament. The various Associations of local authorities invite Members to become Vice-Presidents and many subsequently seek their aid, notably to press for changes in legislation. All the Associations also have Peers as Vice-Presidents: the County Councils seem to rely heavily on the nine Peers who hold this office. John Temple (Con. Chester) and Peter Mills (Con. Torrington) occur twice in the table overleaf; the former through the A.M.C. and the R.D.C.A. and the latter through the R.D.C.A. and the N.A.P.C. In addition, Ronald Lewis (Lab. Carlisle) is a member of the Council of the R.D.C.A. but not a Vice-President. Since local government is concerned with the detail of legislation it is important for the Associations to have a sympathetic Member on a Standing Committee that is dealing with a local government Bill. A larger number of Vice-Presidents increases the chance that this will happen. Even so, any individual Vice-President may not support his Association's viewpoint on every clause in a Bill. In particular, a Government backbencher may not be willing to try to put pressure on Ministers. So other ways may have to be used to try and get an Association's view before a Standing Committee. In the case of the A.M.C. if the V-P technique fails, then the list of those nominated to the relevant Standing Committee is carefully studied and a Member who is thought suitable is asked to help. The approach to the Member may be made through his local Town Clerk.

MEMBERS AS VICE-PRESIDENTS
OF LOCAL AUTHORITY ASSOCIATIONS (1971)

Association	Vice-Presidents			
	Con.	Lab.	Lib.	Total
Assoc. Municipal Corporations	12	9[1]	—	21
County Councils Assoc.	—	—	—	—
Urban District Councils Assoc.	8	6	1	15
Rural District Councils Assoc.	16	6	—	22
National Assoc. Parish Councils	4	2	—	6

It is clear that both employers, trade unions and local government are abundantly represented in the Commons. So also are other social groupings. A wide variety of voluntary organisations, actively concerned to influence state policy on particular issues, have their headquarters in London and are in regular touch with one or more Members. What is more natural than for an Association for the Prevention of X or the Encouragement of Y to ask a Member, interested in these objectives, to become a Vice-President or to serve on an Executive Committee? This is a desirable extension of the representative nature of the House of Commons, for it enables Members to put the viewpoint, not merely of constituencies, but also of specific ideals and causes. Frequently these are matters that do not arise in party political controversy. A sectional pressure group must not be regarded as something evil or even sinister; it is merely a body of persons which endeavours to make its opinions effective. Whether pressure is improper or undesirable depends on the methods used to achieve influence, and the process

---

[1] Includes Stephen Davies Ind. Lab. Merthyr.

of lobbying those elected to a legislature scarcely deserves condemnation. The wider the range of Members' interests and the fuller their information, the better can Parliament perform its function as the Grand Inquest of the Nation. There is a danger that unorganised opinion will go by default, but this is unlikely to happen in the House of Commons where normally some Member is always ready with an opposing argument.

An exhaustive analysis of the extent to which Members are connected with the myriad of voluntary associations would need a separate book. Clearly, these bodies have very different purposes. The simplest classification is between the selfish groups and the 'do-gooders'. The Institute of Directors seeks to achieve economic advantage for a limited section of the community, while the R.S.P.C.A. may fairly be termed altruistic. But this distinction is open to challenge. A body such as the Association of British Chambers of Commerce or the National Union of Manufacturers may urge that business prosperity is vital to the well-being of our society as a whole. Further, there could well be disagreement on whether professional, religious and other organisations were selfish in their objects—for example, the Association of University Teachers, the Lord's Day Observance Society and the Automobile Association. A fuller classification of pressure groups would recognise the distinction between purely economic interests, professional aims, women's organisations, regional and ethnic groups, governmental organisations including the local authority associations, religious bodies and humanitarian associations. All such bodies attempt to claim the attention of Members. Some associations manage to form all-party groups of Members who feel affinity to their particular cause: e.g. the National Council for Civil Liberties. A sympathetic Member can be used in many ways. He may speak in the Chamber or in committee using material supplied by the association. A Member can put down questions designed to attract public attention, if not a favourable response. Alternatively he may arrange for a deputation to meet a Minister. Also many of the Bills introduced by backbenchers through the ballot or under the Ten-Minute Rule are inspired by organisations with an axe to grind. Another useful move is for an association to have close links with one or more Members who belong to the appropriate backbench 'subject' committees in each party. Geoffrey Wilson (Con. Truro 1950–70), who was closely associated with the Roads Campaign Council,[1] an organisation which tries to persuade the Government to spend more money on road construction, was also for many

---

[1] See 'M.P.s and the "Roads lobby" ', by William Plowden in Barker and Rush, *The Member of Parliament and his Information*, pp. 69–95, for full discussion of this pressure group.

years an officer of the Conservative backbench committee on transport. There is nothing new in these contacts between the Commons and the outside world. A century ago Bagehot recorded that there were said to be 200 Members for the railways in the present Parliament (1866–68). Most Members welcome close links with a few organisations which reflect their personal interests. The briefs provided by outside organisations are a valuable source of material on which speeches and questions can be based: it follows that a brief is of greater value to a Member if its circulation is restricted. Further, these specialised topics provide a useful focus of activity on the backbenches: if a newcomer can establish that he has mastered subjects X and Y, even if X and Y are highly specialised, this is a good basis on which to build a wider parliamentary reputation.

Members are a natural target for public relations activities. Little luncheon parties and dinner parties are arranged at which it is hoped to gain the sympathy of one or two Members for a particular cause. On a more lavish scale, Members may be invited to go on trips abroad to visit a country whose government is worried about its public image in Britain: this tends to happen most often with right-wing military style regimes. A group of Members were invited to Greece in 1968. After the separatist movement in East Pakistan had been crushed in 1971, three Members led by Mrs. Jill Knight (Con. Birmingham, Edgebaston) were invited by the Pakistan Government to visit the area before arrangements were completed for the journey of the official parliamentary delegation led by an ex-Minister of Overseas Development, Arthur Bottomley.[1] It was notable that the official delegation was more critical of the Pakistan authorities than were the Members who had been on the private visit; the difference was not a party difference because both groups included Conservative and Labour Members. If Members accept invitations they lay themselves open to the insinuation that their opinions have been affected by the hospitality received, but to imply that performance of *parliamentary* duties had been influenced by hospitality would be a breach of parliamentary privilege.[2]

---

[1] Labour Member for Chatham 1945–50, Rochester and Chatham 1950–59 and Middlesbrough East since 1962.

[2] In the Christmas recess 1964 William Warbey (Lab. Luton 1945–50, Broxstowe 1953–55, Ashfield 1955–66) visited North Vietnam and his hotel bill in Hanoi was paid for by the Fatherland Front, a Communist organisation. This fact was noted by *The Spectator* and *The Daily Telegraph* in commenting on Warbey's support for the North Vietnamese government. Warbey complained that the articles constituted a breach of privilege by suggesting 'he was not a witness of truth but a bribed spokesman for a foreign government'. His complaint was rejected. The Solicitor-General advised the House that no breach of privilege had been committed because the articles related to Warbey's general political activities and not specifically to his actions as a Member of Parliament. H.C. Deb., Vol. 707, cols. 43–4 and Vol. 709, cols. 576–642.

Are these activities around Parliament really of much use to pressure groups? Their impact is limited by the restricted influence of backbenchers. Well-established professional, industrial and local government interests negotiate directly with Whitehall, but they still think it useful to be able to have their case understood and stated in the Commons. Members must, of course, be persuaded, for they cannot be instructed. Trade unions who make payments to Members realise that their parliamentary representatives will not submit to specific mandates. If there is a divergence between the claims of a pressure group and the policy of his party—a Member will rarely vote against his party. Sir Ian Fraser,[1] when President of the British Legion, was sometimes criticised at Legion meetings for failing to press its full demands in the House. On one matter that deeply concerned the Legion, the abolition of the separate Ministry of Pensions, Sir Ian did vote against the Conservative Government. Should the clash between pressure group and party be direct and acute, a Member can be expected to abandon the group. Yet it must not be assumed that contacts with Members are of little value. An organisation likes to feel that it has a channel through which views can be made known to Parliament; it is good for the morale of the organisation and improves its status. Perhaps a contact will facilitate anticipation of future government action. On minor matters it is always possible that a Minister will adjust his policy in response to a well prepared argument, perhaps presented in private. Pressure group links with Members are of much importance on questions like Sunday observance and abortion which traditionally fall outside the attentions of party whips. They are also potentially influencial on any issue where the Government is divided or in process of making up its mind; the classic example of this situation is the work of a group of backbench Conservatives, headed by John Profumo,[2] who persuaded the Churchill Government to accept the idea of commercial television.

What induces Members to busy themselves at the behest of pressure groups? Is it certain that the motive is always altruistic? Venality can exist in any powerful assembly and there are at least three means through which Members conceivably could use their parliamentary status for personal advantage. One, a Member with business connections who enters the Government might try to use his position for the benefit of his past—and possibly future—business associates: such conduct would be unanimously condemned as corrupt

---

[1] Conservative Member for St. Pancras North 1924–29, 1931–37 and for Lonsdale, subsequently Morecombe and Lonsdale, 1940–58.

[2] Member for Kettering 1940–45 and Stratford 1950–63: on this topic see H. H. Wilson, *Pressure Group: the campaign for commercial television* (Secker and Warburg, 1961).

and reprehensible. Two, a Member may obtain by means of his parliamentary status information not generally available and use it for financial advantage. If the information were a Budget secret, or otherwise covered by the Official Secrets Act, for a Member to act on it would clearly be wrong. If, however, a Member merely gained an impression that Ministers were likely to make some move, perhaps to check inflation or deflation, how far would it be blameworthy if he took action accordingly? In private enterprise fortunes are normally made by anticipation of the market. Three, a Member might urge a policy or personal case on a Minister or on his parliamentary colleagues that would be to the benefit of himself or his associates. This happens all the time and it is here that the line between proper and improper conduct is most difficult to draw. If an ex-miner speaks on the need for safety in mines or if an ex-teacher argues that teachers should have higher pay—this can be regarded as part of the process of representation. But if a Member takes some action in Parliament as a result of a specific payment then his behaviour is unethical. According to the Select Committee on Members' Interests: 'The distinction to be drawn is between advocacy of a cause for a fee or retainer and the advancement of an argument by a Member who, through a continuing association with an industry, service or concern from which he may draw some remuneration, is able to draw upon specialist knowledge of the subject under debate'.[1] So a Member who speaks as an *ad hoc* advocate for a public relations firm is on the wrong side of the line, but a Member who speaks as a result of a long association with a trade union or some aspect of commerce or industry is beyond reproach. In the latter case the Member's sincerity is not in question and if the nature of his interest is known all suspicion is removed.

In 1968 the *Sunday Times* published a report from the public relations firm of Maurice Fraser to the Greek Government which stated that a backbench Member associated with the firm was working behind the scenes to influence other Members. Later the backbencher concerned was revealed to be Gerald Bagier (Lab. Sunderland, South). As a result of an all-party agreement the Commons then established a Select Committee to review the whole question of Members' interests.[2]

There are existing rules which attempt to prevent Members from abusing their position. The Commons have a Standing Order that no motion to impose a charge on public revenues may be proceeded with save by the consent of the Crown: this prevents backbenchers from introducing measures that would be of direct financial benefit to their constituents or some other limited group of persons. A Member cannot vote in a division if he has a financial interest in the outcome. This rule

---

[1] 1969–70 (57) para. 110.   [2] H.C. Deb., Vol. 780, cols. 1630–39.

is a splendid declaration of principle which is wholly inoperative due to its interpretation by Speaker Abbot in 1811: 'To be prevented from voting an interest must be a direct pecuniary interest and not in common with the rest of His Majesty's subjects'. So for a vote to be disallowed the interest must be *individual*. A Member could not vote for a resolution granting a pension uniquely to himself: he can vote for a benefit to a group of persons, perhaps shareholders, that includes himself. Granted this interpretation of the rule, it is not surprising that there is no record of a Member's vote being disallowed on a public Bill.

A convention also exists that a Member who joins in a debate should declare an interest if he has one. But the convention is weak and is not always observed partly because no clear guidance is available on what constitutes an interest for this purpose. Since 1967, Liberal Members have kept a voluntary register of their business interests which is open to inspection. Entries are made under three headings; directorships of companies, other outside bodies from which regular income is received and other unremunerated professional or business activities. A suggestion by the Liberals to other parties that they should keep similar registers has been ignored.

The 1969 Committee on Members Interests examined the Liberals' register but decided that to put some such arrangement on a formal compulsory basis involved insuperable difficulties. Eric Lubbock (Lib. Orpington 1962–70) in a minority report argued that Members should make a full disclosure of personal financial circumstances through publication of income-tax returns. The majority of the Committee felt this to be an intolerable invasion of privacy. They also seemed to fear that if anything less than the Lubbock proposal were adopted, then Members would be able to dodge through the rules: 'cumbrous, inquisitional machinery is likely to be evaded by the few Members it is designed to enmesh'.[1] Yet the Committee recognised the dangers arising from public relations activities and accepted that it would be improper for a Member to advocate a cause in the House as a consequence of payment. Barristers already have a firm convention that they will not join in debate in the House on any matter with which they have already had some professional connection. There is no reason why a similar standard of behaviour should not be accepted by other professions, including public relations. Another means of control would be to require public relations firms to make a formal statement to Parliament of their link with Members. Such a provision would involve certain difficulties of definition but legislation on these lines does exist in the United States.

---

[1] 1969–70 (57) para. 78.

The Committee's solution to the problem was to set down a code of conduct for Members embodied in two resolutions:

(1) 'in any debate or proceeding of the House or its committees or transaction or communication which a Member may have with other Members or with Ministers or with servants of the Crown, he shall disclose any relevant pecuniary interest or benefit of whatever nature, whether direct or indirect, that he may have had, may have or may be expecting to have:

(2) that it is contrary to the usage and derogatory to the dignity of this House that a Member should bring forward by speech or question, or advocate in this House or among his fellow Members any bill, motion, matter or cause for a fee, payment, retainer or reward, direct or indirect, which he has received, is receiving or expects to receive.'

The wording of the resolutions is tough and comprehensive. The Select Committee cannot be accused of evading the problem. Nevertheless, the case for a register of interests is very strong.[1] The arguments against it rest on Members' right to privacy and the complexity of operating a Lubbock-style scheme. But anyone who enters public life as an elected representative cannot expect to enjoy the same degree of seclusion as other persons. In any case, the amount of detail required to provide a reasonable standard of knowledge of Members' interests is much less than Lubbock required. It does not matter how much a Member receives from a particular source. What matters is the existence of a financial link. So income-tax returns need not be published; all that is needed is a list of sources of revenue. The complexity issue is related mainly to what the Inland Revenue describes as 'unearned income' especially shareholdings. Some people buy and sell shares frequently. Investors in unit trusts do not know necessarily how their money is distributed. So to maintain a register of Members' shareholdings would be a continuous task: no doubt it would be consulted infrequently and it could easily be inaccurate or incomplete. One method of simplification would be to limit the register to shareholdings above a certain size, say £1,000 in current market value. My view is that share ownership should be omitted from a register of interests to achieve simplicity and parliamentary acceptance. So also could broadcasting and authorship under a Member's own name for these activities are public knowledge.[2] With these exceptions a register should list for each

---

[1] It was argued before the Committee by William Hamilton (Lab. Fife, West) and Mr. Andrew Roth, author of *The Business Background of M.P.s.*

[2] Other points of detail would arise. Should spouses be included? If they are not, an obvious loophole is provided. Yet to include them would create insuperable difficulties. A Member may not live with his wife—or her husband. A spouse could have good reason for complaining at the requirement. In any case the authority for the register would presumably be a resolution of the House so that the interpretation

Member the organisations from which he receives remuneration or benefit (no amounts needed). A record on these lines would do much to meet the objections relating to complexity and privacy and would also cover the sort of case which has aroused disquiet in the past.

It is impractical to suggest that Members should not derive benefit from their parliamentary status. Through belonging to the Commons a Member may find that new opportunities in industry or commerce come his way. A firm may feel that the presence of a Member among its directors gives added respectability and inspires confidence. A public relations organisation may find it useful to have a Member who will give advice on the state of public or parliamentary opinion. All this is not under challenge. The concern is not with what a Member does outside Parliament but with what he does within it, so that if he has a personal financial reason for doing what he does there—then this fact should be known.

The Select Committee's idea of a code of conduct would be an acceptable alternative to a register of interests. Unfortunately no such code has been adopted and the Report has not even been debated. After the 1970 Election the new Leader of the House, William Whitelaw (Con. Penrith), commented that the second of the two proposed resolutions[1] would prevent sponsored Members from speaking on trade union matters.[2] It is clear from the Report that the Committee did not intend to impose any limitation on sponsored Members but the effect of the resolutions it proposed does not seem to match the intention. Meanwhile no reason has been officially advanced for not adopting the first resolution on the declaration of interests. As a result Members are still subject to less clear restraint than local councillors: section 76 of the Local Government Act, 1933, requires a member of a local authority to declare any financial interest he may have in relation to business that comes before his council. Why has nothing been done by the Commons? Perhaps there is a feeling that the House should not over-react to a small-scale irritant. Perhaps there is a wish to let sleeping dogs lie.

At present, the rules of the Commons by themselves play but a small part in establishing a standard of conduct for Members. Far

---

of the regulations could remain wholly a matter for the Commons. A Member's spouse could not be required to submit to a resolution of the House.

Another question is how widely the register should be published. Should it be a parliamentary paper or be held in the Commons' Library solely for consultation by Members? Any type of restricted publication would arouse criticism. If Members are entitled to know the interests of their colleagues, why should members of the public not know the interests of their elected representatives?

[1] p. 182 *supra*.   [2] H.C. Deb., Vol. 805, col. 214.

more important are four other factors: the traditions of British public life, the prevalence of the non-conformist conscience, the overriding demands of party loyalty and the resistance of the Civil Service to claims for special treatment. Of these, it is arguable that the impartiality oft he Civil Service is the most effective safeguard. Members have influence, but they do not command the power of the executive: if they wish to seek favours, they must negotiate with those who can make decisions. It is significant that Mr. Stanley directed his activities towards Ministers and not backbenchers.[1] Men who enjoy economic security are less likely to abuse a position of authority for personal gain, and if Members do not suffer pressing financial needs an element of strain is removed. To quote Walter Elliot in a debate on Members' pay: 'There is also a tendency towards the "kept men" in this House, and a House composed entirely of "kept men" would be dangerous, especially if men are kept by bodies able to pay more than the State is willing to pay for their services. . . . We pay a cashier very much more than other people . . . because we put a heavy strain on his honesty which it would be dangerous for us to make too heavy.'[2] The Commons is no longer a largely patrician assembly and it is important to recognise that possibilities of temptation exist; in addition, the scope for temptation widens as the machinery of state plays an increasing role in the direction of the nation's economy.

The level of probity in British public life is extremely high: public responsibilities are kept separate from private interests. Yet there is no room for complacency if this reputation is to be maintained. So Members should be compelled to make a public return of organisations which provide them with payments or benefits. It is possible that this requirement would force a few Members to leave the House but the departure of Members who felt business privacy to be more important than the quality of parliamentary life is a loss that could easily be sustained. Even the adoption of the Liberals' voluntary register by other parties would be an advantage since a Member who was shown subsequently to have concealed an interest would be an obvious target for criticism. The influence of money will never be wholly eliminated by regulations, but that is no reason why regulations should not be used to make underhand dealings more difficult. It is not enough that the conduct of elected representatives should be honourable; it should also be seen to be honourable. The frank declaration of Members' interests would be good for society as a whole and good for Parliament.

---

[1] Cf. Report of the Lynskey Tribunal 1948–49 Cmd. 7616, xviii.

[2] H.C. Deb., Vol. 530, col. 75. Walter Elliot was Conservative Member for Lanark 1918–23, Scottish Universities 1946–50 and Glasgow, Kelvingrove, 1924–45 and 1950–57. The problem of the remuneration of Members is discussed in Ch. 2.

CHAPTER 10

MEMBERS AND THE PUBLIC

Parliamentary Privilege

To commence an examination of the relationship between Members and the general public with an outline of parliamentary privilege may seem a little strange. But the essence of privilege is to grant special rights to a limited category of people. Any privilege given to Members must elevate their position in the community and distinguish them from other persons, at least in legal terms. The rights claimed by Parliament seek to ensure that parliamentary business is carried on without improper interference. In earlier centuries the Commons were afraid of the Crown; now the threat to independence is seen as coming from other quarters, notably the Press.

At the opening of a new Parliament Mr. Speaker goes to the Upper House to receive royal assent to his election. The Speaker then lays claim to the undoubted rights and privileges of the Commons—freedom of speech in debate, freedom from arrest, freedom of access to Her Majesty and for the most favourable construction to be placed on the proceedings of the Commons by Her Majesty. Each year these privileges are duly confirmed by Her Majesty, but the privileges of the Commons do not depend upon the will of the Crown. Some of the rights of the Commons, e.g. freedom of speech,[1] have been incorporated in statutes and the House also claims that its privileges are unwritten law, to be determined by itself through reference to its own precedents. By a resolution passed in 1704, however, the House agreed that it should not extend its privileges beyond those which already existed.

Only one of the rights specifically named by the Speaker is of major significance—namely freedom of speech. The desire that 'their proceedings may receive from Her Majesty the most favourable construction' is an echo of earlier centuries. The right of access to the royal person is not to be exercised individually by Members but belongs to the House as a whole which, acting collectively, may submit an Address to the Crown through the Speaker.

Freedom from arrest applies only to civil suits. It does not apply to criminal cases or to detention under emergency legislation.[2] When a

---

[1] Bill of Rights, 1689, S. 9.

[2] See report of the Privileges Committee on the detention of Captain Ramsay, Conservative Member for Peebles 1931–45; 1939–40 (164) iii.

Member is arrested the House expects to be informéd immediately: on July 2nd 1970 Mr. Speaker reported the imprisonment of Miss Bernadette Devlin (Ind. Mid-Ulster).[1] The protection of Members in relation to civil matters is limited to the duration of the parliamentary session and forty days before and after the session. Since 1869 this has been of diminished importance, for in that year imprisonment for debt was abolished and Members are not protected from distraint on their goods. If Members are to carry out their parliamentary duties it is essential that they should enjoy physical liberty. With exceptions, the duty of Members to attend the House is expected to have priority over other official obligations. Thus Members are exempt from jury service. In 1938 the House decided that an order to a Member, Duncan Sandys, who was also a Territorial Officer, to attend a military court of enquiry constituted a breach of privilege.[2]

Associated with freedom from arrest is the right of freedom from molestation when entering or leaving the Palace of Westminster. Each session the Commons make a Sessional Order in the following terms:

> 'That the Commissioner of the Police of the Metropolis do take care that during the Session of Parliament the passages through the streets leading to this House be kept free and open and that no obstruction be permitted to hinder the passage of Members to and from this House, and that no disorder be allowed in Westminster Hall . . .'

This Order helps to protect Members from organised lobbying by large crowds and authorises the police to give priority to Members' cars in the vicinity of Parliament Square.

Easily the most important privilege claimed by the Speaker is freedom of speech. The Bill of Rights enacted that 'The freedom of speech and debates or proceedings in Parliament ought not to be impeached or questioned in any court or place out of Parliament'. Members thus have absolute protection against any action for slander that might arise out of what they say in Parliament. Originally it was essential for the Commons to insist on this right to protect them, not from

---

[1] H.C. Deb., Vol. 803, col. 43.

[2] The court was seeking to discover how he had obtained certain confidential information. Sandys had already complained in the Commons that a Minister had put pressure on him to disclose the source of this information and the House had agreed to refer the matter to a committee. It followed that the order of the military court was an attempt to anticipate, and thereby interfere with, the proceedings of a parliamentary committee. H.C. Deb., Vol. 337, col. 2237: Sandys has been Conservative Member for Norwood 1935–45 and for Streatham since 1950. For further discussion of this incident see p. 44 *supra*.

litigation, but from the King. In the days of conflict between King and Parliament, Members were fearful of royal displeasure and this explains why the Commons have insisted on the control of both the admission of strangers to debates and the publication of debates. These precautions were thought of as methods to prevent the King from discovering the opinions of individual Members. More recently secret sessions have been held in wartime when the House discussed confidential defence matters, and to go into private session it is only necessary for a Member to 'spy strangers'; under Standing Order 115 (1971 edition) the question, 'That strangers be ordered to withdraw', is put without discussion.[1]

As the struggle with the monarchy waned the Commons came to tolerate, in practice, the publication of reports of debates. By the middle of the eighteenth century their chief concern was to prevent misrepresentation of what had actually been said in the House. Since 1909 the reports of debates have been the responsibility of an official reporting staff acting under the authority of the Speaker and are sold to the public by the Stationery Office.[2] Legal immunity given to speeches of Members does not apply if a Member publishes his own speech apart from the rest of the debate:[3] immunity is granted if the whole of a debate is published.[4] By the Parliamentary Papers Act, 1840, papers printed by order of the House are privileged as well as faithful copies of them. This Act was passed to reverse the decision in the famous case, *Stockdale v. Hansard*,[5] where the Court held that the report of a statutory body which the House had ordered to be printed was not privileged. Members are still responsible to the House for remarks made in debate, and the House protects its own Members and the Chair from observations held to be improper.

In 1957 the question arose whether a letter from a Member to a Minister could be termed a 'proceeding in Parliament' and thus become privileged. George Strauss (Lab. Vauxhall) had written to the Paymaster-General complaining about the methods used by the London Electricity Board in disposing of scrap cable. The Paymaster-General replied that this was a matter of day-to-day administration and not within his sphere of responsibility; he would, however, arrange for the

---

[1] Naturally, *Hansard* does not record what is said in secret session, but on March 31st 1943, a division took place during a secret session and the form of the question and the way in which Members voted was published. H.C. Deb., Vol. 388, cols. 200–4.

[2] For the history of the printing of parliamentary debates in the nineteenth century see P. and G. Ford, *A Guide to Parliamentary Papers* (Blackwell, 1956), pp. 68–76.

[3] *R. v. Creevy* (1813) 1 M. & S., 273.

[4] *Wason v. Walter* (1868) L.R. 4 Q.B. 73.

[5] 9 A. and E. 1.

views expressed to be made known to the L.E.B. Subsequently the
L.E.B. asked that the critical statements made in the letter to the Paymaster-General be withdrawn: when Strauss refused to withdraw, the
L.E.B., through their solicitors, intimated that a writ for libel would be
issued. Strauss then raised the affair in the Commons as a question of
privilege and it was referred to the Committee of Privileges.

In November, 1957, the Committee reported that the Member's
letter was a 'proceeding in Parliament' within the meaning of the Bill
of Rights, 1689; therefore the L.E.B. and their solicitors, by threatening
to issue a writ were acting in breach of parliamentary privilege.[1] The
Committee reached these conclusions after lengthy deliberations and
with a sole dissentient, the Attorney-General, Sir Reginal Manningham-
Buller.[2] The problem is what does the word 'proceeding' cover? So
far, this has never been precisely defined. In 1939 it was agreed that a
draft of a parliamentary question was a 'proceeding' for this purpose,
and the Attorney-General at that time said he could see 'a possible
construction of "proceedings" which would extend to matters outside
the precincts (of the House) if they were related to what is to happen
in the House.'[3] This comment opened the way for a broad interpretation
and in 1957 the majority of the Committee felt that the meaning of
'proceeding' must be related to modern conditions. As the question
hour is no longer adequate for the matters Members wish to raise,
the practice of writing to Ministers is accepted as an ancillary to questions: it is thus logical to argue that letters should have the same protection as questions. The Commons, however, rejected the advice of
the Committee of Privileges and, in a free vote by a majority of five,
cleared the L.E.B. and its solicitors of all blame.[4,5] Both main parties
were split on the issue, but the bulk of Conservatives opposed the

---

[1] Para. 20; 1956–57 (305) vii.

[2] Conservative Member for Daventry 1943–50 and South Northants 1950–62.
Created a peer 1962.

[3] *Official Secrets Acts*. Select Committee Report, Minutes of Evidence, Q. 121;
1938–39 (101) viii.

[4] H.C. Deb., Vol. 591, cols. 208–346. It might well have been argued that the
L.E.B. had done no wrong because they had not, in the words of the Bill of Rights,
impeached or questioned the Member for Vauxhall in any Court; they had merely
threatened so to do. There is a difference between action and threat of action. But
this issue was largely ignored. Cf. D. Thompson, 'Letters to Ministers and Parliamentary Privilege', in *Public Law*, 1959, p. 13.

[5] This decision left the way clear for the L.E.B. to continue their proposed
legal action, but the matter was dropped. The Minister of Power instituted an enquiry into the original complaint: the subsequent report (1958–59 Cmnd. 605, xvi)
exonerated the Board's staff from improper motives but suggested that the L.E.B.
reconsider whether its staff should be permitted to accept Christmas presents from
scrap metal dealers.

Committee's report while the vast majority of Labour Members supported it. The suggestion that the solicitors of the L.E.B. were also guilty of a breach of privilege caused great alarm in the legal profession. How, it was asked, could solicitors advise their clients fully if so to do might lead to an assertion of breach of parliamentary privilege? As the law is heavily represented in the House, this alarm was probably decisive.

Questions to Ministers are privileged; why not treat letters likewise? The main reason is that questions are public while letters are not. If a Member should make an irresponsible allegation in the Chamber, another Member will always be ready to challenge and probably rebuke him. To make damaging comments about individuals in the Chamber is widely regarded as an abuse of privilege, and Members are most careful when names are mentioned. Letters, enjoying semi-secrecy, are not subjected to the same safeguards. The document that started this controversy, complaining about the commercial practices of the L.E.B., was concerned with the commercial policy of a public body: it arose not from a constituency grievance but from the personal experience of a Member who admitted frankly that he had a slight financial interest in the outcome. Had the Strauss letter been declared privileged, presumably any letter from a Member to a Minister would have become sacrosanct; on this basis, were a Member to send a constituent's letter to a Minister with a short covering note, privilege would seem to extend to the constituent's letter. Whether this is desirable is a matter of opinion. Yet to maintain the distinction between letters and questions is to force Members to put down questions on items that might otherwise be settled by correspondence. The Select Committee which reviewed the whole question of parliamentary privilege in 1967 recommended that letters should receive full legal protection[1] but so far no action has been taken.

Parliamentary privilege has led, in the past, to clashes between Parliament and the Courts. As was seen above in *Stockdale v. Hansard*, the Courts have asserted the right to define the limits of privilege. The Courts admit claims of privilege on any matter where its recognition is necessary for the efficient and dignified discharge of parliamentary functions; so they will not enquire into anything, except crime, that occurs in the Palace of Westminster. Thus when the Commons refused to let Bradlaugh take the Oath because he was an avowed atheist, the Queen's Bench refused to interfere on the ground that this was a matter of the internal management of the House.[2] By application of the same principle Parliament is allowed to disregard the Licensing Acts. In

---

[1] Para 91; 1967–68 (34) xii.

[2] *Bradlaugh v. Gosset* (1884) 12 Q.B.D. 271.

1934 A. P. Herbert challenged this disregard for the law by laying an information against the Kitchen Committee for selling liquor without a licence. But the Court of King's Bench decided that the Licensing Acts could not be applied to Parliament[1] and reference was made to the following passage from *Stockdale v. Hansard:* 'The Commons of England are not invested with more power and dignity by their legislative character than by that which they have as the grand inquest of the nation. All the privileges that can be required for the energetic discharge of the duties inherent in that high trust are conceded without a murmur or a doubt.' It seems pertinent to ask the question whether this uncontrolled consumption can be said to be required for the energetic discharge of the duties of Parliament.[2] But even with the advantage of this special privilege the catering service at Westminster is frequently in financial difficulties.

The Courts agree that Parliament may punish those guilty of contempt,[3] including both Members and other persons. A Member guilty of disorderly conduct may be named by the Speaker and, if he refuses to withdraw, can be suspended for the remainder of the session or for some prescribed period. The House may also have recourse to other forms of punishment of varying severity. An offender may receive an admonition from the Speaker or, in more serious cases, the Speaker will issue a reprimand and the offender will appear before him in charge of the Serjeant-at-Arms. The most drastic punishment is to commit to prison, but the prisoner must be released as soon as the House is prorogued. The Commons may also decide that a person elected to the House, albeit legally qualified, is unfit to sit. All Members are Honourable Members. If, therefore, a Member has engaged in conduct that the House finds dishonourable, he may be expelled. Expulsion does not prevent a person re-submitting himself to the electors, so that it is possible theoretically, as with John Wilkes, for a series of expulsions and re-elections to take place.

The last instance of expulsion was that of Garry Allighan (Lab. Gravesend) in 1947.[4] Allighan's contempt was based on an article in the *World's Press News* in which he alleged that some Members conveyed private and confidential information to newspapers in return for financial reward, or personal publicity, described by Allighan as

---

[1] *R. v. Graham-Campbell, ex parte Herbert* (1935) 1 K.B. 594. The issue had been raised previously in *Williamson v. Norris* (1899) Q.B. 7, but was not then pressed to a conclusion.

[2] A. P. Herbert, *Independent Member* (Methuen, 1950), Chapter 1, especially p. 17.

[3] *Burdett v. Abbot* (1811) 14 East 1, and *The Sheriff of Middlesex's Case* (1840) 11 A. & E. 809.

[4] H.C. Deb., Vol. 443, col. 1198.

'payment in kind'. He also alleged that Members betrayed information when under the influence of drink and that it was customary for newspaper representatives to purchase intoxicants for Members in the expectation of obtaining useful material. The Committee of Privileges found that some of this information was in connection with events at private meetings of the Parliamentary Labour Party; it took the view that the disclosure of such private proceedings was a gross breach of confidence, yet was not, of itself, a breach of privilege. But the Committee also ruled that the receipt of payment by a Member, in return for information obtained through his status as a Member, was a contempt of the House. So Party affairs now share the protection against bribery previously accorded to parliamentary business. Two Members were found to have received improper payments—Allighan himself and Evelyn Walkden.[1] Allighan's conduct was held to be a grave contempt of the House for he had made charges against others in respect of the very matter of which he was guilty himself.[2] Subsequently, the House expelled Allighan and Walkden was reprimanded by the Speaker.

The most recent case of punitive action against a Member took place in 1968 when Tam Dalyell (Lab. West Lothian) was reprimanded by the Speaker; Dalyell had disclosed confidential evidence given to the Select Committee on Science and Technology by the Porton Down Research Establishment which led to its publication in *The Observer*.[3]

Matters of privilege take precedence over other business and are usually dealt with after question-time. Disorders are dealt with as they occur. When a Member raises a point of privilege the Speaker has to decide whether the matter should receive precedence over other business: the Speaker may delay his ruling for 24 hours in order to consider the full implications of a case. If the Speaker agrees to grant precedence, the matter will normally be referred to the Committee of Privileges. Apart from the merits of the case, two conditions must be observed for a favourable ruling; the issue of privilege must be raised at the earliest opportunity and, if some document is complained of, the whole of the document must be handed to the Speaker. If the Speaker refuses precedence to a complaint it is still open to the aggrieved Member to put a motion on the Order Paper, but there is no guarantee that time will be available to discuss it. The purpose of asking for a Speaker's ruling is to ensure priority for the proposal to refer the matter to the Committee of Privileges which is appointed regularly at the commencement of each session in readiness for any issue that may be referred to it.

---

[1] Member for Doncaster: 1941–47 Labour, 1947–50 Independent.

[2] The report of the Committee of Privileges on the Allighan case is a most important document—1946–47 (138) ix.

[3] 1967–68 (357) xii.

The chairman is a senior Minister; it works in a non-party spirit and in a quasi-judicial atmosphere. On average, it has to deal with two cases each session. Usually these refer to a speech or publication which is critical of an individual Member or of Members collectively. Even where an alleged offence is found to constitute a breach of privilege it is normal for the Committee to recommend that no further action be taken. The bark of privilege is worse than its bite. Normally the Committee's reports are unanimous.

It is convenient to divide breaches of privilege into three categories—disrespect to a Member, as such, by a non-member; disrespect to the House collectively, committed either by a Member or a non-member; disobedience to the orders of the House, or interference with its procedure, its officers in the execution of their duty, or with witnesses appearing before committees in respect of their evidence.

Action by the public affecting a Member will not constitute a breach of privilege unless it could have a significant effect on his parliamentary duties. Thus the isolated threatening or scurrilous communication will be ignored. But incitement to collective activity is more serious. A suggestion that readers of the *Sunday Graphic* should ring up Arthur Lewis to indicate that they disagreed with his views about sending relief to Egypt succeeded in putting Lewis's telephone out of action: this was held to constitute molestation and a breach of privilege.[1]

More important cases are those in which it is suggested that some kind of improper pressure has been put on a Member by an organisation. Many Members receive payments from outside bodies, often in return for services rendered. Such arrangements inevitably admit the possibility that payments will cease if, for any reason, relations between the Member and the organisation become strained. When this occurs it is but a short step to suggest that financial pressure has been exerted to affect the performance of parliamentary duties.

The classic case of this kind is that of W. J. Brown. Brown had been the Labour Member for Wolverhampton, West, from 1929 to 1931, and between 1942 and 1950 he sat as an Independent for Rugby. He was also the General Secretary of the Civil Service Clerical Association, and when elected for Rugby he was appointed as Parliamentary General Secretary of the C.S.C.A. at a salary of £1,350 p.a. plus certain other expenses and facilities. This arrangement was open to termination by Brown but not by the C.S.C.A., except in the event of grave misconduct. In 1947 it was alleged that an atmosphere had been created which put pressure on him to alter his views, and that if he did not his position as an official of the C.S.C.A. would be rendered intolerable.

---

[1] 1956–57 (27) vii. Lewis has been Labour Member for Upton 1945–50 and West Ham, North, since 1950.

The report of the Committee of Privileges on this matter suggested that no action was necessary. 'Where a Member voluntarily places himself in a contractual relationship . . . with an outside body he must in general be taken to have accepted its possible termination as a matter which would not influence him in his parliamentary duties and, therefore, must further be taken to require no protection against a *bona fide* attempt by the outside body to bring the relationship to an end.'[1] In addition, if a Member entered into a voluntary agreement with an outside body it was felt to be difficult to argue that the latter was precluded from bringing the agreement to an end so long as the Member remained in the House.[2] The Committee also noted that there was no evidence that the conduct of W. J. Brown had been affected in any way by the C.S.C.A.

It remains, of course, a contempt of the House to attempt to intimidate Members by financial or other means; but to constitute a breach of privilege the threat must be reasonably specific and direct. On the other hand a Member ought not to enter into agreements which make him susceptible to sectional pressures. In the debate on the Brown case the House carried a motion which declared it

> 'Inconsistent with the dignity of the House, with the duties of a Member and with the maintenance of freedom of speech for any Member to enter into a contractual agreement limiting the Member's independence and freedom of action in Parliament . . . the duty of a Member being to his constituents and to the country rather than to any particular section.'[3]

The second broad category of contempts comprises disrespect for the House collectively committed by either a Member or a nonmember. To tell the House a deliberate lie, especially in the context of a personal statement, is a grave form of contempt; a motion of censure in these terms was passed on John Profumo after he admitted that his statement stressing the platonic nature of his association with Miss Keeler had been untrue.[4] Adverse criticism of the behaviour of Members can produce cases under this heading. In 1965 the Committee of Privileges decided that a speech by Patrick Duffy which accused the Tories 'of being half-drunk during debates' was a breach of privilege.[5]

---

[1] Para. 15; 1946–47 (118) ix.   [2] *Ibid.*, para. 18.

[3] H.C. Deb., Vol. 440, col. 365.

[4] H.C. Deb., Vol. 679, cols. 655–66. At the time Profumo was Secretary of State for War, and this incident led to his resignation from the Government and the House. He was Conservative Member for Kettering 1940–45 and Stratford 1950–63.

[5] 1964–65 (129) viii. Duffy has been Labour Member for Colne Valley 1963–66 and Sheffield, Attercliffe since 1970.

The Commons, however, now treat this type of incident more lightly: in 1968 a proposal that a similar comment by Mrs. Winifred Ewing (Scot. Nat. Hamilton 1967–70) should be referred to the Committee was withdrawn after a modified apology by Mrs. Ewing.[1]

The central issue here is how far Parliament should seek to restrain critical comment about itself, especially where such comment is malicious or ill-informed. It is arguable that some restriction is necessary in order to maintain the authority and dignity of parliamentary institutions which form the heart of our system of representative democracy. It is equally arguable that any inhibitions on public discussion are undesirable and that the Commons will not preserve its dignity by being over-sensitive to public criticism.[2] These problems are well illustrated by the crop of privilege cases that resulted from the reimposition of petrol rationing in the winter of 1956–7. An article in the *Sunday Express*, a cartoon in the *Evening News*, some comments in an 'Any Questions' programme and a statement by a prospective Liberal candidate published in a local newspaper were each challenged because they complained of the allegedly over-generous petrol allowances that had been made to Members and parliamentary candidates. The *Sunday Express* article was critical of Members for failing to protest against the discrimination in their own favour; proceeding on a report from the Committee of Privileges, the House summoned the editor, Mr. John Junor, to the bar of the House where he made due apologies. The Junor incident caused uneasiness, inside and outside the House, about how far parliamentary privilege might be used to restrict freedom of discussion: Richard Crossman (Lab. Coventry East) suggested that much newspaper controversy over a decision to raise Members' pay might, strictly speaking, be regarded as a breach of privilege.[3]

The third class of contempts noted above consists of disobedience to the orders of the House, or interfering with its procedure, officers or witnesses. The tampering with witnesses is a serious offence, and includes bribery, intimidation and any attempt to persuade a witness not to give a committee a full and frank statement of opinion derived from facts known to him.[4] This rule applies only to witnesses before committees;

---

[1] H.C. Deb., Vol. 765, cols. 1093–117.

[2] The issue is discussed from the viewpoint of the Press by Colin Seymour-Ure, *The Press, Politics and the Public* (Methuen, 1968), pp. 164–74.

[3] When Sir Charles Taylor (Con. Eastbourne) complained about the *Sunday Express* article the Speaker at first refused to rule that a *prima facie* case of breach of privilege had been made out on the ground that the allegations in the article were insufficiently serious. This view was subsequently over-borne by the general feeling of the House. H.C. Deb., Vol. 563, col. 938 *et seq.*

[4] Witnesses. Select Committee Report; 1934–35 (84) vi.

it does not protect a person who happens to be in communication with an individual Member.[1] Another form of interference with Parliament is disorder. At Essex University in 1968 the proceedings of a sub-committee of the Select Committee on Education and Science were obstructed by disorderly students. After a division, 197 to 110, the House decided to refer the matter to the Committee of Privileges. The Committee reported that the incident was a contempt of the House but 'this is not an occasion on which the House should exercise its penal jurisdiction'.[2]

In recent years there has been growing anxiety over the scope and consequences of parliamentary privilege. Inevitably the matter has low priority and tends to be set aside until a new case arises. There are two aspects of the problem, the nature of privilege itself and the procedure for dealing with alleged breaches of it. The very concept of privilege or private rights is somewhat offensive. Certainly they need justification. And the justification for giving special treatment to Members is not wholly apparent. They have the full protection of the ordinary law against libel and threats. An intimation that an individual or an organisation will not continue to support a Member unless he behaves in a certain way can be regarded as a legitimate warning to an elected representative. The claim that Parliament needs special protection to ensure that its proceedings are not subject to interference is less than convincing: on the two occasions in recent times when business was interrupted—on the sub-committee visit to Essex University and by canisters of CS gas on the floor of the Chamber—the powers of privilege were not used to deal with the offenders. It can be argued that Members are too sensitive to criticism; that items of privilege are raised to attract publicity; that the extent of privilege is ill defined and can be a threat to freedom of speech; that the House, should it take action on a complaint, acts as judge and jury in its own cause; that a 'defendant' summoned before the Committee of Privileges faces no specific charge and is denied legal assistance. The indictment is formidable. In fact, the Committee and the House have become very hesitant about using their powers. No one has been imprisoned by order of the Commons since 1880; although the power is falling into disuse, it still exists and accommodation for prisoners remains available in the Palace.

In 1967 a Select Committee was appointed to consider this whole

---

[1] 1954–55 (112) iii. This Report was on a complaint that the Deputy Assistant Chaplain General, Salisbury Plain District, had threatened a subordinate chaplain with a view to influencing proceedings in Parliament.

[2] Para. 6; 1968–69 (308) xv.

situation; its report proposed major reforms.[1] In a basic challenge to tradition it urged that the expression 'parliamentary privilege' should be abolished; instead the House should speak of its rights and immunities. The Committee argued that the House should use its penal jurisdiction sparingly and only in order to protect the House, its Members or officers from substantial interference with parliamentary duties. Trivial incidents or defamatory statements should be ignored. Where a Member has a remedy in the Courts he should use that remedy and not seek additional protection by trying to involve the authority of the House. Those accused of contempt should be given legal aid in appropriate cases. A more flexible system of punishments was needed; the House should have the right to impose fines as an alternative to imprisonment. The Committee also suggested a number of procedural changes designed to minimise the raising of trivial incidents and to save the time of the House. It proposed that complaints should be raised, not in the Chamber, but directly with the Privileges Committee. If the Committee failed to take action, the aggrieved Member should be able to obtain time in the Chamber to discuss his complaint provided that he could get fifty Members to support a motion asking the Privileges Committee to investigate the matter. Other proposals from the Select Committee were that immunity from jury service should be retained. Members or officers summoned to attend court as witnesses might be ordered by the Speaker to attend the House in priority to the subpoena. The least controversial recommendation was that the House should formally rescind the seventeenth- and eighteenth-century resolutions forbidding publication of debates.

Opinion on these proposals was deeply divided. The Report itself showed something of a split mind. On the one hand it appeared to be a radical document, eliminating the very word 'privilege', modernising procedure and arranging that only incidents of true gravity were to be considered. Conversely, it also sought to extend privilege by granting full protection to Members' letters to Ministers and through the introduction of fines. The proposal that the initial stage of a complaint should be dealt with in committee is open to the objection that publicity is an essential element of justice. Eric Heffer (Lab. Liverpool, Walton) argued[2] that Members require some additional protection against unfounded Press criticism because many Members have insufficient

---

[1] 1967–68 (34) xii. There was almost no overlap between the membership of this Select Committee and the membership of the regular sessional Committee of Privileges appointed to deal with privilege cases as they arise. One of the limitations of the sessional committee is that it never meets unless there is a specific case to consider. The sessional committee being more experienced in these highly technical matters might well have been asked to undertake the general review of the problem.

[2] H.C. Deb., Vol. 786, col. 890.

financial means to enable them to do battle in a lawsuit against wealthy newspaper proprietors. It is notable that opinions on the Report do not correspond with party affiliation. Some Members feel that privilege should be curbed and simplified; others claim that it provides essential safeguards.

The Report was not even considered by the House until July 1969, eighteen months after publication. This debate was inconclusive.[1] Two years later another full discussion was held[2] and the House agreed that publication of its proceedings should not be treated as a contempt of the House! On the critical issues, no decisions were made. One motion proposed that privilege should not normally be invoked where a Member had a remedy in the Courts. A second motion incorporated the proposal in the Report that a complaint of breach of privilege should be considered initially by the Committee of Privileges. Both resolutions were withdrawn due to lack of general agreement. Privilege is regarded as essentially a parliamentary matter, not a party issue nor a government responsibility, so there is a feeling that changes should not be made unless they command general assent.

So the problems remain unsolved. It is important that means should be found to inhibit petty complaints which waste time and damage the dignity of the House, partly because they attract publicity out of all proportion to their importance. Such trivia give journalists a chance to make Parliament look silly. Other reforms are needed to give anyone accused of contempt a fair chance to defend himself. A 'defendant' appearing before the Privileges Committee should be faced with a precise charge and be permitted to have legal representation. Once a hearing before the Committee resembles more closely a normal legal form it is likely that the whole character and extent of privilege would have to be more precisely defined.

The Mass Media

Most backbenchers are almost unknown to the general public outside their own constituencies. Senior Ministers and ex-Ministers are better remembered but few are so widely recognised that cartoonists can dispense with adding names to their likenesses. The ordinary Member is allowed but a minor claim to public attention: his news value is lower than that of a leading sporting personality or a star of show business. His activities in Parliament will be reported in the local newspaper but will be rarely noted in the national press. Publicity will be certain

---

[1] H.C. Deb., Vol. 786, cols. 825–913.

[2] H.C. Deb., Vol. 821, cols. 922–93.

should he be engaged in a lawsuit and, on a lesser scale, if he resigns or dies. But to achieve fame a Member must act in a way to excite the interest of journalists. Thus the public will be made aware of Members with extreme and outspoken views, especially if these relate to an easily-understood issue that provokes an emotional response: a speech on abortion is more likely to be reported than one on the reorganisation of a nationalised industry. A Member who presses for an inquiry into some alleged scandal or who happens to be near the scene of events of international importance will also be featured in the headlines.

With the decline of the public meeting, the effective platforms for expressing opinion have become the printing press and the microphone. Members produce a steady flow of books and articles some of which have a political message and some not. Maurice Edelman (Lab. Coventry, North) is a novelist. Roy Jenkins (Lab. Birmingham, Stechford) has produced important historical and biographical works. Some Members have written about our system of government: outstanding in this class are John Mackintosh (Lab. Berwick and East Lothian) and Ian Gilmour (Con. Norfolk, Central). Other books are political testaments, designed to convince the reader of the validity of a political viewpoint, and these vary in intellectual depth: examples are Anthony Crosland's[1] *Future of Socialism* and Angus Maude's[2] *The Common Problem*. Political pamphleteering is a dying art but Members contribute to periodicals on matters of contemporary interest. In addition, Members talk freely to journalists and may, through them, influence the content of political news and gossip that is published.

In this connection the Lobby correspondents have a pre-eminent role. They are a select band of newspapermen who have the right to enter the Members' Lobby: their task is not to report debates—which is done by a separate corps of journalists in the Gallery—but to gather information to enable them to explain, forecast and generally comment upon parliamentary affairs. Lobby journalists total just over one hundred. National newspapers are allowed a small team of two or even three only one of which would be in the Members' Lobby at any time. As well as the national press, provincial newspapers and the television and broadcasting services are represented in this system. Admission to the Lobby is strictly controlled by the Serjeant-at-Arms. A complex code of etiquette has developed around these arrangements which is summarised in the 'Lobby rules'.[3] The essential point is that a source of

---

[1] Labour Member for South Gloucestershire 1950–55 and Grimsby since 1959.

[2] Conservative Member for Ealing, South, 1950–58 and Stratford since 1963.

[3] These were published for the first time by Jeremy Tunstall, *The Westminster Lobby Correspondents* (Kegan Paul, 1970).

information must never be quoted without permission. Much material thus appears in the Press on a non-attributable formula—'I understand that the Prime Minister intends, etc. . . .'. Lobby journalists gather information from conversation with Members, including Ministers, and at meetings arranged in the Parliament buildings by Ministers and the Leader of the Opposition. The Prime Minister's press officers meet the Lobby twice a day. The Lobby also gets advance copies of important official documents to give time for the preparation of detailed comment.

Relations vary between the Lobby and backbenchers. Members who are ex-journalists may have personal friends in the Lobby. William Deedes (Con. Ashford) is himself an ex-Lobby man. Members who are practising journalists may be treated with reserve since their full-time counterparts will think of them as competitors. Some Members are more likely to have interesting information, notably elder statesmen on the Government side of the House with close contacts with the Cabinet. Another valuable source can be a parliamentary private secretary to a senior Minister. Any Member may have a useful tale to tell when there has been a row at a party meeting. And the flow of information between journalists and backbenchers is not all one way. A Member may be keen to know the views of a Lobby man on the state of opinion in his own party since the latter, as an impartial, experienced observer is in a good position to make an assessment. The Lobby man may well have the latest information about some international crisis or negotiation. Conversely, a backbencher sponsoring a private member's Bill may try to arrange a meeting with the Lobby to explain the purpose and merits of his measure.

Occasionally there has been great bitterness among Members over information leaked to journalists about events at a private party gathering. It was noticed above that this practice led to the expulsion of a Member in 1947.[1] Conservatives have a reputation for being able to keep secrets, but published accounts of the meeting of the 1922 Committee which considered the Profumo affair caused great agitation and letters to *The Times*.[2] Leaks are not necessarily anonymous. An account of a discussion by the Parliamentary Labour Party on the Government's East of Suez policy appeared in the *Daily Mirror* in May 1966; the article was by Woodrow Wyatt. An attempt to censure Wyatt at a subsequent P.L.P. meeting was defeated.[3] It was claimed that Ministers talked to the Press on the traditional non-attributable basis to ensure

---

[1] p. 190 *supra*.

[2] June 23rd, June 29th, July 3rd 1963.

[3] Colin Seymour-Ure, *The Press, Politics and Public* (Methuen, 1968), p. 224. Woodrow Wyatt was Labour Member for Birmingham, Aston 1945–55 and Bosworth 1959–70.

that their own version of an argument was published; other Members should therefore not be blamed for writing in the Press. Thus 'leaking' often has an ulterior motive—to ensure that a particular viewpoint secures favourable publicity. A leak can produce a biassed, partial report which can be corrected only if the other side of the case is supported by another leak. These situations lead to familiar arguments about confidentiality. One view is that an element of secrecy is essential for full and frank discussion of delicate issues: the contrary view is that democracy demands that decisions be made in a public manner and that secrecy is merely a convenience to smooth the path of those in positions of authority.

Members have an ambivalent attitude towards publicity. They enjoy it and sense that favourable exposure can give political advantages. Equally they fear that well-publicised adverse material can be damaging. Perhaps they over-estimate both the gains and the losses. Radio and television are now the most pervasive of the mass media; the microphone is at least as influential as an editor's pen so it is natural that Members should be sensitive about the character of political programmes. In particular they have been concerned about the effect of broadcasting upon Parliament: it was seen as a competitor which could detract from the authority of Parliament as the centre for public discussion of affairs of state. In the post-war period a rule evolved with the agreement of the main political parties that prohibited broadcast discussion of any topic due to come before Parliament in the next fortnight.[1] This '14-day' rule against the anticipation of debates became inoperable during the Suez crisis and was subsequently abandoned. Today the rule seems so curious and anti-democratic as to be inexplicable. Yet there was real fear amongst Members that were items on the parliamentary agenda to be discussed first on the radio, the debates at Westminister could be prejudiced and certainly would become less important. Clearly, parallels can be drawn between this restriction and eighteenth-century attempts to prohibit publication of debates.

Since the era of the 14-day rule there has been a remarkable increase in broadcast discussion of current affairs. Inevitably this has aggravated the problem of securing political balance in programmes. The British Broadcasting Corporation is acutely conscious of the need both to maintain its independence and to arrange a fair presentation of controversial matters. Party political broadcasts are arranged through the national party organisations and rarely concern back-benchers. However, the growth of discussion and interview programmes, especially on sound radio, has greatly increased the opportunities for Members to come to the microphone. In the year ending March 31st

---

[1] For fuller discussion see my *Honourable Members* (Faber, 1959), pp. 175–7.

1956 there were 401 broadcasts by Members on B.B.C. Sound and Television: in the year ending March 31st 1970 the corresponding figure was 2,099, made up from 513 appearances on television, 1,297 broadcasts on home radio and a further 289 broadcasts on overseas services.

Selection of those who participate is made by producers of individual programmes. To some extent Members choose themselves. One who has been active in relation to a constituency problem, e.g. unemployment, is likely to be invited to speak on local radio or a regional television programme. The sponsor of an important private member's Bill will be asked to explain and defend it on the national network. A similar invitation may follow the putting down of a parliamentary question felt to be newsworthy. Members known to be specialists in a particular field will be in demand if their specialism comes into the headlines and so will those who have travelled abroad to a zone of conflict or disaster. And those who develop a reputation for being stimulating and fluent will be asked back more often than those who are thought to be dull. Thus invitations to broadcast are decentralised and depend on many factors. Were no supervision arranged, it could happen, quite by chance, that Members from one party enjoyed an unduly high proportion of opportunities to broadcast—at least in the short-term. So the B.B.C. maintains a private tally of the number of appearances by Members.[1] If it seems that one party has enjoyed an advantage in recent months, then corrective action is taken. Immediately this raises the question of what is a fair ratio of broadcasts between the parties. My impression is that the B.B.C. follows no precise rule. Government supporters taken as a group are allowed more appearances than their opponents. Liberals are treated more favourably than other back-benchers in recognition of the fact that their strength in the Commons under-represents their support among the electorate as a whole. A Member belonging to a party which is a minority cause in the region which embrances his constituency is also likely to score an above-average number of broadcasts, e.g. Conservative Members from Wales and Labour Members from the South and West of England. Such imbalance cannot be avoided if a regional or local programme includes political discussions with representatives of the main parties.

From time to time there are inevitable complaints of bias at the B.B.C. Since these come from both Conservative and Labour sources, one is tempted to conclude that the scales are well-balanced. A Member who is dissatisfied with a particular programme may voice the matter

---

[1] The tally includes broadcasts on all subjects, political and otherwise. Thus a Member joining a discussion on sport, art or religion is counted. Mention of Members' speeches or other activities in news bulletins is excluded.

with the B.B.C., but more often he approaches his party Whip. The Whips' offices have a close liaison with the B.B.C. which could be regarded almost as an extension of the 'usual channels'. The Labour Party tends to get more excited about balance in broadcasting than the Conservatives; indeed, the Conservative Whips have tended to play down complaints by their own backbenchers.

The need for fair treatment of all opinions takes on a different form when a party is split on a major issue. In these circumstances spokesmen for opposite attitudes within the same party should be given the opportunity to put their views. Such programmes may be irritating to party leaders since they emphasise differences among their followers. On the Common Market neither of the main parties were united. A senior Labour Member, a pro-Marketeer, complained to the B.B.C. that most broadcasts on the subject were between a Conservative pro-Marketeer and a Labour Member opposed to the E.E.C. link and that this arrangement tended to give a false impression of the state of opinion in both Parties. The B.B.C. accepted that the criticism was valid and the point was kept in mind when organising subsequent programmes.

The touchiness of the relationship between politics and broadcasting is illustrated again by the issue whether parliamentary debates should be televised or transmitted on the radio.[1] A continuous live programme would be impossibly expensive at least for television having regard to the size of the potential audience. The practical alternative is that an edited version of the day's proceedings in the Chamber should be produced fairly late each evening when the House is sitting. Whether such a programme should be arranged has been argued intermittently at least since 1963. The following paragraphs concentrate on the television alternative because this constitutes the bigger challenge to parliamentary traditions.

The case for televising Parliament is that it would be good for democracy and good for Parliament. Electors, it is claimed, have every right to know what Members are doing on their behalf at Westminster: the most modern means of communication should be used to facilitate this knowledge. Respect for Parliament is widely held to be in decline. To counteract this tendency Parliament should promote maximum publicity for itself. Television would enable everyone to see Parliament as the central forum for the discussion of public affairs. The prospect that noisy, angry scenes in the Chamber when shown in countless homes would do little to enhance the reputation of the Commons can be

---

[1] Robin Day, *The Case for Televising Parliament* (Hansard Society, 1963), puts one view. The objections are set out by Allen Segal in an appendix to Bernard Crick's *Reform of Parliament* (Weidenfeld & Nicolson, 1964).

countered by the argument that the presence of the cameras should make Members behave better. In any case there is no reason why the style of Members' behaviour, be it good or bad, should be concealed from the public. Nor is there any reason why television should interfere with Parliament in a physical sense. Modern cameras are compact and highly sensitive, so little change would be needed in the lighting and the cameras themselves need not be obtrusive.

Those who object to televising Parliament have to show that the project differs materially from newspaper reporting and the daily sound programme 'Today in Parliament'. Of course, there are major differences. The television audience would be much larger than that for the present fifteen-minute radio report. The moving picture and the participants' own voices must make a far more forceful impact than an announcer's voice or a newspaper item. An angry row in the Chamber looks fairly tame in cold print the next morning; on the screen the same evening it would be more impressive. But all such considerations are a matter of degree, impossible to measure, easy to over-estimate. The editor of a televised programme would certainly bear a heavy responsibility. His task would be not only to secure a fair balance between parties, between frontbenchers and backbenchers and between different viewpoints within a party; he would have also to judge whether to include any slightly bizarre incidents. The danger is that if unusual and therefore newsworthy incidents were always covered, then some Members might 'act up' to try and get themselves shown on television. There are other difficulties too. If the television *Hansard* were to attract a considerable audience it could not be shown later than 10.30 p.m. but this would be too early to permit inclusion of the main winding-up speeches between 9 p.m. and 10 p.m. It would also be impossible to show an extract from question-time without considerable editing. Questions are not put orally in the Chamber to save precious minutes and those present follow the rapid proceedings with the help of the Order Paper.

Opponents of television fear that its introduction would interfere with the work of the Commons because there would be pressure to change both procedure and the timetable to meet requirements of the media. Apart from the prospect that some Members would perform so as to try and catch the eye of the television editor, there is the likelihood that even frontbenchers would adapt their speeches to the mass audience: a Minister presenting a major Bill might summarise its contents and the Government's reasons for proposing the measure in five to seven minutes before going into the normal full explanation at second reading. Members are worried also by the thought that the Chamber would sometimes be seen almost empty, especially on a Friday. This could lead to complaints that Members were absentees, not doing the job they were paid to do. It is doubtful if many more Members would attend debates merely to provide background for a television picture;

if they did so the result might be neglect of important public business or of constituency problems.

These considerations are unsatisfactory for two reasons. First, they are based on supposition: it is impossible to foretell what the effects of television might be. Second, if changes in Parliament were caused, is it inevitable that the results would be unfortunate? The case against television seems to assume a degree of perfection in existing arrangements. Would it matter if times of sittings were adjusted? Would it matter if a Minister addressed the viewing public for five minutes out of a speech lasting half an hour or longer? And perhaps the most likely outcome is that, after an initial consciousness of novelty, Members would largely ignore the cameras.

The first full discussion in the Commons on the televising of its proceedings took place in 1965 on a motion by Thomas Iremonger (Con. Ilford, North).[1] The following year a Select Committee reported that continuous live broadcasting was impracticable and undesirable; that a 'feed' of proceedings could be supplied to the broadcasting organisations which they could edit; that an experiment on closed circuit should be conducted which would help the House to reach a decision.[2] The Leader of the House, Richard Crossman, proposed a motion in November 1966 that such an experiment be arranged. The Chief Whips of all parties favoured the proposal and, although a free vote was allowed, there was wide expectation that the motion would be carried. In fact, it was defeated by a single vote.[3]

DIVISION ON THE TELEVISION EXPERIMENT: 1966

	Labour	Conservative	Others	Total
Ayes	78	45	7	130
Noes	62	67	2	131

While the greatest weight of outright objection came from Conservatives, there was a marked lack of enthusiasm among Ministers. Crossman's opening speech was lukewarm.[4] No senior Minister supported

---

[1] H.C. Deb., Vol. 713, cols. 1033–133.

[2] 1966–67 (146) xvi.

[3] H.C. Deb., Vol. 736, cols. 1606–732. On such a close vote the decision becomes a matter of accident. Two Labour Members who intended to fly back to their Scottish constituencies returned unexpectedly to the House because their flight was cancelled due to fog. They then voted against the television experiment.

[4] *The Times* commented 'Mr. Crossman's official role might have been as marriage broker for the cameras. In the event, . . . he sounded more like a misogynist addressing a band of backsliding monks.' (November 25th 1966.)

him in the division. Perhaps Ministers' views were affected by the contemporary political situation. The Government had recently suffered heavy criticism due to the economic restraints it had felt forced to impose owing to the balance of payments deficit. Cameras in the Chamber would have given extra publicity to these protests and could have given benefit to the Opposition. In general, it is probably true that television would harm rather than help the Government. Opposition shouts of 'Resign, resign', would be heard throughout the country whenever unpopular economic measures were announced.

The House of Lords conducted an experiment with closed circuit television in February 1968. Three months later the Commons had a similar exercise with sound radio. Results of both appeared to be inconclusive and no positive action followed.[1] In November 1969 the attempt by Robert Sheldon (Lab. Ashton-under-Lyme) to obtain another broadcasting experiment on closed circuit failed when the requisite hundred Members were not present to force a vote on his motion.[2] The issue was again raised in relation to the historic debate on the Common Market but the Services Committee rejected a proposal for a radio broadcast by six votes to four.[3]

Many Members are suspicious of innovations in the conduct of parliamentary business. On changes which involve publicity they are doubly sensitive. Since the broadcasting question has become a subject for free votes, the attitude of the House is highly unpredictable. In these circumstances Ministers will tend to leave the matter alone if they can.

---

[1] A sub-committee of the Services Committee recommended that public broadcasting of parliamentary proceedings on sound radio only should be permitted. But nothing was done. Services Committee: ninth report, *The Experiment in Radio Broadcasting* 1967–68 (448) xii. A later report by the full Committee considered that 'present financial circumstances preclude any recommendation for expenditure on a project which is known to be controversial': 1968–69 (48) xv. See also H.L. Deb., Vol. 300, cols. 1069–123.

[2] H.C. Deb., Vol. 791, col. 1617.

[3] 1970–71 (510).

CHAPTER 11

POLITICAL PROMOTION

The aim of a party in opposition is to acquire power; the desire of the party in power is to retain office. Ambitions of the invividual are related to those of his group, and politicians, excited by their intense consciousness of the pursuit of power, are activated also by visions of personal advancement. Probably almost all new Members aspire to ministerial rank, although conventions of modesty limit the publication of their hopes; it is not unknown for older Members, especially Conservatives, to refuse office perhaps for financial reasons. Most Members do spend the whole of their parliamentary career on the backbenches, for the number of posts available is sufficient to accommodate only 20–28% of the Government supporters if the Government has a bare plurality in the House, and the ratio diminishes as the size of the majority increases. This is a vital safeguard to the independence of the legislature. A government could use the patronage at its disposal to quell objection to its policies, and the limitation of patronage in this country has been closely linked with the growth in the independence of the Commons. The total of ministerial posts is closely controlled by legislation, and the Select Committee on Offices of Profit expressed disquiet about the rise in the number of parliamentary private secretaries— Members who act as unpaid and semi-official assistants to Ministers— lest this should lead to a further growth of official influence on the backbenches.[1]

Even so, the chance of a Member obtaining some ministerial rank during his parliamentary career is fairly good. Of course, the proportion who achieve office will depend on political circumstances: if one party is in office for a long uninterrupted period, the amount of ministerial experience on the Opposition benches will dwindle. For this reason alone it is arguable that regular alternation of parties in power is good for the health of democracy. When the party majority in the Commons changes regularly the number of Members with ministerial experience will be high. The table opposite shows the extent of ministerial experience in the main parties in 1970; this is shown also as a percentage of the size of the party group in the Commons at the particular time. Whips, as members of the Government, are included in the figures. Parliamentary private secretaries, who do not receive an official salary, are excluded. The figures show that rather more than one-third of

---

[1] Report, para. 24; 1940–41 (120) iii.

Members become Ministers, at least for a short period. Those fortunate enough to represent a safe seat have a chance of office that is roughly evens. Yet, the ambitions of Members are not always satisfied. Not only backbenchers can feel frustrated but also junior Ministers. It is easy for one who is a centre of attraction in his own constituency to overrate himself, and new Members may not appreciate the range of qualities that are required for ministerial office. Also they may not at first be aware of the intensity of the competition for preferment or the pressure of talent on the backbenches seeking occupation.

MINISTERIAL EXPERIENCE OF MEMBERS: 1970

Number who held or had held office

	Before the election	After the election
Conservatives	80 (30%)	111 (33%)
Labour	138 (40%)	97 (35%)

There are various means through which claims to recognition can be advanced. Members tend to concentrate their attention on particular topics so that their contributions to debate may be well informed. They will attend the party committee(s) dealing with their special interests; one who shows much ability and energy at these meetings may subsequently be elected an officer of a committee. This is a small step forward but it can lead to greater things. Personal qualities are further displayed in the Chamber itself, and an aspirant to office must first prove himself in debate. Opposition Members have a greater freedom of manoeuvre in this regard; the Government is always facing them and may be attacked on any suitable opportunity. Government supporters may offer constructive criticism of their leaders, but they should not afford comfort to the enemies of their party. Alternatively, they may counterattack those on the Opposition benches, but this technique does not easily build great reputations for so often it leads merely to a restatement of the Government's case, with an addition of some party polemics. Yet there are exceptions to this rule. Iain Macleod's victory in 1952 in a debating duel[1] with Aneurin Bevan assisted his early promotion to become Minister of Health. If a Member on the Government benches hopes for promotion he is ill advised to challenge a Minister on a major item of policy, for political memories are uncomfortably long. A sortie in the wrong division lobby can be damaging to personal

---

[1] H.C. Deb., Vol. 498, col. 886 *et seq.* Macleod was Conservative Member for Enfield 1950-70; Bevan was Labour Member for Ebbw Vale 1929-60.

prospects: equally, as Lord Butler has observed,[1] the careers of political leaders have often been advanced by colourful rebellion or resignation.

The first step up the ladder for many Members on the Government side of the House is to become parliamentary private secretary to a Minister—the common abbreviation is P.P.S. This is entirely a personal arrangement between a Minister and a backbencher; as noted above, the position carries no payment and it has no official status.[2] Most Ministers—but not junior Ministers—have a P.P.S., and the general function of the latter is to act as an additional pair of ears and eyes for his Minister and so keep him informed of trends of opinion in the Commons. But it is not possible to generalise in detail about the tasks of a P.P.S. because Ministers vary in the extent to which they invite assistance. A Minister may require little more than the arranging of 'pairs' for him when a two-line whip is in operation and a division is expected, thus allowing the Minister to be absent from the House. At the other extreme a Minister may not only wish for full reports on backbenchers' views but will invite comments on projected developments in Departmental policy. It is usual for a P.P.S. to attend the party committees concerned with the functions of his Minister. His presence serves to give these meetings a greater sense of importance; knowing that they will be privately reported, Members may speak with greater care and a heightened sense of responsibility. A P.P.S. should also be well informed on developments in Opposition policy in relation to his Department so that he can forewarn his Minister of probable lines of attack in future debates. Members with a minor matter to raise in relation to a Department may decide to see the P.P.S. as an alternative to putting down a question. It follows that a good P.P.S. can probably save his Minister a lot of trouble in the House. To do so he must be well liked and it is a help if his Minister is also well liked. And if a P.P.S. is known to enjoy his Minister's confidence he may get access to more information: the House is shrewd in its assessment of personal relationships and is aware that his role varies from nominal to influential. In the Department the position of the P.P.S. is delicate. He has no official standing yet he may be frequently closeted with the Minister and be on terms of some intimacy with him. To do his work effectively he must have access to an amount of 'inside' information, and he may be present

---

[1] In his autobiography, *The Art of the Possible* (Hamish Hamilton, 1971), p. 29. Conservative Member for Saffron Walden 1929–65. Now Master of Trinity College, Cambridge.

[2] But in the Conservative Party the Whips appear to have exercised some supervision over these appointments. According to Julian Critchley (Con. Rochester and Chatham 1959–64 and Aldershot since 1970), his nomination as a P.P.S. was forbidden in 1961 by the deputy chief whip 'on the grounds that he believed me to be insufficiently "sound".' *The Times* December 22nd 1970.

when important policy matters are under discussion. Often he has modest accommodation in the Department and may see copies of all correspondence between Members and his Minister. The nature of the task makes it an admirable training ground for office-holders, but it also imposes severe limitations which may hamper future prospects. A P.P.S. must never speak in the Commons upon the work of the Department with which he is associated; outside the House he may so speak if he has an official brief. On other matters the P.P.S. is free to act as he chooses but should show restraint; if he is critical of another Department the Minister concerned may feel a temptation to complain to *his* Minister. In addition, the doctrine of collective responsibility which binds Ministers to support each other on all occasions has tended also to engulf the P.P.S.s. These restrictions taken together may inhibit the development of a parliamentary reputation and it is arguable that an ambitious politician is wise to avoid this role. Only five of the 1970 Conservative Cabinet had had this type of apprenticeship and in four of these cases the Minister served was, or subsequently became, the Prime Minister.

Another avenue to political promotion is the Whips' office. Ministerial Whips, of course, are members of the Government: Opposition Whips have high expectation of office if their party comes to power. An Opposition Chief Whip may well become the Leader of the House if his party wins an election. A Government Chief Whip normally achieves Cabinet rank. Edward Heath (Con. Bexley) is the first Chief Whip to become Prime Minister. Since 1906, 40% of Whips have been promoted to departmental office and one in nine have reached the Cabinet. In the past there has been a generous distribution of honours, baronetcies and knighthoods to former Conservative Whips.[1]

The greatest opportunity for Members to gain promotion comes when a new Government is formed. If political conditions are unsettled, if the electorate favour the Opposition at each general election, the rise and fall of Ministers will be rapid. But the composition of the Cabinet when the Opposition comes to power is greatly influenced by the membership of its previous Shadow Cabinet, the alternative government, which largely consists of ex-Ministers. While a place in the Shadow Cabinet offers great hope of future ministerial office it is also a position which the average backbencher is unlikely to attain. The Shadow Cabinet is responsible for guiding the Opposition's policy in the Commons and it provides the party's major spokesmen over the whole range of government activity.

When in Opposition the Conservatives arrange a system of

---

[1] F. M. G. Willson, 'Some Career Patterns in British Politics', *Parliamentary Affairs*, Vol. XXIV, pp. 33–42.

frontbench spokesmen on a two-tier basis. The Shadow Cabinet, sometimes known as the Leader's Committee, is supported by 'junior
shadows' who together with the Party Whips form the Shadow Government. All these appointments are made by the Leader with whom
ultimate authority resides. Under Edward Heath this organisation was
associated with policy groups which were planning ahead for the time
when the Party returned to power.[1] The size of the Shadow Government
has varied. When Heath first became Leader in 1965 it contained 72
names, including nine Whips. After the 1966 Election came a dramatic
cut: the Shadow Cabinet was reduced from 21 to 16 (including two
Peers) and second-rank spokesmen in the Commons fell from 42 to 13.
The change was made partly to produce a more compact fighting force
and partly to avoid the appearance of any wide commitment in relation to
the personnel of the next Tory Government so that all younger Conservative Members would feel that they had a more equal chance of office.

The Conservative Leader is elected for an unlimited term, which
ends either in death or resignation. Before 1965 the actual choice was
made as a result of informal consultations amongst senior members o
the Party out of which a new Leader 'emerged'. The choice was then
ratified by a formal electoral college composed of all Members and
Peers who received the Conservative Whip together with all prospective
candidates adopted by constituencies and the Executive Committee of
the National Union of Conservative and Unionist Associations. The
emergence of the Earl of Home[2] as Leader and Prime Minister in 1963
caused dissension in the Party and Iain Macleod and Enoch Powell
refused to serve in the new Cabinet. In 1965 the Conservatives adopted a
new system so that Members alone elect the Leader through a complex
system of voting. To succeed on the first ballot the leading candidate
must have an absolute majority of the votes cast and a 15% lead over
his nearest rival. If no one satisfies these criteria, fresh nominations are
invited and new candidates as well as the original ones can contest
a second ballot. On this second round an absolute majority i.e. 50%
of the votes cast is sufficient to secure election. If no one satisfies this
stipulation, the candidates entered for the second ballot go into a
third ballot conducted on the single alternative vote system so that the
candidates with the lowest number of first preference votes are eliminated
until someone has acquired 50% of the votes cast. This complex
arrangement was adopted because of Tory suspicion of making important decisions by voting. In particular there was a fear that a close

---

[1] See p. 49 *supra*.

[2] Conservative Member for Lanark 1931–45, 1950–51 and Kinross and West
Perthshire since 1963: in the Lords as Earl of Home 1951–63 when he renounced the
Earldom.

vote could split the Party, that election by simple majority could leave a large minority dissatisfied. To meet these fears, the nature of a winning majority was carefully defined and provision made for new and compromise candidates to enter the contest if the first ballot failed to produce a result.

So far this system has been used once. On the resignation of Sir Alec Douglas-Home in 1965 the vote was:

Edward Heath	150
Reginald Maudling	133
Enoch Powell	15

These figures, in formal terms, failed to produce a result because although Heath had an absolute majority he did not have a 15% lead over his nearest rival as required by the rules. However, Maudling and Powell withdrew from the contest and Heath became Leader. Perhaps this will produce a pattern for the future and Conservatives will come to feel that their rules are a little too sophisticated. It does seem unlikely that anyone who achieves an absolute majority on the first ballot will fail to be elected.

Labour backbenchers hold annual elections for the posts of Leader and Deputy Leader[1] when their Party is not in office. The successful candidate is required to win a majority of votes cast; if no one obtains a majority, the candidate with the lowest vote drops out and a second ballot takes place. Between 1922 and 1960 the re-election of the Leader was unopposed, but his initial election has always provoked a keen contest. The first Chairman,[2] Keir Hardie, obtained the position in 1906 by a majority of one: in 1922, MacDonald's majority over Clynes was five: in 1935, Attlee won a triangular fight against Morrison and Arthur Greenwood on the second ballot: in 1955, Gaitskell defeated Bevan and Morrison: in 1963, Wilson defeated Brown after James Callaghan had been eliminated on the first ballot.

When Labour is called upon to form the Government the Monarch invites the Leader to become Prime Minister and the annual elections cease. To date, no Labour Prime Minister has died while still at Downing Street, or resigned leaving his Party with a majority in the Commons. After the 'emergence' of Macmillan as Prime Minister the Labour Party issued a statement to indicate that should a Labour successor be sought for a Labour Prime Minister, the Parliamentary Labour

---

[1] In 1970 the Parliamentary Labour Party agreed that the office of Deputy Leader should go into abeyance when the Party is in office. This will obviate any claim to a *de facto* position of Deputy Prime Minister.

[2] The term Leader was not used until 1922: R. T. MacKenzie, *British Political Parties* (Heinemann, 1955), p. 306.

Party would first proceed to elect a new Leader who would then be ready to accept the invitation of the Crown to take office.[1] If the Labour Leader dies or becomes incapacitated during an election campaign, the Labour Members of the recently dissolved Parliament elect a new Leader.

It is notable that the Deputy Leader may well fail to succeed his chief. Arthur Greenwood became Deputy Leader in 1935 although Morrison, not Greenwood, had been runner-up to Attlee in the election for the Leadership. In 1955, Morrison, then Deputy Leader, was passed over in favour of Gaitskell as the successor to Attlee. In the 1963 election to choose a successor to Gaitskell, Brown was defeated by Wilson, in spite of the fact that a few months earlier he had defeated Wilson in a contest for the Deputy Leadership. By both precept and custom Labour Members have full freedom of action when the Leadership is vacant.

Two factors affect the choice of Leader—personal qualities and policy attitudes. Gaitskell v. Wilson in 1960 and Gaitskell v. Anthony Greenwood[2] in 1961 were clear cases of a fight between the right and left wings of the Labour Party, then deeply divided over the issue of nuclear disarmament. Personality and policy each played some part in the 1963 election of Wilson, but personality was decisive.

A Labour Shadow Cabinet is composed of the Parliamentary Committee of nineteen, the Leader, Deputy Leader, Chairman and Chief Whip, three Peers and twelve other Members, all elected annually by Labour Members. Other Members, notably ex-Ministers, may be invited to meetings at the discretion of the Leader. The Labour Leader also nominates a Shadow Government which includes all members of the Parliamentary Committee but is much larger; in 1970 it numbered 74. In the Shadow Government a small number of Members are allocated a watching brief over each Department and are responsible for presenting their Party's case on cognate issues. The distribution of responsibility is entirely within the discretion of the Leader and carries no guarantee of appointment should Labour win power. When Labour is in Opposition, therefore, a process of election helps to determine both the colour of Party policy and the selection of its spokesmen. A comparison of the voting figures at the annual elections can be used to show whether advocates of particular policies are gaining or losing in popularity, and this imposes on the Labour Leader and Shadow Cabinet a type of pressure unknown in the Conservative Party. Thus Michael Foot[3] was elected to the Shadow Cabinet in 1970 in spite of the

---

[1] *The Times*, January 22nd 1957.

[2] Member for Haywood and Redcliffe 1946–50 and Rossendale 1950–70.

[3] Member for Plymouth, Devonport 1945–55 and Ebbw Vale since 1960.

fact he had not been a member of the previous Labour Government. The procedure is highly democratic but it has drawbacks. The contests aggravate personal rivalries and factional differences among Labour Members. Every autumn the distribution of responsibility in a Labour Shadow Cabinet becomes a matter of uncertainty and speculation.

The Prime Minister, whatever his party, has unfettered discretion in the selection of his Cabinet. He may consult with senior colleagues and the advice of the Chief Whip is often sought in filling minor posts. A Minister may make suggestions for filling the junior post(s) in his Department. There are also various political considerations which affect the choices made. A Conservative Premier had a Liberal National element in his team until 1962. A Labour Premier must allocate some positions to representatives of the trade union movement and the Co-operative Party. Room must be found for a female element in any government; usually there is a woman in the Cabinet. The Secretaries of State for Scotland and Wales should represent a constituency within their territory otherwise nationalist sentiment will be offended.[1] The Cabinet also needs adequate representation in the House of Lords. Above all, it will help the authority of a government with its own political supporters if the Ministers are felt to encompass a wide range of opinion so that various groups in the party may feel that their views are represented when important policy decisions are made.

It is also for the Prime Minister to determine the general structure of his government. The size and nature of the Cabinet have varied considerably in recent years and have reflected the needs of the time as interpreted by successive Prime Ministers. In war it is usual to have a small Cabinet from which many Ministers in charge of Departments are excluded; during the period 1916–18 and for a part of the last war the Cabinet consisted almost entirely of Ministers without departmental responsibilities. Even in peacetime there should be an upper limit to the size of the Cabinet if it is to be an effective body, and the formation of new ministries since 1939 has led to the exclusion of the less important Ministers from the Cabinet. The three Service Ministers were omitted from the Cabinet in 1946 and were replaced by the Minister of Defence responsible for co-ordination of all the Armed Forces. More recently further Departments have been amalgamated, both to smooth the path of inter-departmental co-operation and to help to reduce the size of the Cabinet. As Departments grow bigger there is also a tendency to increase the number of Ministers at each Department. The older

---

[1] Conservatives encounter insuperable difficulties in finding Members with adequate ability and experience who represent Welsh constituencies. In 1970 neither of the Ministers at the Welsh Office had a Welsh seat: they were Peter Thomas (Conway 1951–66 and Hendon, South, since 1970) and David Gibson-Watt (Hereford).

pattern of a Minister in the Cabinet supported by a Parliamentary Secretary has long since gone. In the new conglomerate Departments, e.g. Trade and Industry, there are Ministers nominated as responsible for a sector of the Department under the overall direction of the Secretary of State. Another level of appointment has developed considerably in numbers, the Minister of State, who might be described as a senior Junior Minister, although in terms of status is of full ministerial rank. For purposes of statistical analysis it is convenient to group these intermediate positions together under the designation of non-Cabinet Ministers.

The table below shows the totals of Members occupying official positions in four recent governments. As the figures exclude Peers they do not show the full size of these Cabinets which were—1950 eighteen, 1960 twenty-one, 1965 twenty-three and 1970 eighteen.

MEMBERS IN THE GOVERNMENT
(excluding Peers)

Year	1950	1960	1965	1970
Prime Minister	Attlee	Mac-millan	Wilson	Heath
Cabinet Ministers	15	17	21	15
Non-Cabinet Ministers	13	11	22	16
Junior Ministers	24	27	31	21
Whips	9[1]	9[2]	15	12
Law Officers[3]	4	3	2	3
Totals[4]	65	67	91	67

It was noted above[5] that the Ministers of the Crown Act, 1964, increased the permitted maximum of Members of the Commons who could hold office in the Government from 70 to 91. The Wilson administration had a record number of Ministers. The Heath administration has returned to the more traditional size. The figures in the table still

---

[1] Plus three unpaid Whips.

[2] Plus five unpaid Whips.

[3] It is often the case that one or both of the Scottish Law Officers belong to neither House of Parliament.

[4] The totals exclude the Second Church Estates Commissioner who, although not a member of the Government, does hold office under the Crown.

[5] p. 13.

underestimate the number of Members associated with the Government because parliamentary private secretaries are not included; these number about 30. So the number of Members who owe special loyalty to the Government is approximately 100 and in the Wilson period the figure was even higher.

There is no fixed pattern of political promotion. When senior positions become vacant there is a tendency to appoint those who have shown high competence at a lower level of the pyramid. Yet there are a few cases where a backbencher has achieved direct advancement to full ministerial status, Iain Macleod as Minister of Health in 1952, Aubrey Jones (Con. Birmingham, Hall Green, 1950–65) as Minister of Fuel and Power in 1955 and John Davies (Con. Knutsford) as Secretary of State for Trade and Industry in 1970. When Frank Cousins (Lab. Nuneaton 1965–67) was appointed Minister of Technology a seat had to be found for him in the Commons. If a party achieves power after a long period in Opposition there must be an inadequate supply of former Ministers to fill all senior positions. The youngest Cabinet Minister in recent times was Harold Wilson, appointed President of the Board of Trade in 1947 at the age of 31 after only two years in the Commons spent as a junior Minister.

New Members cannot expect to be asked to join the Government immediately, and for those in Opposition hope must be deferred until after a general election. If their party is in office, how long must they wait? The general answer is that a Member who has sat on the Government backbenches for seven years has a steadily diminishing prospect of promotion. It is probably advantageous for a Member to enter the Commons when his party is in a minority, for this allows a few years of freedom on the Opposition backbenches in which to gain experience and the beginnings of a reputation. Then on the morrow of electoral victory there are many posts to be filled at a time when the flush of new Members on the winning side have not the necessary experience. But a Member first returned when his party gains power is less happily placed. After an interval he may be thought ready for office but by then the political pendulum may have swung back and installed his opponents; alternatively, if his own party remains in the ascendant, only a trickle of junior ministerial vacancies will arise for which there will be many well placed competitors. Then, of course, not every Member accepts a Government post when it is offered to him: 26 Members told the Boyle Committee that they had refused to accept junior ministerial office for financial reasons.[1] Following the publication of the Boyle Report in December 1971, the salary of junior Ministers was raised from £5,000 p.a. to £8,500 p.a., i.e. £5,500 is the ministerial

---

[1] 1971–72 Cmnd. 4836 p. 59.

emolument to which is added £3,000 of the parliamentary salary. Before this increase there is no doubt that the financial position of some junior Ministers was uncomfortable and, since they were deprived of the opportunity to augment their incomes by commercial and other activities,[1] they were frequently worse off than backbenchers.

Not all junior Ministers reach Cabinet level. Some do not show the requisite ability; some lose interest in ministerial life because they can gain greater financial rewards elsewhere; some quit over disagreements with their colleagues; some fall out when the political pendulum swings against their party; some leave because of ill-health or, occasionally, because of personal disgrace. The path to the Cabinet room is commonly long and hazardous; F. M. G. Willson has shown that between 1868 and 1958 a Cabinet Minister on taking office could look back, on average, to fourteen years' service in the Commons.[2] Members of the 1964 Wilson Cabinet had served an average of sixteen years in the Commons before achieving Cabinet rank: this is a reflection of the long years Labour had spent in Opposition between 1951 and 1964. The average for the 1970 Conservative Cabinet was only eleven years because the Party had been out of office for a shorter period. The message is clear: if the more promising of new Members are not given an early opportunity of junior office, a future shortage of experienced Ministers is a serious probability.

For the individual there is a significant element of luck or accident in public life. Had Parliament not passed legislation in 1963 to permit the renunciation of peerages, through pressure by a Labour ex-Member, the Earl of Home could not have become Conservative Prime Minister in 1963. With another Prime Minister in 1963 the Conservatives might not have lost the Election of 1964 and there might have been no vacancy in 1965 to be filled by Edward Heath. The smile of fate and a safe seat are great aids towards high office but they are by no means sufficient conditions to ensure it. The Commons plays a decisive part in judging the fitness of those called upon to lead in our national life; a Member who is not well respected is less likely to receive an appointment and a Minister who is not a success in the House is ill placed to receive further promotion. Yet it is difficult to explain how the House chooses its leaders. As Harold Laski wrote 'the selective function of the House of Commons is the most mysterious of all its habits'.[3]

---

[1] Peter Emery (Con. Reading 1959–66 and Honiton since 1967) told the Commons in 1970 that a junior Minister in the new Conservative administration had been forced to sell his London home because of the loss of income suffered through joining the Government. H.C. Deb., Vol. 805, col. 904.

[2] Cf. *Political Studies*, Vol. VII, p. 227. This calculation excludes Peers and exceptional war-time appointments.

[3] *Parliamentary Government in England* (Allen and Unwin, 1938), p. 158.

Conditions of work in the House are sufficiently intimate for it to be acutely conscious of personalities and most Members have decided views on the qualities of other Members. Sincerity, good-humour and respect for the Commons as an institution assist the construction of a favourable reputation, while Members who appear self-centred and to crave publicity rank low in the estimation of their colleagues. A Member with great achievements to his credit before he enters the House will find that his past is of little help to him, for in the House every new Member is equally a beginner. In debate, mastery of a subject and facility with words are important but what is felt to be the inspiration of a contribution is important too. Hearts are judged as well as minds. While it is possible to suggest factors that inhibit success, the aspiring Member cannot find an infallible prescription to achieve it. Every Government contains men with a wide variety of qualities, some of which may be antithetical; each period of time may require a different type of leadership. The path to high office is an incalculable journey and many of those who seek greatness with the fullest determination are among the most disappointed.

CHAPTER 12

WHAT FUTURE FOR BACKBENCHERS?

The Threat to Parliamentary Institutions

Disillusion with parliaments is international. No longer do we speak proudly of Westminster as the Mother of Parliaments. So many of the legislatures created in ex-colonial territories on the Westminster model have withered as the new sovereign governments have showed themselves unwilling to tolerate political opposition from their compatriots. At home, criticism of Parliament is so well established as to be traditional. Twenty years ago Professor Keeton wrote a book on *The Passing of Parliament* and Christopher Hollis (Con. Devizes 1945–50) in similar vein entitled his volume *Can Parliament Survive?* The common line of argument has been that real power rests with the executive, with Ministers and civil servants, so that Parliament is left merely to record formal approval of decisions made elsewhere and the Commons accept this situation like a flock of sheep because they submit to the influence of the Whips. This analysis is too simple but it is widely believed.

More recently new forces have been at work. During the greater part of the nineteen-sixties, British Governments were notably weak governments. Their policies were often obviously unsuccessful. Their performance at by-elections or in opinion polls was either poor or disastrous. In the 1964–66 Parliament the stability of the Government was in constant doubt because of its minute majority in the Commons. This image of weakness reflected on Westminster and was also reinforced by Westminster as it exercised the natural and proper function of criticising Ministers. Yet Parliament was never able to dismiss a discredited Government, which is again a demonstration of impotence. For the public, the amount of political information and commentary also grew steadily through radio and television. In some measure, familiarity breeds contempt. Elections have been fought amidst unparalleled publicity. Party leaders of both main parties have aroused expectations they could not realise. Inevitably the public become discontented and cynicism flourishes. The feeling grows that there is little difference between the parties, perhaps because both compete for the support of the middle-of-the-road voter, perhaps because politicians are bereft of principles. In the nineteen-fifties the phrase 'Butskellism' was coined by *The Economist* to indicate the similarity of views between R. A. Butler and Hugh Gaitskell. It is notable that no journalist has attempted to link the names of Heath and Wilson in similar fashion; the differences between our contemporary leaders are visibly greater. Nevertheless, it is true that parliamentary politics are consensus politics in so far as the issues which divide Members are less strong than the issues which unite them. Resentment at this Establishment solidarity is fed by the current movement to criticise or resist authority—a tendency which has also led to the nomination of committees of enquiry into almost every branch of our political institutions, including parliamentary procedure.

Whether this impulse to denigrate is a serious threat to the British Parliament is highly dubious. A wish to criticise is not necessarily a wish to destroy. Parliament may be widely described as a 'talking-shop' but there is no movement to replace it. At elections any candidates with extreme opinions, Right or Left, gain few votes. And as Ian Budge has shown, politicians are even less critical or our democratic procedures and institutions than the public as a whole.[1] The number of potential career politicians attracted by the existing system shows no sign of diminishing. To judge *depth* of public feeling is difficult and tends to defeat orthodox questionnaire techniques. The present state of opinion probably reflects no more than a fashionable and healthy scepticism about Parliament rather than a deep-rooted malaise.[2] Parliament is sufficiently vigorous to withstand challenge while modernising itself. And this is a far happier condition than an easy acceptance of tradition that leads to stagnation and decay.

Meanwhile the urge to resist authority has produced a variety of ideas with conflicting motives. The fear that Ministers have become too autocratic and powerful because of their docile majority in the Commons has stimulated interest in the concept of a written constitution which would safeguard individual rights.[3] Such a constitution would have to be legally superior to ordinary laws. It would have to be especially difficult to amend in order to be protected from the displeasure of any Cabinet; this could be achieved by requiring, say, a 2/3 majority in both Houses of Parliament or perhaps a referendum. The interpretation of the constitution would be a matter for the Courts. The scheme is popular with some right-wing lawyers for it would increase the power of judges. It is not popular with politicians and is quite contrary to British tradition. Its chances of adoption are nil.

More widely-voiced is the claim that there should be wider opportunities for public participation in government. One consequence has

---

[1] *Agreement and the Stability of Democracy* (Markham, Chicago, 1970), Ch. 4.

[2] For example, Max Nicholson, *The System* (Holder, 1967).

[3] O. Hood Phillips, *Reform of the Constitution* (Chatto and Windus, 1970) and G. W. Keeton, *Government in Action in the United Kingdom* (Benn, 1970).

been attempts at 'direct action'. Another is the demand that major issues should be decided by popular referenda. Direct action is essentially an undemocratic programme followed by political groups which seek a dramatic confrontation with authority or which are unlikely to succeed through lobbying or the traditional electoral process. The referendum idea is founded on a primitive breed of democratic theory and has a conservative impetus—conservative with a small 'c'—due to the human tendency to fear change that is not obviously beneficial. International experience of referenda is that they tend to give a negative response to proposals to alter the law. Inevitably, demands for referenda arise when those who oppose change are confident that majority opinion is on their side, e.g. on capital punishment or entry into the Common Market. Thus to urge a popular vote on a particular question is just as much a political tactic as a sortie in direct action.

It is the referendum concept that has greater support. Relatively few people are keen to take part in political demonstrations which may involve a clash with the police. Many people will favour, at least in theory, the idea of having a direct voice in major political decisions. Proposals for referenda can take various forms. The extreme version is that certain questions should be put directly to the electorate and that their votes should be decisive. Thus Parliament would be completely replaced. A compromise plan advocated by Wedgwood Benn (Lab. Bristol S.E.) was for a national advisory referendum to be held on the Common Market. Philip Goodhart (Con. Beckenham) wrote a book with a similar theme[1] and actually organised a referendum in his constituency. Three polling stations were kept open for a fortnight so that the voters of Beckenham could express their views. The whole enterprise was organised and paid for by Goodhart: it was not sponsored by the local Conservative Association. Goodhart promised that the opinions of his constituents would weigh more heavily with him than pressure from the Whips. But the result produced no such conflict, with a narrow majority in favour of entry into Europe on a 10% poll. Mrs. Sally Oppenheim (Con. Gloucester) had a ballot form sent to each voter in the city. A 50% response produced an anti-Market majority of 4,286 in a total vote exceeding 30,000. Mrs. Oppenheim duly followed this lead. David Walder (Con. Clitheroe) distributed 26,000 leaflets, one to each household in the constituency, asking for opinions; only 82 written replies were received. Referenda were held in other areas, some sponsored by organisations opposed to the Common Market. Nearly 50% of the voters in Middlesbrough West took part in a local poll which showed more than a 2 to 1 majority against entry

---

[1] *Referendum* (Stacey, 1971).

into Europe. John Sutcliffe, the Conservative Member for this highly marginal constituency, accepted the verdict as a reinforcement of his own convictions. At Hastings a 3 to 1 majority against the market was recorded in a 25% turnout but the local Conservative Member, Kenneth Warren, followed the principles of Burke and voted in support of Government policy. Where a referendum does attract a high level of participation, the independence of the local Member is challenged for there must be a strong demand that his vote in the Commons should follow the balance of local opinion: in the case of a national referendum as proposed by Wedgwood Benn the moral authority of Parliament itself would be undermined.

The case against this form of mass participation can be stated briefly. If people are to be asked to answer a question about what type of public policy they prefer—the first task is to frame the question. On almost all issues it is impossible to phrase it in a way which is both unambiguous and adequately summarises the issue at stake. It is not unknown for pressure groups to cast questionnaires in a form that tends to produce the desired responses. Political choice is rarely a matter of stark alternatives. Instead of either black or white, many people prefer an intermediate shade of grey. Again, unless an issue can be wholly separated from other political questions, reactions of voters may result from feelings that have little to do with the immediate problem. A poll on Sunday opening of licensed premises in Wales is perhaps separable from other matters; a vote on a major item of Government policy is not. Many people might have voted against the Government's intention to join Europe because of dissatisfaction over rising prices or unemployment. The general experience of referenda, and Beckenham was quite typical, is that turnout is low, much lower than at ordinary elections. This may be due simply to apathy but it may also be that many electors are unwilling to give an opinion on a particular issue, either through indecision or from a feeling of inadequacy. Clearly, if policy decisions were made by mass referenda, the average level of understanding of those who decided would be lower—often much lower—than if decisions are made by elected representatives who have the time, opportunity and responsibility to study public affairs. From a democratic standpoint this may seem a dangerous argument. If the right to join in decision-making is to be a product of understanding or formal education, why have universal suffrage? The answer must be that representative democracy combines the value of consultation with all and the value of decision by the few who are judged by the many to be competent to decide public policy for a limited period. And if the few are not allowed to decide on capital punishment or the Common Market—why should they decide anything? A referendum is fundamentally opposed to the concept of representation. Parliament is right to resist referenda in the interests of self-preservation.

The Tasks of the Commons and the Purpose of Reform

Much disillusion with Parliament arises from a lack of public knowledge of what elected representatives do. Misunderstanding is not surprising since Parliament makes little effort to explain itself. Indeed, it would be virtually impossible to organise any official public relations work on behalf of Parliament since Members would not agree about its content. The tasks performed by the Commons are complex, not simple; although continuous, they vary in importance from time to time; some of the most influential activities are concealed, quite deliberately, from public view.

Members, collectively, discharge five functions. The Commons support and maintain a Government. They provide a pool of talent from which national leaders are drawn and help to choose these leaders. In debates they reflect public opinion, may help to educate it and forge links between public opinion and public policy. They have the formal responsibility of agreeing to new legislation and they influence its content. Finally, Members undertake scrutiny of executive action and thereby help to safeguard individual rights. My view is that these tasks are performed more vigorously than ever before—with one exception. To substantiate this claim each function will be briefly reviewed.

The need for Members to maintain a government in office is frequently overlooked. Yet this task is vital if society is to enjoy stability and if those entrusted with executive authority are to be responsive to the popular will. The duty to maintain a government is not, of course, a duty to any particular group of Ministers: the requirement is to sustain an acceptable team of people to take charge of executive functions so that communal business can be carried on. The usual criticism is that this duty is carried out too well; that Ministers supported by party loyalty and discipline are only too secure. In this century it has been rare for the continued existence of a government to be threatened by the Commons. Since Government backbenchers have no desire for an early general election, they must use informal party machinery if they wish to challenge their leaders. When the fortunes of the Labour Government were at a very low ebb in the spring of 1969 an assorted group of Labour backbenchers did make an effort to replace the Prime Minister. They tried to have the issue discussed at a meeting of the parliamentary party but the Chairman, Douglas Houghton (Sowerby), refused to accept a motion of no confidence in the leadership unless it attracted 120 signatures—i.e. that it stood a high chance of success. Since this level of support was not forthcoming, the revolt distintegrated and Wilson remained in office. But the outcome might have been different had the Members concerned been more fully agreed amongst themselves on who was the alternative Prime Minister. An Opposition challenge to a Government is formal and carried through in the Chamber and the division lobbies. Even here the Opposition may give covert assistance to Ministers, when the Government majority is low, so long as the Opposition does not wish to force an election.[1]

Political selection of leaders was discussed in the previous chapter. Sometimes the role of backbenchers in the process is formal and obvious as with the election of party Leaders and the Executive of the Parliamentary Labour Party when Labour is in Opposition. Yet all the time backbenchers are involved informally as they assess and re-assess the qualities of their colleagues. Reputations constantly rise and fall. Some Members are seen to acquire greater confidence or fuller mastery over particular subjects while others seem to become erratic, grow old or develop interests which divert them from parliamentary business. Such evaluation is casual and uncoordinated yet it plays a part in deciding whether a Member gets an invitation to join a government. Subsequent promotion or demotion of a Minister is also affected by his reputation with Government backbenchers. In the Conservative Party family ties and personal relationships used to be highly influential in the distribution of ministerial office. Now this pattern is fading. The Heath administration is almost devoid of the genealogical links that were to be found in the Macmillan Government. Instead, backbench opinion has become more significant, notably in the election of the Party Leader.

The third function, the relationship between Parliament and public opinion, quite inevitably arouses the most controversy. Anyone who holds strong opinions may be dissatisfied if his views are not shared by a majority of Members. A matter which agitates an individual may be virtually unnoticed by Parliament which has only time to consider a limited range of public issues. To expect Westminster to provide more than an imperfect and partial reflection of opinion is unrealistic. Yet few debates stem from the enthusiasm of an individual Member, for the stimulus that determines how private members' time shall be used comes largely from voluntary organisations.

Bernard Crick has argued that Parliament is a continuous election campaign.[2] This is an over-simplification, yet Members' behaviour often does justify the description. It is natural for them to become heated and intense when deeply controversial decisions are at stake, but most attempts to score party debating points are trivial and time-wasting. Perhaps Members engage in political jousting because it is customary and may advance a personal reputation. To believe it will win many votes is a delusion. The vast majority of electors pay little heed to what occurs in parliamentary debate. Indeed, the one task which Parliament performs less effectively today is the ability to educate opinion: the

---

[1] pp. 81–2 *supra*.

[2] *The Reform of Parliament* (Weidenfeld and Nicolson, 1964), p. 194.

Grand Inquest of the Nation no longer gives much of a lead to the nation. Chapter 10 showed how far this activity has been taken over by the mass media, notably radio and television. As the new media are more widely available than printed reports of parliamentary debates, the change is no loss to the public; the damage is to the status of Parliament. However, the Commons still have a vital educational task—to educate each other, not excluding Ministers.

Legislation is central to the work of the Commons. But an assembly of 630 Members cannot itself frame legislation. Preparatory research work and preliminary discussion with interested parties and those with specialised knowledge must be done elsewhere by smaller groups of people. The task for Parliament is to accept, reject or perhaps amend the heads of proposals prepared in this way. The Government often seem to resist very reasonable criticism by Members of legislative proposals. Occasionally, Ministers have struck a bargain beforehand with a pressure group and feel unable to break the agreement; this situation is inimical to the democratic process. More often it may be that the *amour propre* of Ministers or their senior advisers may be damaged if they admit the validity of arguments put forward by critics. Since the main confrontation in debate is normally between Ministers and the Opposition Front Bench, discussion on a controversial Bill contains elements of a gladiatorial combat. Any retreat or second thoughts by Ministers may look like weakness or a victory for their opponents. The smaller the party element in legislation, the easier it is for parliamentary pressure to secure changes. On the other hand, Ministers should not always be blamed for resisting amendments. Popular ideas often involve spending money and Ministers must retain responsibility for the total of public expenditure. Further, in a complex measure an apparently useful amendment may have wide implications and create difficulties or anomalies in the administration of the whole Act. So attempts by Members to change legislation are commonly unsuccessful. Yet the extent of parliamentary influence on the final form of an Act is under-estimated. No fewer than 15 changes were made in the Leasehold Reform Bill 1967 through backbench initiative.[1] The Trade Descriptions Bill 1968 was amended in both Lords and Commons. Many such changes are technical and originate from the activity of pressure groups. Other successful amendments, e.g. on the Race Relations Bill 1965 and the Immigration Bill 1971, involve important policy issues. So the role of Parliament in legislation remains vital. Ministers are forced to explain and defend their proposals; sometimes they agree, or are forced, to alter them. And as was

---

[1] Memorandum by Edward Rowlands (Lab. Cardiff, North 1966–70) to the Select Committee on Procedure. 1970–71 (538) Appendix 17.

shown in Chapter 7, initiative comes not only from Ministers: private members' legislation in the 1966 Parliament achieved a new peak of importance.

The fifth function noted above, the scrutiny of executive action, is increasingly a matter for the committee rooms. Here the backbencher has greater freedom because the party element is allowed to fade within a select committee. Again, on personal cases and constituency matters, the significance of party diminishes. As shown in Chapters 6 and 8, this whole area has occupied much more backbench energy in recent years. The growth of Members' role as welfare officers, the appointment of the Parliamentary Commissioner for Administration and the experiment of specialised committees all indicate a determination to protect individual rights and to extend the element of surveillance over the actions of permanent officials. From all these endeavours the sum total of visible benefit may be modest. Yet the value of a watch-dog is always immeasurable: the watch-dog may do little, but what would happen were he to be withdrawn?

Modest steps to achieve greater efficiency in the Commons have been taken through recent reforms in parliamentary procedure. Some changes were highly technical: the modernisation of financial business reduced the element of what Emrys Hughes called 'mumbo-jumbo'.[1] The more flexible rules governing emergency debates make it easier for Members to give immediate attention to contemporary crises. Time in the Chamber is saved by the innovation of Second Reading Committees and by taking part of the committee stage of the Finance Bill in Standing Committee. Time of Members has been saved by reducing the size of Standing Committees and this has helped to release Members to serve on the extra committees concerned with the scrutiny of executive action. One reform that failed was the idea of morning sittings in the Chamber to deal with issues of second-rank importance: Members found this inconvenient and the extra opportunity offered was felt to be totally unexciting. To succeed, procedural reform must both reflect the wishes of Members and preserve the balance between Government and Opposition. The danger in streamlining procedure is that it restricts the ability to debate so that it becomes easier for Ministers to get their business through the House. For the Opposition, the possibility of causing delay by protracted discussion is an important weapon. So streamlining should not be taken too far. The reforms made since 1966 have kept a careful balance: little has been done to ease the work of Government Whips but some fresh means have been found to made backbenchers more productive.

---

[1] Emrys Hughes: *Parliament and Mumbo-Jumbo* (Allen and Unwin, 1966). Hughes was Labour Member for South Ayrshire 1946–69.

The impetus to reform in the Commons is still strong. The Procedure Committee report issued in August 1971 entitled *The Process of Legislation* contained no fewer than 28 suggestions for further change.[1] Naturally, these varied in scope. Some were minor or technical. Others constituted a major challenge to existing practice. Among the proposals were the establishment of both pre-legislation and post-legislation committees. The former would consider relatively non-controversial issues with small financial implications and would prepare the way for a future Bill. The latter would consider the difficulties, legal and administrative, of the practical operation of a recent Act. On private members' Bills, the Procedure Committee urged that the ballot be held before the summer adjournment to give more time for the preparation of Bills coming forward through this channel. Also the first ten Members to be drawn should be given assistance with drafting their Bills. Other ideas were that explanatory memoranda should be issued to help Members to understand the purposes and effect of a Bill; that it should be possible to commit a Bill in part to a Standing Committee and in part to a select committee; that time in the Chamber could be saved by having a vote on Third Reading without debate; that the terms of reference of the Select Committee on Statutory Instruments be made more flexible. Taken together these reforms, if implemented, would strengthen significantly the role of the backbencher in legislation.

The direction of change is significant. Yet it does not mean that backbenchers are moving towards a dominant place in national decision-making. Ministers, the leaders of the majority party, will retain the initiative in policy and responsibility for administration. The role of backbenchers is to influence, not to command. And influence cannot be subjected to precise measurement. Certainly, the impact of Parliament will vary. A newly-elected Cabinet, a successful Cabinet, a united Cabinet will enjoy unquestioned loyalty from its supporters. It has nothing to fear in Westminster. But a team of Ministers, losing popularity in the country, that demonstrably fails to deal with urgent problems and which gives evidence of internal disunity—such a body can be forced to pay more attention to parliamentary opinion. The greater influence of Labour backbenchers in 1968–69 is an indication of the contemporary weakness of the Wilson Cabinet. Ministers and ex-Ministers will sometimes tell an academic enquirer that they have never changed a major policy decision as a result of backbench pressure. Such testimony is unimpressive. What does 'major' imply in this context? What is a minor matter to a Minister may seem very important to other people. Politicians may feel it is damaging to self-esteem and a confession of weakness to admit that one has surrendered to critics:

---

[1] 1970–71 (538).

this is an admission that politicians may be expected to avoid. Further, when a decision is altered a number of factors can be at work. It may be possible to show that urgent administrative or technical considerations required a change of policy and so to argue that parallel political pressure from Members was purely fortuitous. One other approach to the extent of backbench influence is purely speculative: what might have happened were it not for backbench opinion? Members do not always campaign for change; instead they may wish to keep the *status quo* at a time when some Ministers favour a policy upheaval. Thus inaction by the Cabinet may contain some element of backbench victory. Under the Wilson Government the failure to reach agreement with the Smith regime in Rhodesia and the continued ban on arms sales to South Africa are possible examples of this situation. Such influence cannot be clearly proved. To repeat, influence is immeasurable.

Backbenchers on the Government side of the House can often hope to affect a Cabinet decision. Since the time of Sir Anthony Eden, the Chief Whip has been present at Cabinet meetings to report when necessary on the state of parliamentary opinion. This fairly recent innovation is a tribute to the Commons. The views of the Chief Whip may be reinforced or contradicted by representations made through the recognised spokesman for the Government backbenchers—the Chairman of the 1922 Committee or the Chairman of the Parliamentary Labour Party. Patrick Gordon Walker, after substantial Cabinet experience, has stated that the argument that 'our fellows will not stand it' is persuasive with Ministers.[1] Serious backbench disquiet is normally reflected in the Cabinet itself. There is a gulf between Ministers and their parliamentary supporters in terms of status, salary and experience; there is no great difference in terms of political philosophy. So backbench rebels may well have some ministerial sympathy. From this basis it can be urged that the influence of Members is not too weak but too strong—that Cabinets retreat too easily from necessary but unpopular policies. Developing this theme Ian Gilmour has argued that while Members feel restraint when a vote is taken and to some extent in debate in the Chamber, they are otherwise wholly free to lobby and cajole.[2] Since the vital discussions take place in private, their freedom to influence is little impeded.

Two factors inhibit further growth in the role of backbenchers. One is the amount of energy Members are willing to give to parliamentary duties. If Members spend substantial time on professional or

---

[1] *The Cabinet* (Cape, 1970), p. 63. Gordon Walker has been Labour Member for Smethwick 1945–64 and Leyton since 1966.

[2] *The Body Politic* (Hutchison, 1969), pp. 270–5. Gilmour is Conservative Member for Norfolk Central.

commercial activities, then their political work must suffer. Morning sittings and the idea of prelegislation committees, both encouraged by Richard Crossman in 1966, both foundered on lack of backbench support. Higher parliamentary salaries should ease this problem by lessening economic pressure on Members to seek additional income. The second constraint is party loyalty. The more Members accept the wisdom of their party leaders without challenge, the weaker Parliament must be. Each prospect of rebellion gives added life to the Commons. Yet it is idle to expect Members to cast aside regularly the shackles of party discipline. They are constrained not simply by blandishments or threats from Whips or by fear of hostile constituency reactions. Members are conditioned to act in party terms: almost each new Member arrives at Westminster after many years of political activity in support of his party. To vote against one's associates, if it means voting with traditional opponents, is to act contrary to a life purpose. Most Members will do this rarely and after hesitation. The hold of party is strong and will remain. Nevertheless, Members will be effective as backbenchers only if they think of themselves as backbenchers and not as potential Ministers.

The conclusion must be that procedural rules are less important than the mode of parliamentary behaviour. Of course, procedure can frustrate, inhibit and impede more effective legislative action. But what matters in even a reformed framework of procedure is what Members allow themselves to do. If they are to gain more freedom, it will not come from more rebellions but because the parties agree that more questions are decided on a non-party basis. Certainly free votes will not apply to issues where party views clash, nor can they be allowed where there are major implications for national expenditure. Yet there are still many questions that could be submitted to the personal judgement of Members. It would strengthen Parliament were this to happen more often.

The Future and the Status of Members

To speculate about the future of Parliament when writing in 1971 is to invite being overtaken by events. During the sixties the stimulus for change came largely from Members themselves. During the seventies it may well come from outside. One possibility is Ulster. Another is that Lord Crowther's Commission on the Constitution may open the way for adjustments in the system of government which will affect both Lords and Commons. Entry into the European Economic Community is not yet certain but, without question, it would leave a mark on Parliament.

The effects of entry into Europe would be twofold. First, there would be the need for Parliament to develop machinery to keep abreast of the flow of directions from Brussels which apply to Britain. Second, there would be the consequences that come from sending representatives to the European Parliament at Strasbourg. Westminster might find the European link an awkward experience. Directions coming from the Community cannot be rejected or amended. So the sovereignty of a legislature in a member-country is restricted. National Parliaments within the E.E.C. vary in the extent to which they discuss E.E.C. policy; the legislatures in Belgium, the Netherlands and Western Germany are more active than those in France, Italy and Luxembourg.[1] One assumes that the British Parliament would join the former group and that Members will wish to scrutinise the edicts coming from Brussels both to inform themselves and to be in a better position to influence future European policy through the British representatives in the Council of Ministers and the European Parliament.

On entry into the E.E.C. Britain would send 36 representatives to the European Parliament. The Treaty of Rome (Article 138) contains provisions for this body to be directly elected. The European Parliament adopted a proposal for direct election in 1960 but as the Council of Ministers took no action the scheme remains a dead letter. So the election remains indirect and stays with the parliaments of the member-countries: in Britain it is likely that this would be done through 'usual channels' with the 36 places being divided between the parties roughly in proportion to their strength in the Commons. Those nominated to Strasbourg cannot send deputies; they attend in person or not at all. Meetings are held between eight and ten times a year. They last almost a week. Much of the work is done in specialised standing committees. British representatives to this body would develop much closer links with parliamentarians from Europe. To belong to the European Parliament is to impose a heavy strain on the time and energy of Members; the commitment could consume almost 100 days a year, allowing some time for travel and preparatory work. How many Members would be willing to devote so much time to this task, bearing in mind that the European Parliament is essentially an advisory body?[2] The present scale of expenses allowed for attendance at Strasbourg is approximately £16 per day: at this rate Members should not be out-of-pocket in terms of what they actually spend but the sum is not sufficient to compensate for any substantial loss of professional earnings. Further, would electors be happy for their Member to spend so much

---

[1] Michael Niblock, *The E.E.C.: National Parliaments in Community Decision-Making* (Chatham House: P.E.P., 1971).

[2] It can dismiss the European Commission, the powerful executive of permanent officials, by a 2/3 majority in a vote of no confidence. So far this has not happened. Indeed, it seems an unlikely possibility.

time in Europe? Already there have been cases where European politicians have suffered because their local electors felt themselves neglected through work in Strasbourg.[1] British constituencies should not take a narrow view because the 36 representatives would have a vital role to play in forming a link between Westminster and Strasbourg and in keeping the British public informed about developments in European policy.

Looking further ahead, would association with Europe cause a fresh fall in the status of the Commons and an accompanying decline in the quality of Members? If status is related directly to the extent of legal power, this is an obvious possibility. Yet the range of matters that, in the foreseeable future, may be subject to European regulations and directives occupy but a small part of the energy and attention of Parliament. At the same time Parliament would have a new task as guardian of British interests in the European context. Indeed, if some of the odium that now surrounds our national government for failure to promote economic prosperity could be shifted on to Europe, the standing of British politicians could be improved.

It is common in human affairs to romanticise the past and to urge that things are not so good as they used to be. Thus the calibre of Members is sometimes said to have deteriorated in the last few years because party discipline has eradicated individuality. The idea is not new. When Lord Morley asserted in 1923 that the private Member was a shadow of what he had been at the end of the previous century, he was reminded by Mr. Birrell that W. E. Gladstone had said the same in the eighteen-eighties when arguing that the post-1832 period constituted the Golden Age.[2] To attempt any action to improve the quality of Members must involve training or restriction on selection and would encounter serious difficulties as the Rowntree Trust discovered in 1971. The Trust had the idea of making available to each party a small number of bursaries that could be given to prospective candidates, who would thus have economic freedom to prepare themselves for parliamentary life, partly by constituency work and partly by assisting the research activities of their respective parties. The scheme broke down after negotiations with the political parties over the crucial question of how these fortunate people should be selected.

How can the quality of Members be judged? No precise evaluation can be made for there is no agreement on how quality should be measured. The formal educational qualifications of Members are higher than ever before. The amount of attention paid by Members to public policy and constituency problems grows steadily. Few Members would

---

[1] Stephen Holt, *The Common Market* (Hamish Hamilton, 1967), p. 79.

[2] H. J. Laski, *Reflections on the Constitution* (Manchester U.P., 1951), p. 30.

now agree with Commander Bower that a Member should be able to keep abreast of current affairs by studying the press for half an hour each day; that the greater part of a Member's correspondence did not require serious personal attention; that on many days there was no need to attend the Commons while on other days only a perfunctory visit was required.[1] But in spite of the fact that Members' lives become more exacting, there are more parliamentary aspirants than ever before. Each vacancy in a safe seat produces a flood of would-be Members. Selection committees may not always make wise choices but any selection process should give better results if a wider range of candidates is available. On this kind of objective evidence it appears that the calibre of Members and their sense of duty is rising, not falling. Ability in debate is impossible to measure. However, the newer Conservative Members are dull orators, possibly because they follow the fashion set by their leaders.

The performance of backbenchers is largely influenced by the way in which they approach their duties. For this purpose they can be divided into four fairly definite categories—the useful party Members, the good constituency Members, the individualists and the part-timers. The first group covers those who make some impact on the House through specialising on particular topics; they will probably hold office on the appropriate party backbench committee; in opposition, they will be prominent on any Standing Committee considering a Bill that comes within their range of expertise; on the government benches, many will become parliamentary private secretaries. They will rarely join in party revolts. They are the obvious candidates for promotion to ministerial office. The good constituency Members devote more time to local causes and personal cases. Their questions and speeches in the House will have something of a constituency flavour. The individualists are concerned to press items of policy that fall outside the lines of the main party battle. Here are the most colourful personalities who attract above-average publicity. The Liberals and Independents tend to fall into this category. Opinions will differ on which Conservative and Labour Members should be included; among the Conservatives obvious candidates are Sir Gerald Nabarro (Worcestershire, South), Enoch Powell (Wolverhampton, S.W.) and Norman St. John Stevas (Chelmsford), while the strongest Labour contender for inclusion is Leo Abse (Pontypool). The part-timers are those Members who combine other activities with their parliamentary duties, perhaps as company directors, at the Bar or in journalism.

These four categories are not mutually exclusive. It is possible

---

[1] Conservative Member for Cleveland 1931–45 in a letter to *The Times*, July 24th 1957.

that a Member may fit into more than one. An individualist may well be a good constituency Member. A part-timer may be a useful party Member if he has sufficient energy. And the extent to which a Member is drawn into constituency affairs depends partly on his own inclinations and partly on the nature of the constituency. Those who sit for marginal seats may feel a need to spend more time on local problems than those who represent a safe seat. And a slice of contented suburbia, a peaceful or prosperous rural area will demand less attention than depressed areas or those with special problems, e.g. Ulster. Finally, it is possible, if unusual, for a Member to move clearly out of one group into another. Enoch Powell has ceased to be a useful party man; so has Christopher Mayhew (Lab. Woolwich, East). Some individualists are ex-Ministers who have had serious disagreements with senior colleagues.

There is a growing tendency for Members to think of Parliament as a full-time, or largely full-time career occupation. The proportion of useful party Members and good constituency Members is growing. Eccentricity withers in this climate. The career politician is more interested in the facilities of the Palace of Westminster and how to improve them. He is also more concerned to attain ministerial office since as a backbencher he feels frustrated because he is but on the margins of government; he wants to get into the heart of the system and help to make decisions instead of being a critic. Development of specialist committees has been largely an attempt to relieve this form of tension. So the changing attitude of Members to their role has produced conflicting behaviour patterns. On the one hand, Government supporters—especially when Conservatives are in office—may try to comport themselves as behoves future junior Ministers. At the same time there is a restless fount of energy and ability among backbenchers that demands opportunity to demonstrate their talents.

If it be agreed that the quality of backbenchers is wholly adequate to provide a good supply of future junior Ministers, it is still possible to claim that there are few Members who are obviously destined for high office. Certainly, it is almost unknown for a man of outstanding achievements in industry, trade unionism, science or the arts to come forward for selection. Even should someone of this stature seek a parliamentary seat, it is by no means certain that a constituency caucus would choose him because of the desire to have a Member prepared to spend time on local affairs. Traditionally the House is replete with legal talent; many of the most able lawyers, and therefore the most highly paid, are now reluctant for financial reasons to enter the political arena. A few trade union Members have left the House voluntarily to pursue their careers in the trade union movement or elsewhere. Other Members drop out of public life because they find it impossible to combine business with their parliamentary duties. So men of talent are deflected away from Westminster by pressure from the constituencies and the Whips who demand, respectively, attention and attendance.

But how far does this damage the quality of our leading statesmen? Is it certain, or even likely, that a brilliant scientist or author, a dynamic industrialist or a dominant trade union leader would be equally successful in the world of politics? Political leadership demands an apprenticeship. Men who go straight to the Cabinet without a period on the backbenches may well be insensitive to public and parliamentary opinion. The House of Commons is the place where the arts of leadership and political understanding can be developed. If today senior Ministers and ex-Ministers appear less impressive than formerly— it may be because they are subjected to more critical scrutiny by the mass media. If the gap in quality between senior Ministers and backbenchers seems to have narrowed—in my view the explanation is that backbenchers are of higher standard.

Meanwhile, the Commons remains a strong magnet. Since it extracts a formidable toll from Members, this attraction requires explanation. Probably some candidates have not fully appreciated the exertions that face them should they be successful: this was true of some of the Labour Members first elected in 1945. Monetary reward is certainly not the inducement and even the chance of obtaining a ministerial salary is not very exciting. The level of pay for junior Ministers has been a positive disincentive for some Conservatives. The motive force that supplies an abundance of potential candidates must be a combination of political enthusiasm and a genuine willingness for public service. It is significant that many Members have preliminary experience in local government and that others have a family tradition of participation in public affairs. Once a candidate is elected, these sentiments are powerfully reinforced by the fascination of being close to the centre of great events and by heightened ambition to obtain office. Members who have been in Westminster for many years without achieving prominence are still reluctant to leave. The lure of the House is strong and not easy to describe. A club-like atmosphere is retained and Members know each other by Christian names; the Smoking Room is naturally the best informed centre of political gossip in the land. A real attachment to Parliament extends beyond Members to the staff of the House and to the reporters in the Gallery. It is not restricted to any political party, and I recall the private confession of a former Labour Member that he was more interested in Parliament than he was in socialism.

The charm of Parliament cannot be equated to love of power since most Members do not, and never will, exercise great personal power. The ability to make major decisions about public policy belongs to senior Ministers. What Members may have is influence, the strength of which varies with the political situation. For some, influence is more attractive than power, since it does not carry the same onus of responsibility.

Members have an exacting and unusual task. Their calling provides great variety, opportunity and excitement. Their representative status still enjoins an element of esteem. Responsible opinion recognises that Members perform functions vital to the operation of a democratic system of government. However, contemporary society is decreasingly deferential: overtly ambitious people may provoke mild cynicism or even distaste. Nevertheless, a good constituency Member enjoys respect for what he does, or tries to do, for his locality. This is a gratifying experience and a further attraction of parliamentary life. It would be unwise to begrudge Members this pleasure. The general attitude towards politicians must have an effect on their quality: the higher Members stand in public estimation, the better will the public be served.

SELECT BIBLIOGRAPHY

Official Publications

Parliamentary papers provide detailed information about the work of Parliament. They include *Hansard*, reports of parliamentary and other committees and other official returns.

Books

Specialised studies of Parliament:

A. Barker and M. Rush, *The Member of Parliament and his Information* (Allen and Unwin, 1970).

M. Barnett, *The Politics of Legislation* (Weidenfeld and Nicolson, 1969).

R. Butt, *The Power of Parliament* (Constable, 1967).

D. Coombes, *The Member of Parliament and the Administration* (Allen and Unwin, 1966).

B. Crick, *The Reform of Parliament* (Weidenfeld and Nicolson, 1964).

A. Hansen and B. Crick (eds.), *The Commons in Transition* (Collins, 1970).

R. Jackson, *Rebels and Whips* (Macmillan, 1968).

N. Johnson, *Parliament and Administration* (Allen and Unwin, 1966).

A. Morris (ed.), *The Growth of Parliamentary Scrutiny by Committee* (Pergamon, 1970).

P. Richards, *Parliament and Conscience* (Allen and Unwin, 1970).

P. Richards, *Parliament and Foreign Affairs* (Allen and Unwin, 1967).

Other works on British politics which contain valuable material on the backbenchers:

David Butler's series of volumes on each General Election (Macmillan).

I. Gilmour, *The Body Politic* (Hutchinson, 1969).

W. Hampton, *Democracy and Community* (O.U.P., 1970).

J. Mackintosh, *The Government and Politics of Britain* (Hutchinson, 1970).

N. Nicolson, *People and Parliament* (Weidenfeld and Nicolson, 1968).

A. Ranney, *Pathways to Parliament* (Macmillan, 1965).
C. Seymour-Ure, *The Press, Politics and Public* (Methuen, 1968).
J. Tunstall, *The Westminster Lobby Correspondents* (Routledge, 1970).

Autobiographies and biographies about Members are of varied quality. Those which concern leading political personalities tend to concentrate on their activities as Ministers or Shadow Ministers rather than as backbenchers.

Journals

The following quarterlies regularly publish important articles on Parliament:

Parliamentary Affairs (Hansard Society).
Political Quarterly.
Public Administration (Royal Institute of Public Administration).
Public Law (Stevens).

INDEX OF MEMBERS

Abbot, C. (Speaker), 181
Abse, L., 85, 143n, 147, 149n, 231
Acland, Sir Richard, 162n
Aldritt, W. H., 174
Alligham, G., 12, 50n, 190–1
Amery, L. S., 90
Anderson, Miss M. B. H., 72
Asquith, H. H., 24, 90
Attlee, C. R., 1st Earl, 15, 59, 60, 63, 68, 90–1, 211, 212, 214
Avebury, 4th Baron, *see* Lubbock, E. R.
Avon, 1st Earl, *see* Eden, Sir R. Anthony

Bagier, G. A. T., 180
Baker, P. A. D., 12n
Baldwin, S., 1st Earl, 46, 90
Banks, C., 157
Baxter, W., 69
Beckett, J., 87
Bell, R. M., 48
Benn, A. N. W., 15, 17n, 63, 111n, 221
Benn, W. W., 15, 16, 220
Bennett, J., 103
Berkeley, H. J., 161
Bevan, A., 59, 60, 62, 207, 211
Bevin, E., 23
Birch, E. N. C., 64
Birrell, A., 230
Bishop, E. S., 148
Black, Sir Cyril W., 146
Bonar Law, A., *see* Law, A. Bonar
Bottomley, A. G., 178
Bowen, E. R., 72
Bower, R. T., 230–1
Boyd-Carpenter, J. A., 113
Boyle, Sir Edward C. G. (Baron), 25–32 *passim.*, 48, 215–16
Bradlaugh, C., 189
Brooks, E., 149n
Brown, A. G., 162n
Brown, G. A., (Lord George-Brown) 140, 211, 212
Brown, W. J., 173, 192–3
Burke, E., 154–5, 156, 221
Butcher, Sir Herbert, 87
Butler, R. A. (Baron), 208, 218

Callaghan, L. J., 129, 171, 211
Campbell-Bannerman, Sir Henry, 24
Chamberlain, Sir Austen, 46, 47
Chamberlain, A. N., 90
Churchill, Sir Winston L. S., 25, 85, 90
Churchill, W. S., 20
Clarke, H., 20
Clynes, J. R., 211
Cousins, F., 23, 215
Craddock, G., 59
Crathorne, Viscount, *see* Dugdale, Sir Thomas
Critchley, J. M. G., 208n
Crosland, C. A. R., 198
Crossman, R. H. S., 129, 139, 194, 204, 228
Cunningham-Reid, A. S., 65n

Dalyell, T., 191
Davies, J. E. H., 23, 215
Davies, S., 18, 59, 161, 176n
Deedes, W. F., 48, 199
de Ferranti, B. R. V. Z., 175
Devlin, Miss B., 12, 20, 85, 186
Dilhorne, 1st Viscount, *see* Manning-ham-Buller, Sir Reginald
Donnelly, D. L., 62, 67, 162
Douglas-Home, Sir Alec, 16, 64, 210, 211, 216
Du Cann, E. D. L., 122
Duffy, A. E. P., 87, 193
Dugdale, Sir Thomas, 91
Duthie, Sir William S., 67

Eadie, A., 63n
Edelman, M., 198
Eden, Sir R. Anthony, 68, 227
Elliot, W., 184
Emery, P. F. H., 216n
English, M., 63n, 149n
Evans, S. N., 158
Ewing, Mrs. W. M., 78, 107, 136, 194

Faulds, A. M. W., 130
Fernyhough, E., 59
Fisher, N. T. L., 158, 162
Fletcher, L. R., 63n

Foot, M. M., 59, 85, 133, 212–13
Fraser, Sir Ian, 179
Freeson, R., 171

Gaitskell, H. T. N., 60, 211, 212, 218
Gibson-Watt, D., 213n
Gilmour, I. H. J. L., 198, 227
Gladstone, W. E., 230
Goodhart, P. C., 220
Gourlay, H. P. H., 103
Greenwood, A., 211, 212
Grieve, W. P., 161
Griffiths, P. H. S., 86

Hailsham, 2nd Viscount, *see* Hogg, Q. M.
Hamilton, W. W., 120, 182n
Hamling, W., 172
Hardie, J. K., 211
Harris, R. R., 161
Heath, E. R. G., 14, 49, 62, 64, 65, 68, 209, 210, 211, 214, 216, 218
Heffer, E. S., 196–7
Herbert, Sir Alan P., 85, 148, 190
Higgins, T. L., 158, 159
Hill, J. M., 82
Hirst, G. A. N., 67
Hogg, Q. M., 15, 16
Hollis, M. C., 218
Home, 14th Earl of, *see* Douglas-Home, Sir Alec
Hornby, R. P., 48, 159
Houghton, A. L. N. D., 30, 50, 62, 173n, 222
Howard, Hon. G. R., 159
Howie, W., 173
Hughes, E., 59, 225
Hylton-Foster, Sir Harry B. (Speaker), 70

Iremonger, T. L., 204

Jackson, P. M., 61–2
Jenkins, R. H., 62, 148, 198
Jennings, J. C., 172
Johnson, Dr. D. M., 67
Jones, A., 14
Jones, T. A., 146, 149n, 215
Jowett, F., 127

Kenyon, C., 130
Kerr, D. L., 63n
King, H. M. (Speaker), 70
Knight, Mrs. J. C. J., 178

Lambton, A., 16
Law, A. Bonar, 47
Legge-Bourke, Sir Harry, 132
Lever, L. M., 86
Lever, N. H., 148
Lewis, A. W. J., 78, 107, 192
Lewis, R. H., 175–6
Lloyd, S. (Speaker), 70, 71
Lloyd George, D., 1st Earl, 24, 90
Lubbock, E. R., 181, 182

MacAndrew, Sir Charles, 70
MacDermot, N., 144n
MacDonald, J. R., 90, 211
McGovern, J., 59
MacIntyre, R. D., 74n
McKay, Mrs. M., 158–9
Mackenzie, J. G., 114n
Mackintosh, J. P., 51, 89n, 198
Macleod, I. N., 207, 210, 215
MacManaway, Rev. J. G., 16
Macmillan, H., 63, 64, 65, 211, 214
Macmillan, M. K., 33
McManus, F., 12
MacNamara, J. K., 92, 144n
Mahon, S., 86
Maitland, P. F., 63
Mallalieu, E. L., 71n
Manningham-Buller, Sir Reginald E., 188
Marsh, R. W., 14
Marten, H. N., 158
Maude, A. E. U., 198
Maudling, R., 211
Maxwell-Hyslop, R., 143
Maybray-King, Baron, *see* King, H. M.
Mayhew, C. P., 232
Medlicott, Sir Frank, 157
Mellish, R. J., 62
Mendelson, J. J., 133
Mikardo, I., 126
Mill, J. S., 155
Mills, P. M., 175
Molson, A. H. E., 116
Morris, A., 63n, 144n
Morrison, H. S., 1st Baron, 47, 119, 126, 211, 212
Morrison, W. S. (Speaker), 70

Nabarro, Sir Gerald D. N., 85, 231
Nicolson, N., 157–8
Nutting, H. A., 157

Oppenheim, Mrs. S., 220
Owen, W. J., 44

Page, R. G., 117n
Paget, R. T., 67
Paisley, Rev. I., 85
Pardoe, J. W., 107
Parker, J., 148
Paton, Mrs. F. B., 72
Pavitt, L. A., 63n
Pickthorn, K. W. M., 65
Powell, J. E., 67, 85, 103, 165, 210, 211, 231, 232
Profumo, J. D., 58, 64, 179, 193, 199

Ramsay, A. H. M., 185n
Ramsden, J. E., 48
Redmayne, M., 65
Roberts, M. H. A., 172
Robertson, Sir David, 67
Rowlands, E., 224n

St. Clair, M. A. J., 15, 16
Sandys, D., 44, 186
Sheldon, R. E., 205
Shinwell, E. (Baron), 50
Short, E. W., 172
Silkin, J. E., 61, 62
Silverman, S. S., 59, 148, 161n
Sinclair, Sir George E., 103, 158
Slater, Mrs. H., 55
Smith, J. L. E., 24
Sorensen, R. W. (Baron), 152
Soskice, Sir Frank (Baron), 70
Stansgate, 1st Viscount, *see* Benn, W. W.
Steel, D. M. S., 149n
Stevas, N. A. F. St. John, 85, 231
Stow Hill, Baron, *see* Soskice, Sir Frank

Strauss, G. R., 67, 145, 149n, 170, 187–9
Sutcliffe, J. H. V., 221

Taverne, D., 122, 158
Taylor, Sir Charles, 194n
Taylor, E. McM., 78, 107
Temple, J. M., 175
Thomas, P. J. M., 213n
Thomas, T. G., 172

Vaughan-Morgan, J. K., 48–9

Walden, A. B., 148
Walder, A. D., 220
Walkden, E., 191
Walker, P. C. G., 227
Warbey, W. N., 178n
Ward, Dame Irene, 87
Warren, K. R., 221
Watkins, T. E., 63n
Wellbeloved, A. J., 149n
Whitelaw, W. S. I., 82, 183
Wigg, G. E. C., 63
Wilkes, J., 190
Wilkinson, Miss E., 148
Wilkinson, J. A. D., 20
Wilson, H. G. B., 177–8
Wilson, J. H., 14, 50, 52, 60–1, 62, 63, 86, 211, 212, 214, 215, 219, 222, 226
Wilson, W., 149n
Wolrige-Gordon, P., 161
Worsley, W. M. J., 152, 153n
Wyatt, W. L., 67, 199

Yates, V. F., 59

GENERAL INDEX

abortion, 147, 149, 159–60, 179
Abortion Law Reform Association, 147
Accommodation in the New Parliamentary Building, Services Cttee., 37n
Acts and Bills (excluding incidental references):
  Abortion Act, 1967, 147
  Administration of Justice Bill, 1970, 99
  Appropriation Bill, 56n
  Armed Forces Bill, 1967, 98n
  Bill of Rights, 1689, 185n, 186, 188
  Church of England Assembly (Powers) Act, 1919, 151
  Commonwealth Immigrants Act, 1962, 63–4
  Consolidated Fund Bill, 56n
  Corrupt and Illegal Practices Prevention Act, 1883, 12n
  Decimal Currency Bill, 1969, 101
  Divorce Reform Act, 1968, 146
  Divorce (Scotland) Bill, 1970, 146
  Election Commissioners Act, 1949, 17n
  House of Commons Disqualification Act, 1957, 13, 14, 16, 17n, 18
  House of Commons Redistribution of Seats Bill, 1969, 101
  Immigration Bill, 1971, 103, 224
  Industrial Relations Bill, 1969, 50, 67, 101, 174
  Industrial Relations Bill, 1970, 80n, 82, 86–7, 149n
  Leasehold Reform Bill, 1967, 224
  Licensing Acts, 36n, 87, 189–90
  Local Government Act, 1933, 183
  Matrimonial Causes and Reconciliation Bill, 1963, 147
  Matrimonial Property Bill, 1969, 148
  Mental Health Act, 1959, 12
  Merchant Shipping Bill, 1969, 101
  Ministers of the Crown Act, 1964, 13, 214
  Official Secrets Acts, 43–4, 180
  Parliament Act, 1949, 89
  Parliament Bill, 1911, 61, 62
  Parliament Bill, 1969, 94, 101
  Parliamentary Commissioner Bill, 1966, 139n

Acts and Bills: (*contd.*)—
  Parliamentary Papers Act, 1840, 187
  Peerage Act, 1963, 15, 216
  Police Act, 1964, 108
  Prices and Incomes Bill, 1968, 61
  Race Relations Bill, 1965, 224
  Rent Act, 1957, 104n
  Representation of the People Act, 1949, 12n, 17n
  Retail Price Maintenance Bill, 1964, 49, 64
  Right of Privacy Bill, 1968, 148
  Sexual Offences Act, 1967, 143n
  Statutory Instruments Act, 1946, 117
  Sunday Entertainments Bill, 1968, 146, 159
  Theatres Bill, 1968, 145
  Trade Descriptions Bill, 1968, 224
  Welsh Church Act, 1914, 16
  Welsh Language Bill, 1967, 136n
adjournment motions, 75, 95, 110–13, 169
Agriculture, Sel. Cttee., 129–30, 131–2, 133–4
Allen, Sir C. K., 104n
Allen, V. L., 174n
Amalgamated Union of Engineers and Foundrymen, 172
Annual Abstract of Statistics, 119n
Association of British Chambers of Commerce, 177
Association of University Teachers, 177
Attlee Government, 123, 142, 214
Automobile Association, 177

Bagehot, W., 155, 178
ballots, for bills and motions, 142, 144–5, 226
Bank of England, 124
Barker, A., 40n, 42, 43, 53n, 83n, 153n, 165n, 177n
Barnett, M. J., 104n
Barry, Sir Charles, 34
Bartholomew, D. J., 92n
Berrington, H. B., 92n
bills:
  drafting of, 145

241

bills: (_contd._)—
  government, 95, 96, 97–105
  private _see_ private bills
  private members' _see_ private members'
    bills
  unballoted, 142–3
Birmingham Post, 161
Borthwick, R. L., 135n
Bowring, Nona, 105n
Bradlaugh v. Gosset, 189n
British Broadcasting Corporation, 123,
  200–2 _see also_ broadcasting; tele-
  vision
British Legion, 179
broadcasting, 198, 200–5, 218
broadcasting of debates, 202–5
_Broadcasting of Proceedings in the House
  of Commons_, Sel. Cttee., 204
Brown, R. G. S., 105n
Bryce, J., 1st Viscount, 155
Budge, I., 219
Bulmer-Thomas, I., 55n
Burdett v. Abbot, 190n
Butler, D. E., 49n, 160n
Butt, R., 49n
by-elections, 14, 74

Cabinet:
  backbenchers and, 43–4, 89–94
  chosen by Prime Minister, 213–15
  size, 213–14
Cable and Wireless Ltd., 124
Campaign for Nuclear Disarmament, 67
Campion, Sir Gilbert, 107, 117
candidates:
  age, 12
  disqualification, 13–18
  nomination of, 17
  religious affiliation, 23
  selection of, 18–19
  trade union, 21–2
capital punishment, 68, 81, 144, 146–7,
  148, 157, 159, 161
Carbery, T. F., 173n
'catching the Speaker's eye', 77
Central Electricity Board, 123
Chairman of Committees (and Chairman
  of Ways and Means), 70–3, 149, 150
Chamberlain Government, 110
Chester, D. N., 105n
Chiltern Hundreds, 14
Church and State, 16, 151, 152
Church Estates Commissioner, 107, 152,
  214n
Church of England, 16, 67–68, 150–2

Church of England Measures, 67–8, 95,
  150–2
Churchill Government, 179
Civil Service, 14
Civil Service Fulton Committee, 121, 138
Civil Service, Members and, 30, 43, 109,
  116, 120–1, 137–41, 167–70, 183–4 _see
  also Agriculture_, Sel. Cttee.; _Educa-
  tion and Science_, Sel. Cttee.; Estimates Cttee.; Public Accounts Cttee.
Civil Service Clerical Association, 192–3
Clark, Sir Andrew, 137
Clarke, P., 17n
clergy, disqualification of, 16–17
Clergy Disqualification, Sel. Cttee., 16
commercial television, 179
Commission on the Constitution, 228
committee stage of bills, 98–103, 134–5,
  146, 149, 150
committees:
  financial, 115, 118–22
  legal, 115, 116–18
  regional, 134–6
  select, 115–36
  standing, 53, 72, 78, 98, 100–1, 102–3,
    176
Common Market _see_ European Economic Community
Commonwealth Parliamentary Association, 42, 88
Comptroller and Auditor-General, 118–
  19, 139, 141
Confederation of British Industry, 175
confidential information, 43–4
conscience, issues of, 67–8, 93, 143n,
  144–9, 152, 157, 159, 160–1, 179 _see
  also_ free votes; P. L. P. conscience
  clause
Conservative Group for Europe, 49
Conservative Party:
  abstention from voting, 63, 64
  backbenchers' committees, 46–9, 51,
    93, 177–8
  candidates, 19, 20
  discipline, 58, 59, 63–6
  Leader, 46, 47, 55, 65, 210–11, 223
  Leader's Committee, 210
  Monday Club, 48, 54
  1922 Committee, 46–7, 158, 199, 227
  policy groups, 49, 210
  regional groups, 47
  Shadow Cabinet, 46, 47, 49, 209–10
  25 Club, 49
Conservative Research Department, 43,
  47, 49

Consolidated, Fund, 118, 139
constituencies:
 boundary changes, 19n
 Members and, *see* Members, constituencies and
constitutional reform, proposals for,
 219–21
contraception, 149
Coombes, D., 125–6
Co-operative Party, 53, 213
 sponsorship of candidates, 22, 172–3
correspondence, Members', 165–71, 187–
 9, 196
Council of Europe, 40, 42
Council of Ministers, 229
courts, and privilege, 185–6, 187, 189–90
Crichel Down, 91, 137–8
Crick, B., 99n, 121n, 128, 202n, 223
crown contracts, 17
Crowther Commission, 228

Daily Mirror, 199
Daily Telegraph, The, 178n
Day, R., 202n
debates:
 adjournment, 75, 110–13
 anticipation of, 200
 broadcasting, and televising of, 202–5
 character of, 83–7, 94–7
 official report *see* Hansard,
 procedure in, 77
 publication of, 187, 196, 197, 200 *see
  also* Hansard
 time available, 76–7, 94–7
defence policy, 59–60, 92, 93, 96, 133 *see
  also* nuclear disarmament
delegated legislation, 75, 95, 96, 104–5,
 116–18
Delegated legislation, Sel. Cttee., 105n
Deputy Speaker, 70–3, 149, 150
Dicey, A. V., 89
divisions, 56, 57, 77n, 79–83
divorce reform, 146, 147, 148, 149,
 159–60
Dod's Parliamentary Companion, 22n
Draughtsmen's and Allied Technicians
 Association (D.A.T.A.), 173–4

Eaves, J., 104n
Ecclesiastical Committee, 151
Economist, The, 92n, 218
Education and Science, Sel. Cttee., 129,
 130, 195

election(s):
 corruption practices, 12
 expenses, 21–2, 172–3
 petitions, 17
 see also by-elections
Elections, Sel. Cttee. (1950), 16n
emergency debates, 75, 110–11, 114n, 225
Epstein, L. D., 157n
Essex University, 195
Estimates Committee, 44, 115, 118–22,
 128–9, 134
 sub-committees, 120, 128–9
European Commission, 230
European Economic Community, 40
 agriculture and, 130
 attitudes to entry, 49, 67, 92, 174, 202,
  220–1
 effect of entry, 228–30
 P. L. P. attitude to entry, 62, 63, 68
 voting on entry, 61, 62, 68, 158
European Parliament, 229–30
Evening News, 194
Expenditure Committee, 115, 122, 134

filibuster, 146
Finance Bill, procedure for, 98–9, 225
financial control, 95, 97, 118–22, 147
Finer, S. E., 92n
Fisher, Sir N. F. Warren, 31n
Ford, P. & G., 187n
foreign affairs, 88, 93, 95, 96, 111, 114,
 133
'Fourteen Day Rule', 200
free votes, 56, 61, 67–8, 84, 93, 148n, 157,
 158, 160–1, 204, 205, 228
freedom of speech, 185–7, 195
Friend, J., 157
Fry, C. K., 140n
Fulton Committee, 121, 138

general elections *see* election(s)
General Synod, Church of England, 151,
 152
Green Papers, 96–7, 122n
Greengrass, D., 129n
guillotine, 56n, 86–7, 100, 149n

Hampton, W., 153n
Hansard, 38, 77–9, 84, 98, 105, 106, 165,
 187n
Hanson, A. H., 99n, 120n, 121n, 128
Heath Government, 52, 62, 65, 68, 122,
 214, 223
Hewart, Lord, 104n
Hindell, K., 160

Holt, S., 230n
homosexuality, 143n, 144, 149, 159–60, 161
honours, 65, 108, 209
House of Commons:
arrangement of business, 74–6, 203
authority of, 89
Chamber, 34–5, 73
cs gas incident, 195
distribution of business, 94–7
functions of, 222–5
length of sittings, 74, 146, 225
Library, 36, 38, 40–2, 115, 131
secret session, 187
House of Commons (Rebuilding), Sel. Cttee., 34
House of Commons (Services), Sel. Cttee., 26, 35–6, 37–8, 70, 205
House of Lords, 15–16, 213
Houses of Parliament *see* Palace of Westminster

immigration, 160, 165
In Place of Strife, 62, 97
Independent Television Authority, 124
Independents, Members and candidates, 18, 67, 76, 77, 85, 161, 231
Information and the Public Interest, 40n
information services, 38–44
Institute of Directors, 177
Inter Parliamentary Union, 42, 88
issues of conscience, 67–8, 93, 143n, 144–9, 152, 157, 159, 160–1, 179

Jackson, R. J., 58n, 60n, 65n
Jennings, Sir W. Ivor, 46n, 98n, 155
Johnson, N., 105n, 121n, 129n
Judicial Committee of the Privy Council, 17
Junor, J., 194
JUSTICE, 138

Keeler, Miss Christine, 64n
Keeton, Professor G. W., 218, 219n
Kirkaldy, H. S., 30
Kitchen Committee, 36n, 190

Labour Party:
annual conference, 60, 62, 156, 160
benevolent fund, 33
Parliamentary *see* P. L. P.
research department, 43
Laski, H. J., 127–8, 148, 216, 230n

Lawrence, Sir G., 30
Lawrence Committee, 27, 30, 32
Leader of the House, 75–6, 152
League of Empire Loyalists, 157
legislation:
drafting of, 101
passage of, 75, 95, 96, 97–105, 224–5
Liberal Party, 18, 81, 40, 231
broadcasting, 201
discipline, 54
register of Members' business interests, 181, 182, 184
life peers, 15n, 16, 57n, 146
Lobby correspondents, 198–9
lobbying, 176–7, 186
local authorities, 130
Ombudsman for, 140, 141
local authority associations, Members and, 175–6
local party associations, Members and, 18–19, 156–63
Lock, G., 40n
London Electricity Board, 170, 187–9
London Passenger Transport Board, 123
Lord Great Chamberlain, 35, 37
Lords Commissioners of the Treasury *see* Whips
Lord's Day Observance Society, 177
Lynskey Tribunal, 184n

MacKenzie, R. T., 211n
Mackenzie, Professor W. J. M., 30
Macmillan Government, 141, 214, 223
maiden speeches, 85
majority, age of, 12
Management of Local Government Cttee. (Maud), 151n
Manor of Northstead, 14
mass media, 197–205, 224 *see also* press, the
Maud Committee, 151n
Members:
absenteeism, 57
accommodation, 34–8
age of, 19–20, 161
attendance allowance, 25
attendance in the House, 74, 79–83, 186, 196, 203
business connections, 174–5, 179–84, 189
calibre, 230–1, 232
change of party allegiance, 162
code of conduct, 182–4
committee work, 42, 53, 58, 78, 83–4, 102–3, 176, 225

Members: (*contd.*)—
  constituencies and, 19, 26–7, 39, 43,
    45, 54, 57, 65, 66, 71, 72, 83–4, 96,
    99, 109, 112–13, 114, 138–40, 149,
    Chap. 8 *passim*, 189, 231, 232 *see
    also* questions
  correspondence, 165–71, 187–9, 196
  disorderly conduct, 86–7, 190
  disqualification, 12, 14–16, 17–18
  educational background, 21
  expenses, 25–7, 28
  expulsion of, 190–1
  facilities for, 24, 25–7, 34–43
  future role of, 228–30
  honours awarded to, 65
  information services, 38–44
  interests, 45, 53–4, Chap 9 *passim*, 189
  interviews with constituents, 38, 165–6
  literary activities, 198
  local government experience, 22, 164,
    166, 233
  Ministerial experience, 206–7
  occupational background, 21–2, 28, 33
  parliamentary experience, 19
  participation in parliamentary busi-
    ness, 77–9
  pay, 24–31 *passim*, 184, 228
  pensions, 31–3
  private earnings, 29–30
  promotion, 89, Chap 11 *passim*, 231,
    232
  qualification of, 12–18
  re-election of, 19
  register of interests, 181–4
  religious affiliation, 22–3
  research assistance, 26
  secretarial assistance, 26
  severance pay, 33
  social life, 87–8
  'surgeries', 165–6
  tax allowances, 27
  time spent on public affairs, 29
  trade union, 173–4, 213, 232
  trade unions' sponsorship of, 21–2, 43,
    53, 172, 174, 179, 183
  travel abroad, 42–3, 88, 115, 120, 124,
    131–2, 178, 201
  welfare officer role, 160, 164–71, 225
  see also candidates
Members' *Expenses* Sel. Cttee. (1953–54),
  25
Members' Fund, House of Commons,
  31–2, 33
Members' *Interests* (*Declaration*), Sel.
  Cttee., 173n, 180–3

Menhennet, D., 40n
Ministers:
  Members and, 89–94, 167–70
  nationalised industries and, 124, 125–6
  number in Commons, 13
  parliamentary private secretaries and,
    208–9
  party committees and, 45, 46, 47, 50,
    52
  pay, 28, 65, 215–16, 233
  responsibility of, 91, 137–8, 141
  selection of, 213–16
  statements by, 95, 105–6, 110
  see also Cabinet; questions
Ministers' Powers, Cttee., 104n, 116n
minority parties, 11, 18, 77
Mitchell, T., 17n
Moral Rearmament (M. R. A.), 161
Morley, Lord, 230

'naming a Member', 87, 190
National Council for Civil Liberties, 177
National Union of General and Munici-
  pal Workers, 172
National Union of Manufacturers, 177
National Union of Mineworkers, 53, 172
National Union of Teachers, 172, 173
nationalised industries, parliamentary
  control, 108, 122–6, 137
Nationalised Industries, Sel. Cttee., 115,
  123–6
Niblock, M., 229n
Nicholson, M., 219n
Normanton, E. L., 121n
North Atlantic Treaty Organisation, 42
nuclear disarmament, 60, 67, 160, 212

oath of allegiance, 74, 75
Observer, The, 191
Office of Manpower Economics, 29, 31
Offices or Places of Profit under the Crown,
  Sel. Cttee., 16, 206
official publications:
  availability of, 38–40
  privilege and, 187
Official Secrets Acts, Sel. Cttee., 44, 188n
Ombudsman *see* Parliamentary Com-
  missioner for Administration
Opposed Bill Committee, 150
Opposition Whips, 30, 55
Overseas Aid, Sel. Cttee., 129, 132, 134

pairing, 57, 58, 66, 80, 82, 208
Palace of Westminster, 34–8, 87, 189–90
Palmer, J., 100n

Parliamentary Affairs, 116n, 129n, 135, 209n

Parliamentary and Scientific Committee, 53–4

Parliamentary Commissioner for Administration, 117, 138–41, 167, 170, 171, 225

Parliamentary Commissioner for Administration, Sel. Cttee., 115, 139, 140

Parliamentary Elections (Mr. Speaker's Seat), Sel. Cttee., 71

Parliamentary Labour Party (P. L. P.), 49–53, 227
   abstention from voting, 60, 61, 81, 97
   area groups, 46, 53
   conscience clause, 60, 61
   Deputy Leader, 211–12
   discipline, 50, 54, 59–63, 65–6, 67
   E.E.C. and, 62, 63, 68
   Leader, 50, 51, 53, 211–12, 222
   Liaison Committee, 61–62
   Shadow Cabinet, 50, 51, 212–13
   Standing Orders, 59–60
   subject groups, 46, 51–3, 93, 177
   'Tribune' Group, 53, 54, 92

parliamentary private secretaries (P.P.S.), 45, 51, 58, 63, 78, 93, 152, 199, 206, 208–9, 215

Parliamentary Privilege, Sel. Cttee., 195–7

parliamentary privilege *see* privilege

parliamentary questions *see* questions

participation *see* public participation

Partington, M., 116n, 129n

party committees, 45–54, 207, 208 *see also under* Conservative Party; Parliamentary Labour Party

party discipline, 11, 13, 50, 54–68, 80, 82, 91–4, 103, 155, 163, 179, 222, 228, 230

party leaders, 89–90
   election, 210–12, 223

party meetings, leaks of information from, 191, 199–200

party organisation, members and, 43

party political broadcasts, 200

Paterson, P., 18n

patronage, 14, 17, 57n, 65, 66, 206, 223

Patronage Secretary, 55

peerage:
   disqualification for Membership, 15–16
   renunciation of, 15, 216
   see also life peers

pensions, *see* Members, pensions

Pensions for Members of the House of Commons, Sel. Cttee., 31n

Personal Bills, 72

Phillips, O. Hood, 219n

Pinto-Duschinsky, M., 49n

Pitt, D., 160n

Platt, D. C. M., 28n

Plowden, W., 177n

Political Quarterly, 40n, 125n, 160n

Political Studies, 51n, 216n

Popham, G. T., 129n

Porton Down Research Establishment, 191

Post Office, 124, 126

Prayer Book Measures 1927 and 1928, 151, 152

prayer card, 73

'prayer' debates, 104–5, 117

press, the, 197–200
   and privilege, 185, 190–1, 192, 194, 196–7

pressure groups, 43, 103–4, 145, 147, 172–9, 223, 224

Prices and Incomes Board, 14, 30

Prime Minister, 89–90
   patronage powers of, 13–14, 57n, 66, 89, 213–15

Private Bills, 72, 95, 149–50

private members' bills, 30–1, 56n, 58, 75, 95, 101, 114, 142–9, 159–60, 177, 225, 226
   motions, 58, 67, 75, 92, 95, 114, 142
   time, 68, 142, 223

privilege, 36n, 63n, 87, 173–4, 178, 185–97

Privileges, Committee of, 12n, 15, 87, 174, 185n, 188–9, 191–2, 193, 195–7

Privy Councillors, 73, 86
   precedence in debate, 77

procedure, reform of, 222–8

Procedure, Sel. Cttee (1945–46), 117, 119
   (1956–57), 98n
   (1958–59), 80, 128
   (1964–65), 65, 82, 120, 128
   (1966–67), 99n, 111, 117n
   (1968–69), 121
   (1970–71), 107n, 224n, 226

Procedure relating to Money Resolutions, Sel. Cttee., 98n

proportional representation, lack of, 11

Public Accounts Committee, 115, 118–19, 120

Public Administration, 105n, 129n, 140n

Public Bill Office, 143, 145

Public Expenditure: A New Presentation, 40n

Public Law, 128n, 188n
public opinion, Members' pay and, 29, 33
public participation, 219–21
public relations activities, Members and, 178, 180–4
Publications and Debates, Sel. Cttee., 36n
Pugin, R. W., 34

qualified privilege, 170–1
Queen's speech, 94, 95, 148n
questions, 41, 75, 78–9, 83, 95, 105–10, 138, 167, 169, 177, 188–9, 203
    admissibility and framing of, 107–8
    nature of, 108–9
    private notice, 105–6, 110
    replies to, 108–110
quorum, 56–7

Race Relations and Immigration, Sel. Cttee., 129, 130, 134
radio *see* broadcasting
Ranney, A., 18n, 161n
'recall', the, 162
referenda, use of, 220–1
regional committees, 134–6
Reid, G., 121n
Remuneration of Ministers and Members of Parliament (Lawrence Committee), 27, 30, 32
reports, debates on, 96–7
Review Body on Top Salaries, 25–32 *passim*, 215–16
R. v. Creevy, 187n
R. v. Graham-Campbell — ex parte Herbert, 36n, 190n
Rhodesia, 64, 66, 67, 159, 227
Richards, P. G., 39n, 43n, 67n, 68n, 127n, 128n, 149n, 159n, 200n
Roads Campaign Council, 177–8
Robson, W. A., 125n
Roth, A., 174–5, 182n
Rowntree Trust, 230
Royal Society for the Prevention of Cruelty to Animals, 177
Rush, M., 18n, 40n, 42, 43, 53n, 83n, 153n, 165n, 177n

Science and Technology, Sel. Cttee., 54, 129, 131–2, 134, 191
Scott, Sir Giles G., 35
Scottish Affairs, Sel. Cttee., 129, 132, 134, 136
Scottish Grand Committee, 102, 134–5
Scottish Nationalists, 18, 136

Scottish Standing Committee(s), 102–3, 135
Scrutiny Committee *see Statutory Instruments*, Sel. Cttee.
Second Reading Committee, 98
Seebohm Committee, 99
Segal, A., 202n
Select Committees, 115–36
    Chairmen, 30
Select Committees of the House of Commons, 122n
separation of powers, 13
Serjeant-at-Arms, 35, 37, 73, 86, 190, 198
servicemen as candidates, 14
Seymour-Ure, C., 194n, 199n
Shadow Cabinet, 43, 51, 209–10
    Conservative Party, 46, 47, 49, 209–10
    Labour Party, 212–13
    party committees and, 46, 47, 50
Shell, D. R., 129n
Sheriff of Middlesex's case, 190n
Sinn Fein candidates, 17n
Smith, Ian, 64, 227
Society for the Protection of the Unborn Child, 147
South Africa, arms sales to, 64–5, 92, 227
Speaker, 69–73, 74
    choice of, 69–71
    duties of, 35, 69, 76, 77, 79–80, 85, 86, 106, 107, 110, 111, 112, 146, 190, 191
Speaker's Panel, 30, 72–3
specialised committees, 126–34, 225
Spectator, The, 178n
Standing Committee(s), 53, 72, 78, 98, 100–1, 102–3, 176, 225
Stanley, S., 184
Statutory Instruments, 75, 95, 96, 104–5
Statutory Instruments, Sel. Cttee., 115, 116–18, 226
Stockdale v. Hansard, 187, 189, 190
Stokes, D., 160n
Study of Parliament Group, 9, 117n, 128
Suez Canal, 63, 92, 93, 157, 158, 200
Suez Group, 63, 92
Sunday entertainment, 146, 159–60
Sunday Express, 194
Sunday Graphic, 192
Sunday observance, 146, 159, 179
Sunday Times, 180
Supply, Committee of, 75, 95
Supply Days, 95, 96, 120

Table, The, 17n
television, 198, 200–5, 218

Ten-Minute Rule Bills, 97, 143–4, 177
theatre censorship, 144, 145, 149
Thompson, D., 188n
Times, The, 15n, 24n, 26n, 41, 63n, 82, 85, 86n, 92, 171n, 174n, 199, 204n, 208n, 212n, 231n
Torrey Canyon, 130–1
trade unions:
  Labour Party and, 53
  sponsorship of Members, 21–2, 43, 53, 172, 174, 179, 183
Transport and General Workers Union, 172, 174
Treaty of Rome, 229
Tribune, 92n
Tunstall, Jeremy, 198n

Ulster Unionists, 47
unballoted bills, 142–3
Unionist Agricultural Committee, 45
United Nations, 40
Unopposed Bills Committee, 150
'usual channels' *see* Whips

Vice-Chamberlain of the Household, 55, 58, 74
voluntary organisations, Members and, 176–8; *see also* pressure groups
Vote of censure, 95
Vote Office, 38–9
voting:
  abstention from, 60, 61, 63, 64, 81, 97, 159
  by proxy, 82
  see also divisions; free votes

Wason v. Walter, 187n
Welsh Grand Committee, 135–6
Welsh Nationalists, 18
Welsh Standing Committee, 102
Wheare, Sir Kenneth, 133
Whip (documentary), 45, 56, 57, 80–1, 82
  resignation of, 67, 157, 158
  withdrawal of, 57, 59, 60, 62, 65, 158
Whips, 13n, 37, 46–7, 50, 52, 54–68, 76, 77, 82, 129, 142, 151, 152, 154, 155, 163, 202, 206, 208n, 213, 220, 225, 227, 229
  appointment of, 55
  Opposition, 30, 68, 209
  promotion of, 209
White Papers, debates on, 96–7
Williams, P. M., 160
Williams, R., 129n
Williamson v. Norris, 190n
Willson, F. M. G., 209n, 216
Wilson Government, 50–1, 62, 81, 94, 96, 99, 124, 126, 129, 133, 146, 147, 174, 214, 216, 226, 227
Wilson, H. H., 179n
Wiseman, H. V., 99n, 120n, 128, 129n
Witnesses, Sel. Cttee., 194n
women:
  as Deputy Speaker, 72
  as Temporary Chairmen, 72
  as Whips, 55
  Members and candidates, 20
  ministerial office and, 213
World Press News, 190

Younger Committee, 148